You Want to Do What with PHP?

YOU WANT TO DO
WHAT
WITH PHP?

Kevin Schroeder

MC PRESS

MC Press Online, LLC
Ketchum, ID 83340

You Want to Do What with PHP?
Kevin Schroeder

First Edition
First Printing—September 2010

MC Press offers excellent discounts on this book when ordered in quantity for bulk purchases or special sales, which may include custom covers and content particular to your business, training goals, marketing focus, and branding interest.

MC Press Online, LLC

    Corporate Offices
    P.O. Box 4886
    Ketchum, ID 83340-4886 USA

For information regarding sales and/or customer service, please contact:

    MC Press
    P.O. Box 4300
    Big Sandy, TX 75755-4300 USA

For information regarding permissions or special orders, please contact:

    books@mcpressonline.com

ISBN: 978-158347-099-2

About the Author

Kevin Schroeder, Technology Evangelist for Zend Technologies, is well-versed in a wide variety of technologies pertinent to both small- and large-scale application deployments. He has developed production software using PHP and many other languages, including ASP, HTML, Java, JavaScript, Perl, SQL, Visual Basic, and occasionally C. Kevin also has extensive experience as a system administrator on Linux, Solaris, Windows, and other platforms on scales of a single server up to several hundred servers on installations ranging from a few to millions of users. He has spoken at several conferences and is co-author of *The IBM i Programmer's Guide to PHP* (MC Press, 2009). In his spare time Kevin races Ferraris, with a dismal win record in his Honda. He can be found online at *www.eschrade.com* speaking in the first person.

Acknowledgments

With a new book comes a new round of acknowledgments. But how does one write creatively when the same people deserve thanks? The answer, it seems, is obvious. Write it in the style of Medieval literature and read it with an English accent.

Toward the beginning of the fourth age of man, the author emerged from Dallas, a great city of men. As was told in *History of the World: Part II*, our hero journeyed from his homeland, where he had been sired by Randy the Great and Irene the Peaceful. Also left behind was his sister, Melanie the Foolish, who had become great in the cutting of hair and the curling of rocks. To this day, the explanations of both the reason for this curling and the mechanism for how these rocks were curled have remained a mystery.

Throughout the hero's journeys, several persons made an impact on his quest. Among these were Mark, the former King of the realm of Titus 2, with his queen, Debbie the Wise; Jennifer and Bob, the Lady and Lord of the North. . . of Dallas; and David, King of the Castle of the Glen, with his wife, Marsha the Sweet.

During the preparation for this great dissemination of knowledge, many people came to know and love our hero and were loved in return. Whilst a complete list has never been discovered, much evidence has been found in the Annals of Facebook of what relationships may have transpired during this period. The Earls and Countesses Buckley and Bruner were chief among the correspondent's contacts here. The stronghold of Fort Dana, whose ruler went by the name of a greeting, contributed mightily to the correspondence.

There too was a court jester known to be in association with the author king who went by the name of Chad. This jester was also known by the names Chadly, Chaddrack, Chadzilla, Chaddanooga, Chaddle, Chaddar, Chadderwocky, Chadbacca, and Chadawan the Learner. Other known accomplices to our hero's exploits were Tom the Brave, former Commander of the Guard; A. J. the Scot, of whom the people spoke well even though he wore no pants; and Tim the Riddler.

Throughout these days, children sang songs of the hero king's greatness. Chief among them were Caroline, offspring of Duke and Duchess Reid and Gay Lynn, sister of the Baron and Baroness Doug and Libby; Annie, Eli, and Liddy of the Earl and Countess Bruner; Kayla, Zack, and Bing of the Earl and Countess Buckley; and Kendall and Avery of Craig, Tender of the Bar, and Katie (who had taken pity on him). Together they sang a chorus of mirth and merriment at our hero's presence.

In the beginning of the journey, our hero, the author, had bested many squires and knights for the hand of the lovely Laurie, known throughout the land for her beauty. Many lands were conquered with her guidance, and she was instrumental in the benevolence purveyed upon the people during the period of our hero's reign.

And through it all, o'er our hero's journey from kind serf to benevolent king, he remembered the true Lord of the Land.

Contents

Introduction

Surveying the landscape of books about PHP makes for a dizzying venture. There are books about PHP everywhere, and for good reason. PHP runs a significant portion of the Internet, and for that reason you will find a wide range of books out there that speak directly to that topic. What makes this book different?

In this book, I take you through some topics that you may not have thought of using PHP for; other topics are covered in more depth than what you typically see.

To some degree, this endeavor may seem like a diversion. After all, PHP's typical purpose is building Web sites (usually with MySQL), so the topics covered here might seem unimportant to your current work. However, what we're going to do is explore some of the things you *could* do with PHP, with the hope that in examining some of these topics, you'll find applications to which you can apply what you learn here.

The subjects we'll cover are different from what you'll find out there. Instead of considering simply the Web, we'll be looking at lower-level programming in PHP. This may be a bit difficult. Many PHP programmers are focused at a very high level in their application development, working with user interfaces, rich Internet applications, and the like. And why not? PHP really excels at these things. But why not more? That is really the question I have often pondered.

I'm not talking about building the next Quake or a replacement for Microsoft Word. But what about things like building a proprietary data storage mechanism, setting up distributed caching, or connecting to a third-party network service?

These applications are definitely pertinent to what you do. Not only that, but they would be fun to write.

And *that* is a lot of what PHP is about. When it comes right down to it, PHP is fun. You can use it for serious business applications and also for fun side projects. PHP runs some of the top sites in the world, but it can also run that simple blog site your grandma has.

And, really, that is also what this book is about. Writing a book about the fun things you can do with PHP is, itself, fun. The topics I've chosen are ones I think you'll find fun to explore. Several of them I have worked on already; several I have not. (I'll leave it to you to decide which ones I've done already.) But that's what drives me when working with PHP. It has the right combination of fun and seriousness that is the reason why a lot of us got into coding in the first place.

One thing I feel I should caution you about is that any type of book like this is going to be incomplete. Technical manuals can be complete. Novels can be complete. Books like this cannot be complete. Rather than writing a book whose purpose is step-by-step instruction, my goal with this project is inspiration. If you read through this book and think, "Hmm, I never thought of doing *X* that way," then I will have succeeded. Sure, I will provide some step-by-step instructions, but that is not the end goal I have in mind. Although in your day-to-day applications you may not use PHP to build a proprietary data storage mechanism, implement distributed caching, or connect to a third-party network service, after going through this book you should not find these types of tasks overly daunting. And by thinking through some non-traditional PHP topics, you will positively impact your development skill set.

For that reason, I have consciously decided to include fewer topics in this book than what I might have. With a title like *You Want to Do WHAT with PHP?* there is a wealth of possible routes to explore because there are many things people might not necessarily think of PHP as being able to do. Rather than make this book exhaustive, I want it to be thorough. I've read too many books that stop right when they get to the interesting part. My goal is not to have you think, "Wow, that's interesting but totally incomplete," but rather, "Wow, that's interesting. I can't wait for *You Want to Do WHAT ELSE with PHP?!*"

I hope I succeed. If I do, buy a book for a friend of yours. If not, feel free to let me know, as gently as possible. I have intentionally hit on a few tough problems, so there are a lot of details you'll need to wade through. Those details may be overwhelming sometimes. But know that for each example I have tried to delicately balance the need to show a complete example with the need to show an example that can be understandable in print. That is a difficult balance to strike, and the balance will be different for different people.

One last thing before we move on to our topics. You might look at the list of topics and find yourself unable to figure out how they are all related to each other. Well, from a topical standpoint, many of them are not. The commonality comes from the experience I have had as a PHP consultant for Zend Technologies. When doing the type of consulting that I've done, you get to see a lot of different ways that people have done things. Sometimes, you get great new ideas you hadn't thought of, and sometimes you need to educate people about bad practices they've picked up, new or better ways to do things, or just new concepts they hadn't had a need to research before. So, the commonality is that the topics I have chosen are those for which I have seen a need.

That said, I'm quite excited about what you'll get to learn here. Not because I'm a great teacher, but because a lot of PHP developers focus primarily on PHP for the Web. That's a great place to start and a great place to work. But to move forward as a Web developer, learning things that you might not directly use but that can impact your approach is a really good idea. As Albert Einstein stated, "A mind once stretched by new thoughts can never regain its original shape." I hope that in reading this book, your mind changes shape. I know that mine did while writing it.

Kevin Schroeder
May 2010

CHAPTER 1

Networking and Sockets

You can think of this chapter as a foundational chapter in this book. Several other chapters will rely on what you learn here. This chapter also matters simply because although a lot of stuff happens on the network, PHP developers are often insulated from that stuff. For example, PHP's **file_get_contents()** function can return, via the streams API, the contents of a remote Web site just as if it were a local file. The statement:

```
$data = file_get_contents('test.php');
```

functions the same way as

```
$data = file_get_contents('http://www.php.net/');
```

Thanks to the streams API, this type of functionality is identical regardless of the data source, as long as your distribution of PHP supports the specified protocol.

This approach has two upsides: it makes your code much simpler, and it makes your application much faster. Because the entire core PHP functionality is written in C, you get the performance benefit of running compiled code, and compiled C code is always going to be faster than PHP code (unless you've royally messed up your C).

The downside of this approach is that you don't get as much exposure to the underlying layer. In most situations that's not a problem, but occasionally you will need to know some of what goes on "under the covers."

The OSI Model

The best place to start is at the beginning, so let's start there. From your point of view as a PHP programmer, the beginning is what is known as "layer 7."

What I'm talking about here is the Open Systems Interconnection (OSI) model. The OSI model is an abstract concept that defines various layers within a network's architecture. PHP typically takes care of network communications for you, even on the lower layers, but knowing what those network layers are can help you understand why your application does what it does.

The OSI Layers

Figure 1.1 lists the layers defined by the OSI model.

OSI Model	
Layer 7	Application layer
Layer 6	Presentation layer
Layer 5	Session layer
Layer 4	Transport layer
Layer 3	Network layer
Layer 2	Data link layer
Layer 1	Physical layer

Figure 1.1: OSI layers

An important point to note about these layers is that each is built on the other. For example, layer 6 is responsible for transferring data from layer 5 to layer 7, and vice versa. In a typical networked PHP application, you send data from layer 7, the application layer. Layer 7 then passes the data to layer 6, which passes it to layer 5, and so on right down to layer 1. Then, on the other side of the application, when the data is received, layer 1 passes it to layer 2, which eventually bubbles it up to layer 7, where the client (or server) then receives it.

This is not a perfect description, nor is the transition between the OSI layers always perfect. For example, HTTP, being stateless, seems to miss layer 5, the session layer. For this chapter, however, we'll be concerning ourselves primarily with layers 3 and 4, and the preceding explanation is sufficient for the purpose of our discussion.

Let's take a closer look now at each layer of the OSI model.

Layer 7: Application Layer

The OSI layer with which you're probably most familiar is layer 7, the application layer. This layer contains the protocols that supply network services to your applications, such as Dynamic Host Configuration Protocol (DHCP), Hypertext Transfer Protocol (HTTP), Internet Message Access Protocol (IMAP), and Post Office Protocol 3 (POP3). Secure Sockets Layer (SSL) is also part of layer 7.

One way to think of layer 7 is as the last endpoint before data is handled in your application. If you are using a custom protocol or have built a custom handler for an existing protocol, your application will be delving into layer 7.

Layer 7 can also be seen as the payload that all the other protocols are working together to send.

Layer 6: Presentation Layer

You can think of the presentation layer as the raw data that will be passed. While layer 7 provides the structure (e.g., HTTP) that the request needs to follow, layer 6 defines the actual data that is going to be handed off. In other words, layer 6 defines the format of the data that a layer 7 protocol needs to use. ASCII is an example of a layer 6 protocol, as are Unicode and 8-bit Unicode Transformation Format (UTF-8).

Layer 5: Session Layer

From the point of view of HTTP, the session layer, which manages sessions between application processes, is unnecessary. The HTTP protocol is stateless, which means that individual requests don't know anything about any previous or subsequent HTTP requests. There are obviously workarounds, such as sessions, but the network architecture does not handle sessions.

Typical protocols that operate on the session layer are the Network Basic Input/ Output System (NetBIOS), Secure Copy (SCP), and Secure Shell (SSH). On Windows networks, Server Message Block (SMB) — also known as the Common Internet File System (CIFS) — is the protocol typically used for file and print sharing, and SMB is also used by the open-source Samba project. SMB is an example of a layer 6 protocol that uses a layer 5 protocol, NetBIOS, to communicate.

Layer 4: Transport Layer

The transport layer is where we will spend much of this chapter. It is here that the Transmission Control Protocol (TCP) and User Datagram Protocol (UDP) reside. There is a separate TCP/IP model that could be seen as a competitor to OSI, but because we are going to look at the Internet Control Message Protocol (ICMP) and also talk a bit about Internet Protocol (IP), using the TCP/IP model did not seem appropriate for this discussion.

The transport layer takes data provided by the session layer or the presentation layer and encapsulates it in a format that can be sent to the network layer or extracted from the network layer to be passed to the session or presentation layer.

Among the responsibilities of the transport layer are:

- Ports: Virtual endpoints for a packet on a destination machine

- Flow control: Keeping the application from flooding the receiving machine with data

- Error detection and correction

Protocols on the transport layer are not required to handle any of these functions, but many, such as TCP, do.

Layer 3: Network Layer

The network layer is responsible for the actual delivery and routing of transport-layer–level packets to an endpoint. Note that your computer, when connected to a network, does not have a "TCP address"; it has an "IP address." Once an IP packet has found its way to its destination IP address, the data bubbles up to the transport layer, where the port information is handled.

The network layer doesn't care if you're using TCP, UDP, or some other protocol. All it cares about is getting that packet to its endpoint. This layer is actually closer to UDP than TCP in its implementation. TCP requires a connection, whereas UDP does not. UDP is "fire and forget" (with some exceptions). IP is the same way. As long as the packet reaches its destination without error, IP is happy. If a connection is opened to a closed port using TCP, the network layer is indifferent about it. All it knows is that a packet was returned; it doesn't care that the TCP protocol on the server returned a TCP reset to a requested connection on a closed port. All IP cares about is that data is being sent to and from an IP address.

Layer 2: Data Link Layer

The data link layer is responsible for sending data only between devices on the same local area network. Ethernet is an example of a layer 2 protocol; so are Point-to-Point Protocol (PPP) and Serial Line Interface Protocol (SLIP). Media Access Control (MAC) is a sublayer within the data link layer. The MAC protocol is used so that a packet destined for a specific device will be ignored by all other devices on the network.

It is that specificity that enables a hub to work. When a packet comes in to a hub on one port, the hub sends it on to all the other connected ports. The Ethernet devices on those ports will ignore the packet, except for the device for which the packet is destined.

Like a hub, a switch is a data link layer device, but rather than simply broadcasting all packets to all connected devices, a switch learns which MAC addresses are on which physical ports. Based on that information, the switch relays packets only to the physical port on which a given MAC address is known to exist.

Routers are much more intelligent than either hubs or switches. They let you subdivide networks, route packets differently, or choose not to route at all, as is the case with a firewall.

What you will actually notice is that if you are on a multiple-hop network, where your packet is routed through multiple routers, the packet will jump back and forth between layers 2 and 3. In a moment, we'll look at a chart that will help you visualize this behavior.

Layer 1: Physical Layer

I'm not even going to try to explain how the physical layer works because I'd get it wrong. Simply put, what this layer does is facilitate the raw transmission of bits from one machine to another.

Putting It Together

Having reviewed the various layers with some very basic descriptions of what goes on in each one, let's take a quick look at the life of a packet as it goes from your Web server to a browser. Figure 1.2 depicts the flow of this activity.

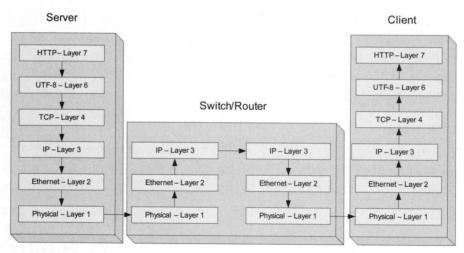

Figure 1.2: Path of a packet

What happens on the server and the client probably makes a fair amount of sense. However, the router part needs a little explaining. First of all, the middle "Switch/ Router" portion of this diagram could be duplicated several times, once for each router through which the packet must pass. But what's actually going on in the router's mind when a packet arrives? Here is that conversation:

Here I am listening on my MAC address 32:95: f6:7a:af:97 (192.168.0.1) and 5d:a4:05:67: e4:5f (192.168.1.1).

What's this? A packet on 32:95:f6:7a:af:97? I love getting packets. Ah! It's from d4:da:01:3f:94:a5. Let's take a look at that IP address. 192.168.0.5? I can handle that! Let's see, where is this packet supposed to go. . .192.168.1.42? Hmm, that's on the 192.168.1.0/24 network.

I know where this packet is supposed to go, so I'll just change the source MAC address to my 5d:a4:05:67:e4:5f. And I know the MAC address to the computer on the 192.168.1.0/24 network (she and I had coffee last week). It's 23:87:82:cc:ab:59. So let's change the destination MAC address to hers.

Almost there. I still have this data, so let's dump that into the new packet and send it on its way. Happy trails, little fella!

The elapsed time for this conversation is most likely measured in nanoseconds.

Routing

In the preceding example, you saw how a router might decide where to send an individual packet. However, you did not see the rules the router used to determine where to send the packet. Those rules are what constitute routing, and while routing is relatively simple for smaller networks, it's a bit of a black art when you're dealing with complex networks.

The thing is, when people think of routing, they often think of how routing is done on the Internet, where multiple routers are all trying to figure out the best way to get an individual packet to where it needs to go. Your local network does not actually work like this. There is no auto-discovery on your local network. At least there shouldn't be. I have never run into a situation where a PHP developer needed to understand a wide area network. But local area networks are quite common. Usually, you won't have to worry about doing too much routing because developers technically should be grouped on their own class C network. However, there may be times when a sandbox or quality assurance (QA) area is needed that should have special rules in place to make sure packets don't get into the wild.

I just referred to a "class C" network. As you are probably aware, only a limited number of IP addresses are available. An IP address, for Internet Protocol Version 4 (IPv4), is a 32-bit number, typically separated into four octets. (I won't be getting into IPv6.) Because each IP address is limited to 32 bits, the maximum number of IP addresses is 4,294,967,296 or 2^{32}.

As you can imagine, simply claiming ownership over certain IP addresses wouldn't work too well. You could do it for your own organization, but as soon as you wanted to communicate with someone else, you would have no guarantee that there would not be an IP address collision somewhere. In other words, you would have no guarantee, for example, that 56.164.2.32 did not exist somewhere else.

This is where the Internet Assigned Numbers Authority (IANA) steps in. This organization is responsible for assigning IP address ranges to various organizations or regions. Typically, it does so by region, although legacy rules permit several private organizations to have their own top-level IP address space, but this is not done any more except for specific needs. The current list of network assignments is available at *http://www.iana.org/assignments/ipv4-address-space/ipv4-address-space.xml*. This list, as you can see if you check it out, contains only class A networks that the IANA has assigned.

There's that word "class" network again. There are five different network classes, only three of which you will be concerned about. Table 1.1 summarizes IP network classes A, B, and C.

Table 1.1: IP network classes			
Class	Bits in network	Bits for hosts	Max hosts
A	8	24	16,777,214
B	16	16	65,534
C	24	8	254

These three classes refer to how many bits in the 32-bit address you can allocate. Network classes are not generally used on the Internet any more, having been abandoned in favor of Classless Inter-Domain Routing (CIDR), but many organizations still follow this method.

The size restriction is managed by something called a subnet mask. What the subnet mask does is tell the router which bits of the IP address belong on which network.

We can actually demonstrate this structure using bitwise operations in PHP. Let's assume that there are three class C networks. They will be 192.168.0.0/24, 192.168.1.0/24, and 192.168.2.0/24. There will also be an IP address, 192.168.2.35. Looking at these numbers, it is easy for us to tell which network the IP address is on. But can PHP tell? Not without a fair amount of work, unless we use bitwise operations on the address. Figure 1.3 shows some code you could use to do netmask calculations in PHP.

```php
// The netmask tells us which parts of the IP address
// are the network and which are on part of the host.
// The bitwise & operation lets us tell PHP which part
// of the IP address we need to be checking.

$netMask    = ip2long('255.255.255.0');
$host       = ip2long('192.168.2.35');
$networks   = array('192.168.0.0', '192.168.1.0',
                    '192.168.2.0');

// Iterate over the networks
foreach ($networks as $network) {

    // Convert the network to a PHP int
    $network = ip2long($network);

    // Check whether the bitwise & produces the same
    // result for both the host and the network
    if (($host & $netMask) == ($network & $netMask)) {
        echo long2ip($host)
            . " is on network "
            . long2ip($network);
        exit;
    }
}

echo "Unknown route";
```

Figure 1.3: Calculating which network a host is on

This code prints out the following result:

```
192.168.2.35 is on network 192.168.2.0
```

At this point, you will either be saying "Aha!" or be starting to see it but not quite there yet. In case you are still working through it, let's add some debug information using the **decbin()** function to the script (Figure 1.4).

```php
// The netmask tells us which parts of the IP address
// are the network and which are on part of the host.
// The bitwise & operation lets us tell PHP which part
// of the IP address we need to be checking.

$netMask    = ip2long('255.255.255.0');
$host       = ip2long('192.168.2.35');
$networks   = array('192.168.0.0', '192.168.1.0',
                    '192.168.2.0');

echo decbin($host & $netMask) . " Host netmasked\n\n";

foreach ($networks as $network) {
    $printNetwork = $network;
    $network = ip2long($network);

    echo decbin($network)
        . " Network ({$printNetwork})\n";
    echo decbin($network & $netMask)
        . " Network netmasked\n";

    if (($host & $netMask) == ($network & $netMask)) {
        echo '\n' . long2ip($host)
            . " is on network "
            . long2ip($network);
        exit;
    }
}

echo "Unknown route";
```

Figure 1.4: Calculating which network a host is on with debug enhancement

Figure 1.5 shows the output that results.

```
11000000101010000000001000000000 Host netmasked

11000000101010000000000000000000 Network (192.168.0.0)
11000000101010000000000000000000 Network netmasked
11000000101010000000000100000000 Network (192.168.1.0)
11000000101010000000000100000000 Network netmasked
11000000101010000000001000000000 Network (192.168.2.0)
11000000101010000000001000000000 Network netmasked

192.168.2.35 is on network 192.168.2.0
```

Figure 1.5: Output with debug enhancement

The first line here is what the host looks like in binary notation once it has been compared against the netmask using the bitwise AND (**&**) operation. What we do after that is take each of our networks and perform the **&** operation on it; if the network matches the netmasked IP address, we have found our network.

Networking then can often go one step further, using a process called subnetting. Subnetting takes place when you take a class A, B, or C network and split it up into non-defined segments. For example, a class C network can have a maximum of 254 machines on it. But what happens if you need to split that network between departments, say marketing and IT, that really have no business touching each other?

You have two options. The first option is to trust that nobody in IT is ever going to do anything to marketing's network. The other option is to split the class C network into two or more subnets. You do the latter by taking some of the additional bits that are left from the original class of the network and assigning them to one of the departments.

Because you are limited to working with bits, you cannot be specific as to how many IP addresses have been assigned to a given subnet. This can be calculated simply by switching one bit at a time from the end of the 32-bit IP address to a zero. On a class C network, that means that the only possible netmask options are those listed in Table 1.2.

Table 1.2: Class C netmasks
Class C netmasks
255.255.255.252
255.255.255.248
255.255.255.240
255.255.255.224
255.255.255.192
255.255.255.128

Subnetmask 255.255.255.254 is also available. But because each subnet needs to have one IP address as the network endpoint and one IP address for broadcasting packets to the subnet, the 255.255.255.254 subnetmask is mostly useless to you.

Let's take our original program for calculating netmasks and add support for subnets as well as netmasks other than for class A, B, or C networks. Figure 1.6 shows the code for the modified program.

```
$host          = ip2long('192.168.0.35');

$networks      = array(
    '192.168.0.0'      => '255.255.255.248',
    '192.168.0.16'     => '255.255.255.192',
    '192.168.1.0'      => '255.255.255.0'
);

echo "Host: " . long2ip($host) . "\n\n";

foreach ($networks as $network => $netmask) {
    $printNetwork = $network;
    $printNetmask = $netmask;
    $network = ip2long($network);
    $netmask = ip2long($netmask);

    echo "Network: {$printNetwork}
          Netmask: {$printNetmask}\n";
    echo decbin($host & $netmask)
        . " Host netmasked: {$printNetmask}\n";
```

```
     echo decbin($network) . " Network\n";
     echo decbin($network & $netmask)
          . " Network netmasked\n";

     if (($host & $netmask) == ($network & $netmask)) {
          echo '\n' . long2ip($host)
               . " is on network "
               . long2ip($network);
          exit;
     }
     echo "\n";
}
```

Figure 1.6: Calculating host/netmask relationship, revised example

Figure 1.7 shows the resulting output.

```
Host: 192.168.0.35

Network: 192.168.0.0 Netmask: 255.255.255.248
11000000101010000000000000100000 Host netmasked: 255.255.255.248
11000000101010000000000000000000 Network
11000000101010000000000000000000 Network netmasked

Network: 192.168.0.16 Netmask: 255.255.255.192
11000000101010000000000000000000 Host netmasked: 255.255.255.192
11000000101010000000000000010000 Network
11000000101010000000000000000000 Network netmasked

192.168.0.35 is on network 192.168.0.16
```

Figure 1.7: Revised example output

Using this calculation, you can now determine the subnetwork on which an IP address resides.

At this point, you might be asking yourself, "As a Web developer, why am I going through this in the first place?" There are several reasons:

- Because you should. Many PHP developers just assume that the network is there without knowing the underlying concepts. Although it may not always be necessary to have that knowledge, it will make you more aware of network-related issues you may encounter.

- The security concept of Defense in Depth posits that a security implementation should have multiple layers. This design lets you add a networking component to your overall security implementation should you need it.

- You could provide different content for people who are on a specific network (e.g., a competitor).

- By understanding some of the basics of networking, you can build better, faster, more secure, more interesting network services. From Web services to your own binary protocols, an understanding of basic network concepts helps you to write better programs.

Reserved IP Addresses

Several reserved IP addresses are regulated by the IANA. These addresses will not be assigned to any given organization. Table 1.3 lists these IP addresses, with their respective CIDR address block and a brief description of their use.

Table 1.3: CIDR address blocks	
CIDR address block	**Description**
0.0.0.0/8	Current network; usually used to listen on all local interfaces.
10.0.0.0/8	Private class A network; you are free to use this address block internally in your organization.
14.0.0.0/8	Public data networks; this is a class A network that is used for transmission of public information. Some examples include telephone service connections and financial transactions.
127.0.0.0/8	Loopback; your local host.
128.0.0.0/16	Reserved, but may have IP addresses granted to a Regional Internet Registry.
169.254.0.0/16	Link-Local; used for local data traffic, such as on a wireless local network, between individuals on the same physical device. You may notice that if your Windows machine does not get an IP address from the DHCP, it defaults to having an IP address on this network.

Table 1.3: CIDR address blocks, continued	
CIDR address block	**Description**
172.16.0.0/12	Private class B network.
191.255.0.0/16	Reserved, but may have IP addresses granted to a Regional Internet Registry.
192.0.0.0/24	Reserved, but may have IP addresses granted to a Regional Internet Registry.
192.0.2.0/24	Used for test applications and documentation references.
192.88.99.0/24	Used when connecting a local IPv6 network to an IPv4 WAN.
192.168.0.0/16	Private network.
198.18.0.0/15	Network benchmark tests.
223.255.255.0/24	Reserved, but may have IP addresses granted to a Regional Internet Registry.
224.0.0.0/4	Used for multicasting.
240.0.0.0/4	Reserved and not really used.
255.255.255.255	Broadcast.

The CIDR address block is simply the netmask stated in a single numerical term that denotes how many bits constitute the network bits. For example, 192.168.0.0/24 refers to network 192.168.0.1 with a netmask of 255.255.255.0.

IP addresses outside this group will be either provided by the IANA or subnetted to you via your Internet access provider.

The UDP Protocol

One of the simplest network protocols is the User Datagram Packet protocol. UDP is a packet in the simplest sense. Your application basically throws the packet onto the network and forgets about it.

There are a few drawbacks to UDP. First, you have no handshake. Because of that, your application has no idea whether the packet has been delivered to the recipient, whereas in TCP it does. The second problem is that there is no error correction. You have error detection through the use of an optional (in IPv4) checksum, but no error correction. If you want error correction or guaranteed delivering of data in UDP, you will need to build it yourself.

One of UDP's biggest advantages is speed. The handshake for TCP can be the cause of a fairly significant amount of overhead. In one test I did several years back examining the performance of KeepAlive in HTTP, I saw a difference in overall performance of the Web server by a factor of 4. In other words, using KeepAlive, the server was four times faster with UDP. While TCP differs in implementation from UDP, this analysis illustrates the potential overhead involved in doing the TCP handshake. Keeping TCP connections open for long periods of time does have drawbacks, but we'll discuss those later.

So, why use UDP? I think that PHP, because it has a shared-nothing architecture, has more use for UDP than other languages that can pool connections. Yes, you could use the **pfsockopen()** function to open up a socket that persists between requests, but because any kind of persistence in PHP is managed on the process level, you could end up easily overwhelming the server to which you are sending data.

Another question is, "When should you use UDP?" In my mind, there are three qualifications. First, does every packet *need* to be received? Second, is speed a high concern? And third, is error correction important? If you answer no, yes, and no to these questions, UDP is a good candidate. You may have other considerations, but these are the basic ones.

What kind of services might be candidates for UDP?

- A cluster-wide hit counter

- A server heartbeat

- Any kind of streaming data

For an example, let's take a look at the first application, a cluster-wide hit counter. The code for our hit counter, shown in Figure 1.8, is quite simple.

```
Hello World
<?php

$res = fsockopen('udp://192.168.0.1:10000');
fputs($res, $_SERVER['REMOTE_ADDR']);
```

Figure 1.8: UDP cluster-wide hit counter

Calling the specified URL produces the output shown in Figure 1.9.

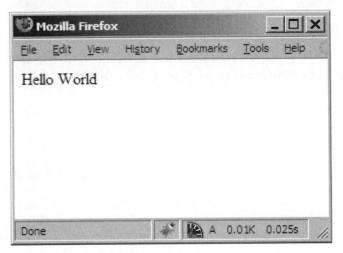

Figure 1.9: Hit counter output

So, it works. And there's no indication of an error and no timeout, even though we have not built our server yet. However, if I open up the Wireshark packet analyzer on my local machine, I see that the packet was indeed sent (Figure 1.10).

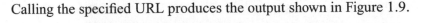

```
⊞ Frame 7 (51 bytes on wire, 51 bytes captured)
⊞ Ethernet II, Src: Usi_94:7e:1b (00:21:86:94:7e:1b), Dst: IntelCor_09:99:af (00:13:20:09:99:af)
⊞ Internet Protocol, Src: 192.168.0.84 (192.168.0.84), Dst: 192.168.0.1 (192.168.0.1)
⊟ User Datagram Protocol, Src Port: 14692 (14692), Dst Port: ndmp (10000)
    Source port: 14692 (14692)
    Destination port: ndmp (10000)
    Length: 17
  ⊞ Checksum: 0x23f5 [correct]
⊟ Data (9 bytes)
    Data: 3132372E302E302E31
```

Figure 1.10: Wireshark output

In the Data portion of this output, you see that the data does not match what we sent. That's because Wireshark prints the ASCII data in hexadecimal. The **REMOTE_ADDR** value in this case was **127.0.0.1**. **0x31** is 1, **0x32** is 2, **0x37** is 7, and so on.

That's our client, and it's very simple. Let's take a look at our server.

The server is a little more complicated. I took a bit of a shortcut by using the **fsockopen()** function on the client because it hid some of the implementation details and also because it works with the "vanilla" PHP installation. With the server — or "aggregator" might be a better term — we have no such luxury.

In the aggregator, we need to make sure that the sockets extension is available and installed. It is included with the default PHP installation, and turning it on is as easy as setting **extension=php_sockets.dll** or **extension= sockets.so**.

There are several things you need to do to create a listening socket for UDP:

1. Create the socket with **socket_create()**.

2. Bind the socket to a specific IP address and port with **socket_bind()**.

3. Read from the socket with **socket_read()**.

If you are somewhat familiar with sockets, you might be wondering what happened to accept, listen, or something of that nature. These functions are used for dealing with connection-oriented protocols. UDP is not such a protocol, so we do not need a separate resource to read from the client socket (because it doesn't exist).

To see how to read data from a UDP socket, let's take a look at the aggregator code (Figure 1.11). Note that the examples are designed to run over the local interface only. The previous example used 192.168.0.1 so the packet could be sniffed off the network.

```
ini_set('error_reporting',0);

$sock = socket_create(AF_INET, SOCK_DGRAM, SOL_UDP);
if (!$sock) die('Unable to create socket');
if (!socket_bind($sock, 'localhost', 10000))
        die('Unable to bind socket');

socket_set_option(
        $sock ,
        SOL_SOCKET ,
        SO_RCVTIMEO ,
        array(
                'sec'           => 1,
                'usec'          => 0
        )
);
```

```
$counter = 0;
$time = time();

while (true) {

        $data = socket_read($sock, 16);
        if ($time < time()) {
                echo "Requests last second: {$counter}\n";
                $counter = 0;
                $time = time();
        }
        if ($data !== false) {
                $counter++;
        }

}
```

Figure 1.11: Reading from a UDP socket

The first socket piece of code we come upon is where we create the socket itself. This is done before binding to a given IP address/port combination. That is how we specify the type that the socket is going to be.

The first **socket_create()** parameter is the address family. This value tells PHP what general type of socket it will be. What we enter here will limit the types of sockets we can create. You *could* say that this parameter specifies the nature of the network layer that will be used. Table 1.4 lists the three available options for the address family.

Table 1.4: Address type constants	
Address family type	**Notes**
AF_INET	The standard IPv4 address. This is the typical 4 octet that you would be familiar with.
AF_INET6	The next-generation Internet protocol. You will typically not be typing in an IPv6 address.
AF_UNIX	A Unix domain socket. Based on the name, you can assume that this family type is used on Unix systems only. It is designed for very fast machine local data transfer.

The second **socket_create()** parameter specifies the type of socket that will be used. There are five options for socket type. Table 1.5 lists the three we will look at here, only two of which you might actually use in a production environment.

Table 1.5: Socket constants	
Socket type	**Notes**
SOCK_STREAM	A sequenced, reliable, error-corrected network stream. TCP is based on this type. Use it if you need packets to arrive in order with guaranteed delivery of data.
SOCK_DGRAM	Used for datagram protocols (i.e., connectionless without guaranteed delivery), such as UDP.
SOCK_RAW	Used if you want to manually build the protocol you want to use. Could be lots of fun, but not all that practical. You can use this type for ICMP-based requests.

The third **socket_create()** parameter sets the actual protocol that will be used to facilitate communications. This is like specifying which level 4, or transport layer, protocol you're going to use. In PHP, we have three options:

- **SOL_TCP** for TCP/IP connections

- **SOL_UDP** for UDP datagrams

- **SOL_ICMP** for ICMP messages

Once we create the socket, we need to tell the operating system where we want it to listen for incoming packets. We do this with the **socket_bind()** function. This function has two required parameters and one optional parameter.

The first required parameter is the socket that will be bound to the IP address. The second parameter is the address to which to bind; this will be either your IPv4 or IPv6 address or the file name for a Unix domain socket. The third parameter, which specifies the port, is optional because not all protocols require a port. The ICMP and Unix domain sockets are port-less and so do not require a port.

The last socket-specific element we specify is how we read the data in to the application. Because this is a UDP-based application, we do not need to get a client-side socket; we only need to read from the server socket. And so we call **socket_read()**, limiting ourselves to 16 bytes of data because the maximum number of characters in an IP address is 15. With UDP, if **socket_read()** is told to read an insufficient number of bytes from the socket, it will fail, returning **false** as a value.

Figure 1.12 shows the test result received with 5,000 requests issued over 10 concurrent connections, using the Apache Benchmark tool (**ab**).

```
Requests last second: 0
Requests last second: 0
Requests last second: 0
Requests last second: 0
Requests last second: 226
Requests last second: 348
Requests last second: 640
Requests last second: 652
Requests last second: 331
Requests last second: 266
Requests last second: 242
Requests last second: 432
Requests last second: 259
Requests last second: 545
Requests last second: 635
Requests last second: 424
```

Figure 1.12: UDP server output

There is one other thing to note in this example. That is setting the timeout. The **socket_read()** function does not have a timeout option, so we set a read timeout on the socket level using **socket_set_option()**. The reason for this timeout is the **0** numbers in the resulting output. Without the timeout set so that **socket_read()** could return without having data, we would have no output for seconds where no data had been retrieved, causing gaps in our data. By setting the read timeout on the socket level, we can do calculations when no traffic had occurred.

In addition, the example uses the **ini_set()** function to turn off error reporting for this test. That's because when a socket timeout occurs, an **E_WARNING** notice is thrown. As an alternative, you could simply suppress errors for the **socket_read()** operation.

The TCP Protocol

In many respects, TCP is the exact opposite of UDP. It has guaranteed delivery (as far as the network is concerned). It has error correction, not just error detection. And it has streaming. With a fair degree of certainty (barring man-in-the-middle attacks), you can be sure that the next packet on a stream did, in fact, come from the same host as the one before. Not only that, but you can be guaranteed that the packet that you are reading is supposed to be the next packet in sequence, whereas with UDP packets can arrive out of order because UDP does not track the sequence of packets.

Those are great benefits, but they come at the price of performance. Compared with UDP, TCP is slower. There is a lot that the protocol needs to do. It needs to establish the connection, which requires at least three packets. The receiver also needs to inform the sender that it has received the data that was sent. If data is lost during the transmission, or if the sender infers that data was lost, the sender will try to retransmit the data until an acknowledgment is received or a timeout is hit.

TCP also manages flow control. In other words, it detects how many packets it can send without overwhelming the receiver. TCP does not wait for an acknowledgment from the receiver that a packet has been received before sending the next. To do so would make TCP immensely slow. Instead, the protocol determines how much data it can send based on responses from the receiver. The sender is responsible for retaining its data until either the receiver indicates that it can handle more in its buffer or a connection timeout occurs.

To initiate a TCP connection, a handshake must occur first. This is done transparently for the application. In PHP, the function responsible for opening the TCP connection typically does not return until the connection has been established with the handshake. The TCP handshake is a three-step process initiated by the client:

1. The client sends a **SYN** packet to the server requesting a connection on a specific port.

2. The server sends a **SYN-ACK** packet to the client, acknowledging the connection request.

3. The client sends an **ACK** packet to the server, acknowledging that it received the acknowledgment.

Once both sides have sent a packet with an **ACK**, the connection is considered open on both sides, and data can be sent. For a connection to exist, two things need to be in place:

- A listening IP address and port on the server
- A receiving IP address and port on the client

The ports that are used are generally divided into three groups:

- Well-known ports: These are ports used for general, important functionality, such as port 25 for Simple Mail Transfer Protocol (SMTP), port 80 for HTTP, or port 443 for secure HTTP (HTTPS).

- Registered ports: These are ports that the IANA manages for usage, typically for a specific protocol that does not have a general application but is important enough that a conflict might occur.

- Dynamic ports: These ports are typically used for private functionality, or functionality that does not need to be exposed to outside applications. Dynamic ports are also used as endpoints for a client.

We make a TCP connection the same way we did a UDP connection. Receiving the connection on the server is done differently, but making the connection is pretty much the same. The only significant difference lies in specifying the protocol used.

In terms of implementation, however, some difference obviously exists with UDP. With UDP, you basically send packets out to the server, hope that they get there, and hope that they get there in order (if that is required). With TCP, you can perform multiple writes to the same sock, and you can be sure that the data arriving at the other end is arriving intact and in order. If that is not the case, TCP tries to retransmit the packets or eventually timeout on the connection.

Let's revisit our hit counter example using TCP instead of UDP. The client script (Figure 1.13) is virtually identical, with the exception of the protocol specified in the **fsockopen()** URL. You can explicitly close the network resource if you like (using **fclose()**), but PHP will also close it automatically during cleanup at the end of the request.

```
Hello World
<?php

$res = fsockopen('tcp://localhost:10000');
fputs($res, $_SERVER['REMOTE_ADDR']);
```

Figure 1.13: UDP cluster-wide hit counter

Figure 1.14 shows the code for the server component.

```
$sock = socket_create(AF_INET, SOCK_STREAM, SOL_TCP);
if (!$sock) die('Unable to create socket');
if (!socket_bind($sock, 'localhost', 10000))
        die('Unable to bind socket');

socket_listen($sock);
$counter = 0;
$time = time();

while (true) {
        $client = socket_accept($sock);

        if ($time < time()) {
                echo "Requests last second: {$counter}\n";
                $counter = 0;
                $time = time();
        }
        if ($client !== false) {
                $data = socket_read($client, 16);
                if ($data !== false) {
                        $counter++;
                }
        }
}
```

Figure 1.14: Reading from TCP sockets

After starting up the aggregator, I ran Apache Benchmark again. This time, the results were quite different (Figure 1.15).

```
Requests last second: 0
Requests last second: 1
Requests last second: 2
Requests last second: 4
Requests last second: 107
Requests last second: 123
Requests last second: 129
Requests last second: 145
Requests last second: 111
Requests last second: 140
Requests last second: 138
Requests last second: 151
Requests last second: 156
Requests last second: 149
Requests last second: 100
Requests last second: 110
```

Figure 1.15: TCP server output

As you can see from this output, the TCP connection was significantly slower than UDP's. This is because the aggregator can receive only one connection at a time using this method. In addition, because the **fsockopen()** is a blocking call and **socket_accept()** is a blocking call, technically only one HTTP request can be served at a time. So, if we have this problem with blocking network requests, what is the solution?

Non-Blocking I/O

Non-blocking I/O means that socket operations will not block if there is nothing for the socket to do. For example, if there is no data for a **socket_read()** operation, the function will simply return rather than waiting for data to become available. You handle non-blocking I/O differently from the way you handle blocking, or normal, I/O. With normal I/O, you might iterate over all the open sockets and call **socket_read()** on each one. Although you can take this approach with non-blocking I/O, this is not how it is intended to be run.

Non-blocking I/O is typically done in conjunction with the **socket_select()** function call. The magic of **socket_select()** is that you pass the function an array of sockets on which you want it to read (or write), and it will provide the sockets that have data waiting at that exact moment. So rather than you waiting for the data, the data is waiting for you.

The **socket_select()** function takes either four or five parameters:

- An array of sockets for reading, passed as a reference. This array will be modified at the end of the **socket_select()** call to contain only sockets that have data to read that would not block.

- An array of sockets available for writing, passed as a reference. If writing to any of the sockets in the list would not block, those sockets will remain in the array reference when it is returned.

- An array of sockets to watch for exceptions, passed as a reference. An example of an exception is out-of-band data. This is data that is from a given client, but not part of the stream.

- The select timeout, or the number of seconds before the call will return, regardless of whether there's data. If the timeout is set to **NULL**, the function will wait indefinitely.

- Optionally, the number of microseconds added to the number of seconds in the timeout.

Figure 1.16 shows our hit aggregator revised to use non-blocking I/O.

```
$sock = socket_create(AF_INET, SOCK_STREAM, SOL_TCP);
if (!$sock) die('Unable to create socket');
if (!socket_bind($sock, 'localhost', 10000))
        die('Unable to bind socket');

socket_listen($sock);
socket_set_nonblock($sock);
$counter = 0;
$time = time();
$sockets = array($sock);

$write = $except = array();
$read = $sockets;
while
  (socket_select($read, $write, $except, 1) !== false) {
        foreach ($read as $client) {
                if ($client === $sock) {
                        $sockets[] = socket_accept($sock);
                } else {
                        $data = socket_read($client, 16);
                        if ($data == false) {
                                $sockets = array_diff(
                                        $sockets ,
                                        array($client)
                                    );
                                socket_close($client);
                        } else {
                                $counter++;
                        }
                }
        }
}
```

```
        if ($time < time()) {
                echo "Requests last second: {$counter}\n";
                $counter = 0;
                $time = time();
        }
        $read = $sockets;
}
```

Figure 1.16: Reading from a non-blocking TCP socket

A few things are of note here. The first is the call to **socket_set_nonblock($sock)**. What this call does is set the socket, on the network layer, to be non-blocking. In this case, we need to do this only on the main socket because we are not doing any writing and the read sockets will be provided only if the socket contains data.

When passing the **$read** sockets to the **socket_select()** function, it is important to also pass the main socket along with every socket you want to have checked. For that reason, we have an array called **$sockets** that is separate from **$read**, which will be modified by the **socket_select()** call. We use this approach so that we can pass **$read** into **socket_select()** and still maintain a master list of sockets.

When the **socket_select()** call returns, **$read** will be an array of all the sockets that have data waiting on them. This may include the main socket if a new connection request has been made. For that reason, the loop includes a check to see whether the socket we're currently looping over is the main socket. If it is, we call a **socket_accept()** on it. This function returns a variable containing the new socket from the client, which we then add to the **$sockets** array so the new socket can have a non-blocking read done on the next iteration over **socket_select()**.

If there is data available on that socket, it will be included in the next iteration in the variable **$read**. Because of that, when we iterate over each of the sockets, we check to see whether the socket is the main socket. If it is *not* the main socket, then it is a client socket and we do a **socket_read()** on it.

We do a type-insensitive comparison on the read data because if **$data** is **false**, it means that an error has occurred and we want to close the socket; if **$data** is an empty string, it means that the client has closed the connection. Either way, we're done with it. So we do an **array_diff()** on the master socket array to omit the closed socket from the array and close it.

The performance benefit of this method becomes apparent when we look at the difference between the blocking I/O method in the previous section and the non-blocking I/O method in this section. Even though our HTTP script is still using blocking I/O, the aggregator is able to handle double the number of requests per second (Figure 1.17).

```
Requests last second: 0
Requests last second: 120
Requests last second: 171
Requests last second: 175
Requests last second: 182
Requests last second: 304
Requests last second: 309
Requests last second: 313
Requests last second: 313
Requests last second: 308
Requests last second: 313
Requests last second: 310
Requests last second: 315
Requests last second: 312
Requests last second: 314
Requests last second: 313
Requests last second: 321
Requests last second: 305
Requests last second: 302
Requests last second: 0
Requests last second: 0
Requests last second: 0
```

Figure 1.17: Non-blocking server output

The ICMP Protocol

The Internet Control Message Protocol is typically used for problem diagnosis and routing purposes. We are all familiar with the ping application. ICMP is the protocol that ping uses to send and receive diagnostic messages back and forth between your machine and a remote host. Although it is not a requirement, machines often will respond to UDP requests on an unbound port with an ICMP message containing a special ICMP code.

Unlike the UDP and TCP protocols, ICMP does not have the concept of a port. There is no port 80 in ICMP. ICMP also, by design, is unreliable. Because it is used for diagnostic purposes, having a reliable protocol is counterproductive. You want to be able to diagnose unreliable machines, right?

What we're going to do in this section is take a look at how you can implement a program that uses ICMP to communicate with other machines.

To build a ping application, we need first to examine the ICMP protocol itself. The protocol is actually very simple, but to understand it you need to be familiar with binary concepts. An ICMP packet is a minimum of eight bytes long with optional data. Because ICMP is connectionless, the data must fit within a single IP frame. Figure 1.18 shows what that frame looks like.

Bits (bytes)	0–15 (0)	16–31 (1)
0 (0)	Message type	Message code
32 (2)	Checksum	
48 (4)	Message ID	
64 (6)	Sequence number	

Figure 1.18: ICMP packet structure

The nice thing is that PHP has a very useful command for handling data like this: **pack()**. Using **pack()**, you can easily read and write binary protocols yourself.

The **pack()** command takes one or more parameters. The first parameter specifies the format, and you use the remaining parameters to substitute into the formatted return value. The **pack()** command is actually very similar to PHP's **sprintf()**, so although you're dealing with binary data, you're working with what probably is a familiar concept to you.

Creating an ICMP packet is as simple as using the following format:

```
'CCnnnA*'
```

Let's break that down a bit. **C** is an unsigned char. A char is basically just an 8-bit value, so it fits in well with our 8-bit message type. Then we have a second **C**, which corresponds to our message code. The **n** is an unsigned short, which is a 16-bit number. That matches well with our checksum, message ID, and sequence number fields, and so we have three **n** values one after another. The last field, **A***, is a space-padded string (in other words, a string). That is exactly what our "optional data" is going to be.

Let's take a look at the code for pinging a host in two stages to make it a little easier. First, Figure 1.19 shows the code that actually makes the ping request.

```
$host = '192.168.0.1';
$message = 'You want to do WHAT with PHP?';
$sock = socket_create(
        AF_INET,
        SOCK_RAW,
        getprotobyname('icmp')
);

$id = rand(0, 0xFFFF);

$packet = pack('CCnnnA*',
        0x08, // Type
        0x00, // Code
        0x00, // Checksum
        $id,  // Unique ID
        0x00, // Sequence Number
        $message // Data
);

if (strlen($packet)%2) $packet .= ' ';
$checkSum = calculateChecksum($packet);
$packet[2] = $checkSum[0];
$packet[3] = $checkSum[1];

socket_sendto(
    $sock,
    $packet,
    strlen($packet),
    0,
    $host,
    0
);
```

Figure 1.19: Sending an ICMP packet

The first thing you might note here is that the **socket_create()** function call now uses the **SOCK_RAW** constant for the socket type. This is so that we can create a raw packet on top of the IP layer. In other words, we are writing data on the same level as UDP and TCP.

To identify message replies, we need to specify a unique ID for this request, which is an echo request. In this case, we create a random number. After that, we use a **pack()** call to build our packet. First, we specify the type of request; **0x08** for an echo request. Next is the optional code. An echo request does not have any subtypes, so we use **0x00**. After that, we put in the checksum, but because at this point we have not built the packet completely, we don't have sufficient data from which to build our checksum, so for the time being we give it a value of **0x00**.

Following the checksum is the unique ID we generated earlier. We'll use this value later to validate the message. After that, we put in the sequence number, which, because we have no sequence, we set to **0x00**. Then, we put in our data. For the purposes of the checksum, our packet needs to fit into 16-bit segments, so we append a space to it if it does not.

At this point, we've built our packet, but we have not done our checksum. That step is handled by the **calculateChecksum()** call. Figure 1.20 shows this function definition. The **calculateChecksum()** function examines all the shorts in the packet, adds them up, and packs the **NOT** bits into a single 16-bit short.

```
function calculateChecksum($packet) {
    $bitsOf16 = unpack('n*', $packet);
    $checkSum = array_sum($bitsOf16);
    $checkSum = ($checkSum >> 16) + ($checkSum & 0xffff);
    $checkSum += ($checkSum >> 16);
    return pack('n*', ~$checkSum);
}
```

Figure 1.20: Calculating an ICMP checksum

Once the checksum has been calculated, we take the first and second bytes, place them into the third and forth bytes in the packet, and send the packet on its way.

A ping is mostly pointless without having some kind of acknowledgment that the ping was received. For that purpose, we're going to use the **socket_recvfrom()** function. Figure 1.21 shows how we implement this. The **socket_recvfrom()** function requires only a socket and a host. The port is not as important, which makes **socket_recvfrom()** a good option here.

```
socket_set_option(
        $sock ,
        SOL_SOCKET ,
        SO_RCVTIMEO ,
        array(
                'sec'      => 1,
                'usec'     => 0
        )
);

$port = 0;
$res
    = socket_recvfrom($sock, $packet, 255, 0,
                      $host, $port);

if ($res === false) die('No reply received');

// First clear off the IP protocol data
$packet = substr($packet, 20);

$data = unpack(
    'Ctype/Ccode/nchecksum/nid/nsequence/C*message',
    $packet
);

if ($data['type'] !== 0x00) {
        die('Type should be 0x00 (Echo Reply)');
} else if ($data['id'] != $id) {
        die('Reply received was not for this request');
}
$packet[2] = pack('C', 0x00);
$packet[3] = pack('C', 0x00);
$checkSum
    = unpack('nchecksum', calculateChecksum($packet));

if ($data['checksum'] !== $checkSum['checksum']) {
        die('Checksum failed');
}
```

```
$replyMessage = '';
foreach ($data as $key => $value) {
        if (strpos($key, 'message') === 0) {
                $replyMessage .= chr($value);
        }
}

if (trim($replyMessage) == trim($message)) {
        echo 'Valid PING message';
} else {
        echo 'PING message failed';
}
```

Figure 1.21: Ping

The first thing we do is set the socket option to time out after one second. If the function has not received a proper packet response from the requested host in this amount of time, it will return false. If that happens, we exit the program with an error.

Next, we strip off the IP data. If data is returned, it will include the IP headers. Because we don't need those, we strip off those 20 bytes.

If we do receive a response, we parse it according to the same packet structure we had before because the ICMP packet structure does not change. However, there is something different about this — it's a lot longer! That's because the result of the **unpack()** operation needs to be able to assign data to an associative array. To read this packet, we take the same format we had before and add names for each format option, separating them with a slash character (/). Upon successful receipt of a valid packet, **$data** contains the values shown in Figure 1.22.

```
array(35) {
  ["type"]=>
  int(0)
  ["code"]=>
  int(0)
  ["checksum"]=>
  int(2470)
  ["id"]=>
  int(64932)
  ["sequence"]=>
```

```
int(0)
["message1"]=>
int(89)
["message2"]=>
int(111)
["message3"]=>
int(117)
["message4"]=>
int(32)
. . .and so on and so forth
```

Figure 1.22: unpack() of ICMP response

The first thing we check is the type, which should be **0x00**, or "echo reply." Next, we check the ID to make sure that the response is being received for the right request. After that, we reset the checksum bytes in the received packet. Why would we do that? Because the checksum was originally calculated without the checksum. So, to check the checksum, we need to check against the data against which the checksum was calculated, which did not contain a checksum.

So, we generate the checksum and unpack it so it is in the same format as the checksum in the original packet. It is upon that that we do our checksum comparison. If the checksum generated by the responding machine is the same as the one we generated, the likelihood of packet corruption is pretty low.

The echo response takes a little bit of work to extract. Because **unpack()** returns data only in a single-digit response, we need to concatenate all the array keys that start with the word **message**. Once we've done that, we take that message and compare it with the original message. If all looks good, we will see:

```
Valid PING message
```

Sending to a Broadcast Address

As I noted earlier, subnets have a reserved IP address for handling broadcast packets. Calculating the broadcast is done by taking the host part of the IP address and turning all the bits on. That is your broadcast address for a given subnet.

For example, my network is 192.168.0.1 with a netmask of 255.255.255.0. That means my broadcast address is 192.168.0.255. Notice that my broadcast address is my inverted netmask bitwise **OR**ed against the host IP address. However, you don't actually need the network IP address to calculate the broadcast address. If you are on a class C network, it *will* be a certain address. However, if you are doing subnetting, you might need to calculate it. And you can do that by using your host IP address. Figure 1.23 demonstrates how to do it using my host address of 192.168.0.35.

```
$host = ip2long('192.168.0.35');
$netmask = ip2long('255.255.255.0');
$broadcast = $host | ~$netmask;

echo 'Host: ' . decbin($host) . "\n";
echo 'Netmask: ' . decbin($netmask) . "\n";
echo 'Broadcast: ' . decbin($broadcast) . "\n";
echo 'Broadcast IP: ' . long2ip($broadcast) . "\n";
```

Figure 1.23: Calculating the broadcast address

This code echoes:

```
Host: 11000000101010000000000000100011
Netmask: 11111111111111111111111100000000
Broadcast: 11000000101010000000000011111111
Broadcast IP: 192.168.0.255
```

The "magic" is in line 3, with the broadcast being **OR**ed against the **BITNOT** of the netmask. In English, we take the netmask and invert the bits so zeros are ones and ones are zeros, and then we apply a bitwise **OR** to the operation. The result will be a value in which the bits are turned on if they are on *either* the left side or the right side of the **OR** operator. Say I'm not on a 255.255.255.0 network but a 255.255.255.192 network instead. My broadcast address will be different because I have a fewer number of bits that I can turn on (Figure 1.24).

```
$host = ip2long('192.168.0.35');
$netmask = ip2long('255.255.255.192');
$broadcast = $host | ~$netmask;

echo 'Host: ' . decbin($host) . "\n";
echo 'Netmask: ' . decbin($netmask) . "\n";
echo 'Broadcast: ' . decbin($broadcast) . "\n";
echo 'Broadcast IP: ' . long2ip($broadcast) . "\n";
```

Figure 1.24: Calculating broadcast address with a netmask

This code echoes:

```
Host: 11000000101010000000000000100011
Netmask: 11111111111111111111111111000000
Broadcast: 11000000101010000000000000111111
Broadcast IP: 192.168.0.63
```

My broadcast IP address on my local subnet, with a netmask of 255.255.255.192, is 192.168.0.63.

Sounds interesting and all, but what is the practical application of this? One example is a heartbeat. Say you built some software that needs to know who is running it. For each installed version of the software, you could have a service running on a certain port and listening for UDP datagrams. The heartbeat monitor would send out a ping using UDP (not ICMP; we'll look at that in a bit). This ping would be received by each server on the network with a service running on that port, or it would be ignored if the service is not running. Upon receiving the UDP packet, the server would respond with an acknowledgment.

To illustrate this functionality, let's look at a simple heartbeat script that we can run on any number of machines that will all detect each other as soon as the service is brought up (Figure 1.25).

```php
$broadcastIP = '192.168.0.255';
$broadcastPort = 10000;

$sock = socket_create(AF_INET, SOCK_DGRAM, SOL_UDP);
if (!$sock) die('Unable to create socket');
if (!socket_bind($sock, 0, 10000))
        die('Unable to bind socket');

socket_set_option(
        $sock ,
        SOL_SOCKET ,
        SO_RCVTIMEO ,
        array(
                'sec'       => 1,
                'usec'      => 0
        )
);

$addr = array();
$time = time();

while (true) {

    $data = @socket_read($sock, 255);
    if ($data !== false) {
            $addr[$data] = 1;
    }
    if ($time < time()) {
        echo "\n";
        foreach (array_keys($addr) as $host) {
                echo "Heard from {$host}\n";
        }
        $time = time();
        $addr = array();
        // Re-announce myself

        $computerName = isset($_SERVER['COMPUTERNAME'])
                            ? $_SERVER['COMPUTERNAME']
                            : $_SERVER['HOSTNAME'];
        $announceSock = socket_create(
                            AF_INET, SOCK_DGRAM, SOL_UDP);
        socket_set_option(
            $announceSock,
            SOL_SOCKET,
            SO_BROADCAST,
            1
        );
```

```
        socket_sendto(
                // The broadcast socket to announce on
                $announceSock,
                // Our name
                $computerName,
                // Length of our payload
                strlen($computerName),
                // Send options. We have none
                0,
                // The IP address to send to
                $broadcastIP,
                // The port to send to
                $broadcastPort
        );

    }

}
```

Figure 1.25: Sending to a broadcast address

What this script does is listen on all local IP addresses (you can't listen on a broadcast address) on port 10000 for incoming datagrams. The **0** in the **socket_bind()** operation is there so that PHP will listen on all available interfaces. From there, we reuse our timeout code to make sure we go through the loop at least once every second.

In the loop, we read incoming packets from the socket and, once a second, pause to echo who we heard from and clear that array for the next round of heartbeats. Because each machine needs to send a heartbeat once a second, this is also a good time to re-announce the machine to the network. This is where we change strategies a little from our earlier UDP hit counter example. Instead of using **fsockopen()**, we use **socket_sendto()**. The reason for this is because Linux does not like sending messages to broadcast IP addresses without the socket being explicitly defined as a broadcast socket. To address that, we tell Linux that it's a broadcast socket via the **socket_set_option()** call.

After setting the option, we can deliver our payload. Because it will be sent to the broadcast address, it will go to all IP addresses in the subnet. Figure 1.26 shows the script in action running on the host "server."

```
Heard from server

Heard from server

Heard from server

Heard from server
Heard from LAPTOP

Heard from server
Heard from LAPTOP

Heard from server
Heard from LAPTOP
```

Figure 1.26: Heartbeat script running on host "server"

As you can surmise from this output, I started the script first on my server. Three seconds later, I started it on my laptop. The output on **LAPTOP** was pretty much the same thing.

As a side note, TCP definitely is not practical for broadcast messages. TCP needs to have two endpoints: one for the server and one for the client. A broadcast message can have multiple clients, so you would end up having a server trying to do handshakes with multiple clients on the same port. That wouldn't work too well. Save yourself the hassle, and use UDP for broadcast messages. If you need to use TCP for something like this, you would need to build a TCP relayer or replayer.

Unix Domain Sockets

Unix Domain Sockets are typically used for low-overhead, local communications. They generally are acted upon just like a normal file. When you read that last sentence, make sure you emphasize the word "generally." Obviously, Unix Domain Sockets don't work on Windows, because Windows isn't Unix. There are some drivers that can allow Unix Domain Sockets on Windows, but don't count on them being installed. It's usually best to stick with what the operating system does natively anyway.

Unix Domain Sockets are implemented on the file system level, which means you have access to many of the security features of your Unix system. Also, because they are on the file system level, Unix Domain Sockets are very fast. You don't have the intermediary of the networking system, on top of the network protocol, that needs to be handled. And because Unix Domain Sockets are local, reliability does not have to have as big of a focus because if the kernel cannot send data reliably between two points within itself, you have bigger problems than data reliability.

In terms of actual speed, it depends on what you're doing. If you're performing simple streaming operations, such as keeping connections open for long periods of time and sending data, TCP keeps up with the Unix sockets. However, if you're doing very short open and closes on a socket, Unix Domain Sockets are about 25 percent faster.

Implementing a Unix Domain Sockets server is actually quite easy. We use the same calls we did when creating TCP sockets. There are only a few lines in our aggregator code that we need to change.

Figure 1.27 shows the code used in the previous examples.

```
$sock = socket_create(AF_INET, SOCK_STREAM, SOL_TCP);
if (!$sock) die('Unable to create socket');
if (!socket_bind($sock, 'localhost', 10000))
        die('Unable to bind socket');
```

Figure 1.27: Connecting to a TCP socket

Figure 1.28 shows the modified code to connect to a Unix socket.

```
$sock = socket_create(AF_UNIX, SOCK_STREAM, 0);
if (!$sock) die('Unable to create socket');
if (!socket_bind($sock, '/tmp/server.sock'))
        die('Unable to bind socket');
```

Figure 1.28: Connecting to a Unix socket

By making this simple change, we can use those Unix Domain Sockets to handle communications between processes on a local machine. This method is often used for interprocess communications. For example, Syslog uses Unix sockets, as do Cyrus, MySQL, and Sendmail. Anything that has an interface that requires simple, local, fast access is a candidate for using Unix sockets.

Conclusion

In this chapter, we have covered some of the things you can do with sockets and PHP. Some of the concepts we've explored are not the typical ones you see with PHP, such as using ICMP. Nonetheless, if you want to better build complex, scalable, or simply more advanced code, these subjects are useful for you to know. And as we go through some of the more advanced topics in this book, you will see how a lot of this "low-level" networking can actually benefit you as you start using PHP for more than building Web sites connected to a database.

Binary Protocols

In the words of game programmer and software entrepreneur John Carmack, "Low-level programming is good for the programmer's soul." What we'll be talking about in this chapter might not technically be "low-level" programming, but PHP developers don't spend time with device layers, kernel instructions, or hardware acceleration. For us, low-level programming means activities such as working with bits or adjusting the saturation of an image. Our work tends to be much wider in scope than that of other programmers, and because of that, we leave much of this type of work to the people who develop libraries for lower-level functionality. But learning some of the basics of lower-level programming can help us to be more thoughtful in how we approach higher-level problems.

The Basics

Most PHP programmers are not very familiar with binary protocols. In my experience, if you have a decent understanding of how to work with a binary protocol, you are in the minority. That's not to say that PHP or Web developers lack an essential skill. Binary protocols — such as Domain Name Service (DNS), Network File System (NFS), and Telnet — just aren't that important to Web developers. Web developers deal primarily with text-based data, such as Hypertext Markup Language (HTML) or Extensible Markup Language (XML). True, we may need to manipulate images using the GD Graphics Library or write data to the file system, but seldom do we actually work with bits and bytes.

The typical Web developer is limited to working directly with HTML, Cascading Style Sheets (CSS), JavaScript, XML, and the like. None of these are binary protocols. None requires you to manipulate data on a byte-by-byte basis. If you're handling anything like that, it is probably limited to some kind of ASCII character, such as a word character (a–z, A–Z, 0–9, and _) or a forward slash (/).

So what we're going to do in this chapter is examine some basic binary protocols to give you an idea of how to work with them. The techniques illustrated here are shown to give PHP developers a *better chance* of being able to apply them. This means that any C developer who reads this and says, "That's not how you should do it," is probably going to be right. But we'll be looking at these solutions in a way that is appropriate for PHP developers.

Hex

The first basic concept we'll tackle is the hexadecimal representation. Examining hex before binary may seem a little counterintuitive, but hexadecimal is the language you will be talking in most. As you saw in the networking chapter, binary operations are definitely important. However, you will be spending most of your time working with hexadecimal values.

As you probably know, hexadecimal is an alphanumeric representation of a 4-bit word and is typically represented with the prefix 0x. A single-digit hexadecimal representation starts with 0x0 (the numerical zero) and goes to 0xF (the numerical 15). The number 16 is represented by 0x10. 17 is 0x11, and so forth. A full byte — that is, a byte with all the digits set to 1 — is represented as 0xFF, or 255 in base 10 notation.

In terms of representing character values, what you use is highly dependent on the character set you are working with. Most likely it will be ASCII or UTF-8, but there have been times when I've had to use EBCDIC, which definitely does not render in the same way as either of those encoding schemes. The network protocol sees no difference between EBCDIC and UTF-8. To the network, it's all hex. Actually, that's not true. It's all binary. Hexadecimal is just the typical length of either the data or the options you'll work with in the protocol. As such, it makes for a good concept to get to know.

Bitwise Operations

The second concept to be familiar with is that of bitwise operations. Use of bitwise operations would seem to contradict my earlier statement about hexadecimal being a major component of binary protocols. And considering the amount of space we're going to spend on bit-based operations, it might also seem as though binary-based work will be more important. However, this is more because my experience has taught me that most PHP developers have a decent understanding of hexadecimal concepts but are less familiar with bit-based concepts.

One of the things you can do with binary-level protocols is pack a lot information into a very small area. In the space of a single character, you could pack 16 options that you could turn on and off at will in combination with other options, validate payload data, or specify the length of a variable-length field.

You may think to yourself, "Couldn't you pack 255 options into a single character?" The answer would be no. You can have 255 options, but you can pack only one of those options into that single-character field. Using bitwise operations lets you have 16 individual options, *each* of which could be turned on in that single byte.

Table 2.1 lists the six individual bitwise operations that are available to you.

Table 2.1: Bitwise operations	
Operation	**Description**
AND	Returns an integer that represents all the bits that are turned on in both numbers.
OR	Returns an integer that represents all the bits that are turned on in either number.
XOR	Returns an integer that represents all the bits that are turned on in one number but not in the other.
NOT	Returns an integer that represents the inverse of the bits in one number.
Shift left	Returns an integer that has the currently set bits shifted *n* places to the left. Existing on bits are either discarded (if on the left) or set to zero (if on the right).
Shift right	Returns an integer that has the currently set bits shifted *n* places to the right. Existing on bits are either discarded (if on the right) or set to zero (if on the left).

Note that I state that the bitwise operations return an integer value. However, the actual value of the integer is seldom of importance to you. In general, it is the individual bits that you are interested in.

Let's examine the individual operators and see what they look like.

OR

First, let's consider the bitwise OR. This operation is represented by the | operator. This operator is different from the || operator, which is used to evaluate a Boolean OR. A Boolean is not the same as a bitwise OR. A Boolean OR returns a Boolean true if one of the conditions evaluates to true. A bitwise OR returns a number when bits in either of the numbers are set to **ON**.

We look at OR first because it is quite common to use the bitwise OR on the client side to pack all our options together. For our examples, we'll pretend to write a server that supports several different versions of a certain protocol. When a client sends a handshake request to the server, it includes the bits of all the individual protocols that it supports. Figure 2.1 shows the code for this example.

```php
define('OPT_V1',    0x01);
define('OPT_V2',    0x02);
define('OPT_V3',    0x04);
define('OPT_V4',    0x08);

echo 'Version 1: ' . writeBits(OPT_V1) . "\n";
echo 'Version 2: ' . writeBits(OPT_V2) . "\n";
echo 'Version 3: ' . writeBits(OPT_V3) . "\n";
echo 'Version 4: ' . writeBits(OPT_V4) . "\n";

function writeBits($num)
{
        return str_pad(
                decbin($num),
                4,
                0,
                STR_PAD_LEFT
        );
}
```

Figure 2.1: Writing bits

This code will print out which bytes are used to represent which version of the protocol:

```
Version 1: 0001
Version 2: 0010
Version 3: 0100
Version 4: 1000
```

As you can see, only one bit is needed for each version.

Let's assume that our client is a little bit old and does not support Version 4 of the protocol. In addition, Version 2 had some problems and so it is not supported. To have the client inform the server of the supported protocols, we would provide a number that represents bits 1 and 3 being turned on (Figure 2.2).

```
define('OPT_V1',    0x01);
define('OPT_V2',    0x02);
define('OPT_V3',    0x04);
define('OPT_V4',    0x08);

$iSupport = OPT_V1 | OPT_V3;

echo 'In hex: 0x' . dechex($iSupport) . "\n";
echo 'In decimal: ' . $iSupport . "\n";
echo 'In binary: ' . writeBits($iSupport) . "\n";
```

Figure 2.2: Reading bits

The resulting output:

```
In hex: 0x5
In decimal: 5
In binary: 0101
```

A few months pass, and the company now needs to support Version 4, but it still does not support Version 2. To do that, we add another bitwise | to our **$iSupport** assignment:

```
$iSupport = OPT_V1 | OPT_V3 | OPT_V4;
```

Our code now prints out:

```
In hex: 0xd
In decimal: 13
In binary: 1101
```

AND

The bitwise AND operation is represented by the **&** operator which, as with the | operator, differs from the Boolean **&&**. What the **&** operator does is return an integer that represents all the turned-on bits that are in both numbers.

This function is more useful on the server side because it lets the server look at the number provided by the client and test each protocol version independently of the other. Let's say the client has sent the packet and the server has extracted the version byte. Figure 2.3's code examines the bits.

```
$clientSaid = 0xD;

echo writeBits(OPT_V3) . ": Version 3\n";
echo writeBits($clientSaid) . ": Client claims\n";
```

Figure 2.3: Examining the bits

This code prints out:

```
0100: Version 3
1101: Client claims
```

A bitwise AND operation on these two values will return a value of **4**, but that doesn't matter at all. What matters is that the operation returns a non-zero number. This value can also be evaluated as a Boolean true and as such can be easily evaluated in an **if()** statement.

Assume the code shown in Figure 2.4.

```
$clientSaid = 0xD;

if ($clientSaid & OPT_V1) echo "Client supports V1\n";
if ($clientSaid & OPT_V2) echo "Client supports V2\n";
if ($clientSaid & OPT_V3) echo "Client supports V3\n";
if ($clientSaid & OPT_V4) echo "Client supports V4\n";
```

Figure 2.4: Example of testing for bits

The server will output:

```
Client supports V1
Client supports V3
Client supports V4
```

XOR

XOR is a bit of an unusual beast for PHP programmers. It stands for Exclusive OR. The exclusive OR works very similarly to the bitwise OR operation. The only difference is that if both bits are set, the operation sets the bit to **0** (zero). In other words, if a bit is set on one side or it is set on the other side, it will be **1**. If a bit is set on both sides, it will be set as **0**.

In terms of how you would use the XOR operator in a binary protocol, there aren't many examples of where it would be used. It is most commonly used for cryptography, but PHP already has so many options for cryptography that there is little point in showing how to use it for that. That doesn't mean we can't look at an example, so Figure 2.5 provides one.

```
$num1 = mt_rand();
$num2 = mt_rand();

$res = $num1 ^ $num2;
echo writeBits($num1) . "\n";
echo writeBits($num2) . "\n";
echo str_repeat('-', 32) . "\n";
echo writeBits($res) . "\n";

function writeBits($num)
{
        return str_pad(
                decbin($num),
                32,
                0,
                STR_PAD_LEFT
        );
}
```

Figure 2.5: Requisite XOR example

This code outputs:

```
00101010101111001111011010011010
01110011101101011110111011010010
--------------------------------
01011001000010010001100001001000
```

Bitwise NOT

You have already seen how the bitwise NOT works, in Chapter 1's example of how to use a bitwise NOT on a subnet mask to get the broadcast IP address for the subnet. For your reference, Figure 2.6 presents that example again.

```
$host = ip2long('192.168.0.35');
$netmask = ip2long('255.255.255.192');
$broadcast = $host | ~$netmask;

echo 'Host: ' . decbin($host) . "\n";
echo 'Netmask: ' . decbin($netmask) . "\n";
echo 'Broadcast: ' . decbin($broadcast) . "\n";
echo 'Broadcast IP: ' . long2ip($broadcast) . "\n";
```

Figure 2.6: Example of a bitwise NOT

And the output is:

```
Host: 11000000101010000000000000100011
Netmask: 11111111111111111111111111000000
Broadcast: 11000000101010000000000000111111
Broadcast IP: 192.168.0.63
```

Hacking a Network Protocol

Just because you see the word "hack" here does not mean we're up to anything nefarious. Hacking, in its truest sense, is simply finding functionality using documented or undocumented means. It can often involve a combination of both, but sometimes sufficient documentation is lacking, which means being creative. And that is where the fun is.

In fact, using a network sniffer such as tcpdump or Wireshark can often be faster than reading the documentation because you can use the programs that are using the protocol you are examining. With your network sniffer up and running, you can store the resulting transactions and replay them in a script to test your code. I don't know about you, but I find that reading Requests for Comments (RFCs) can be mind-numbingly boring. Simply looking at the data stream and making intelligent guesses is often a lot more fun. This may not be true for tasks such as checksum calculations, encryption, hashing, or other complex work, but for many protocol hacks it is.

I have also found that setting up a program to run as an intermediary that simply replays packets back to the server can be a good approach to take. You have many different options for examining various protocols, and you can use those options in conjunction with this type of application. However, I recommend having this kind of program running as the intermediary because you can

1. Start by first simply observing packets

2. Write code that learns how to read the packets and predict how the data can be interpreted

3. Start scripting, or hijacking, communications

We're going to build a packet replayer to support just Transmission Control Protocol (TCP) and User Datagram Protocol (UDP) because looking at these two protocols will cover most of the situations for which you're likely to end up using this code. Plus, once you start getting into the more raw data packets, some of the internals of PHP keep you from having completely full control over your socket. In the vast majority of situations, however, this won't affect you, and so we'll stick to TCP and UDP.

That said, let's look at the start of the replayer program (Figure 2.7).

```php
define('LISTEN_IP',        '0.0.0.0' );
define('REPLAY_IP',        '192.168.0.1' );
define('CLIENT_IP',        '192.168.129.208' );
define('SERVICE_PORT',     53 );
$proto = 'udp';

if ($proto === 'udp') {
        handleUdp();
} else if ($proto === 'tcp') {
        handleTcp();
}

function printBytes($data, $sender, $recv)
{
        echo "\n{$sender}->{$recv}: ";
        $len = strlen($data);
        for ($c = 0; $c < $len; $c++) {
                if ($c % 8 === 0) echo "\n";
                $hex = str_pad(
                        dechex(ord($data[$c])),
                        2,
                        0,
                        STR_PAD_LEFT
                );
```

```
                $char = ctype_print($data[$c])?$data[$c]:' ';
                echo "{$hex}={$char} ";
        }
        echo "\n";
}
```

Figure 2.7: Setting up the packet replayer program

This section of code sets up the application for listening. The **LISTEN_IP** constant specifies the IP address on which the application will listen; we use a value of **0.0.0.0** to specify all interfaces.

REPLAY_IP is the IP address of the destination machine, or rather the machine supporting the protocol we want to examine. You might think we could just get the IP address from the client, but what happens if the server is the originator of the packet? We wouldn't know where to forward it. This would be true for both TCP and UDP.

SERVICE_PORT identifies the port on which we want to listen. If the protocol requires listening on multiple ports (few do; IRC is one exception that allows for multiple ports, but it is not required there either), this code would not work. You probably would need to start looking at non-blocking I/O in that case.

Because the first protocol we're going to look at is DNS, which is a UDP-based protocol, UDP is a good place to start for using the replayer. Figure 2.8 gives you a look at that code.

```
function handleUdp()
{
        $sock = socket_create(
                AF_INET,
                SOCK_DGRAM,
                SOL_UDP
        );
        socket_bind($sock, LISTEN_IP, SERVICE_PORT);

        $buf = '';
        $host = NULL;
        $port = NULL;
```

```
    $lastPort = NULL;
    while (socket_recvfrom(
            $sock,
            $buf,
            1024,
            0,
            $host,
            $port) !== false) {
        switch ($host) {
            case CLIENT_IP:
                    $lastPort = $port;
                    socket_sendto(
                            $sock,
                            $buf,
                            strlen($buf),
                            0,
                            REPLAY_IP,
                            SERVICE_PORT
                    );
                    printBytes($buf, $host, REPLAY_IP);
                    break;
            case REPLAY_IP:
                    socket_sendto(
                            $sock,
                            $buf,
                            strlen($buf),
                            0,
                            CLIENT_IP,
                            $lastPort
                    );
                    printBytes($buf, $host, CLIENT_IP);
                    break;
            default:
                    echo "Unknown host "
                        . $host
                        . "responded!\n";
                    break;
        }
        $host = NULL;
        $port = NULL;
    }
}
```

Figure 2.8: Replayer code for the UDP protocol

The first thing we do is set up the socket, telling it to listen on our **LISTEN_IP** constant and binding to the **SERVICE_PORT** port.

After binding, we are ready to start receiving packets, but before we do that we need to take into account one of the intricacies of DNS. Because DNS is a request/ response protocol, we need to be able to handle bidirectional data. UDP, being connectionless, means that you have to make some assumptions for the response. One assumption is deciding where to send the response packet. What the **$lastPort** variable does is take the port of the last request on the client side, store it, and replay the response packet to that port. You may not need to do this for each protocol, but if you are working with a UDP-based reply/response protocol, you probably will need to do something like this.

The solution for TCP (Figure 2.9) differs a bit because we have the ability to manage our connections without assumptions of endpoints.

```
function handleUdp()
{
  $sock = socket_create(
      AF_INET,
      SOCK_DGRAM,
      SOL_UDP
  );
  socket_bind($sock, LISTEN_IP, SERVICE_PORT);

  $buf = '';
  $host = NULL;
  $port = NULL;
  $lastPort = NULL;
  while (socket_recvfrom(
              $sock,
              $buf,
              1024,
              0,
              $host,
              $port) !== false) {

          switch ($host) {
              case CLIENT_IP:
                  $lastPort = $port;
```

```
                    socket_sendto(
                            $sock,
                            $buf,
                            strlen($buf),
                            0,
                            REPLAY_IP,
                            SERVICE_PORT
                    );
                    printBytes($buf, $host, REPLAY_IP);
                    break;
            case REPLAY_IP:
                    socket_sendto(
                            $sock,
                            $buf,
                            strlen($buf),
                            0,
                            CLIENT_IP,
                            $lastPort
                    );
                    printBytes($buf, $host, CLIENT_IP);
                    break;
            default:
                    echo "Unknown host "
                        . $host
                        . "responded!\n";
                    break;
        }
        $host = NULL;
        $port = NULL;
    }
}
```

Figure 2.9: Replayer code for the TCP protocol

What we have done with this code is basically taken our non-blocking I/O code from the networking chapter, made it blocking by removing the **socket_set_nonblock()** calls, and added a peer connection process. The reason we set it to block is because we simply don't need it to be non-blocking. However, we need to be able to receive data from both the client and the server, so having an **fread()** operation on one socket would not be a valid option. Using **socket_select()** lets us iterate over the sockets that have data waiting on them, regardless of the source, without having to have a timeout on each individual socket.

One of the main differences between the UDP code and the TCP code is that we need to be able to manage endpoints. In other words, when data arrives from one socket, we need to be able to send it to its peer. So when the **socket_accept()** call is made, we automatically connect to the server and pair the resulting socket with the one just received from the main socket. To find the peer socket, we simply do an **array_diff()** on the peer array we created earlier and write the data to the result of that call. But before doing that, we print out the bytes in hexadecimal, with their ASCII-encoded character, so that we can see what was being sent.

Now that we have a basic hacking tool, let's start looking at some protocols.

DNS

Domain Name Service is a relatively simple UDP-based protocol that we can use to make our first attempt at using our tool. You can run DNS over TCP, but because that reduces the scalability to some degree, UDP is generally the transport protocol that is used. To test the tool, we can run a simple DNS lookup.

I am using a virtual machine on my local machine to keep things separate. The command I run is

```
host -t A mcpressonline.com 192.168.129.1
```

This command is asking 192.168.129.1 (the IP address on which the tool is listening) to look up an A (address) record for mcpressonline.com. I specifically ask for the A record because the host has a tendency to ask for a lot of information. The **-t** A flag makes sure we are doing only one lookup.

In our tool, this call prints out the request and response shown in Figure 2.10.

```
192.168.129.214->192.168.0.1:
9c=£ 51=Q 01=  00=  00=  01=  00=  00=
00=  00=  00=  00=  0d=  6d=m 63=c 70=p
72=r 65=e 73=s 73=s 6f=o 6e=n 6c=l 69=i
6e=n 65=e 03=  63=c 6f=o 6d=m 00=  00=
01=  00=  01=
```

```
192.168.0.1->192.168.129.214:
9c=£ 51=Q 81=   80=   00=   01=   00=   01=
00=   02=   00=   01=   0d=   6d=m 63=c 70=p
72=r 65=e 73=s 73=s 6f=o 6e=n 6c=l 69=i
6e=n 65=e 03=   63=c 6f=o 6d=m 00=   00=
01=   00=   01=   c0=ᴸ 0c=   00=   01=   00=
01=   00=   00=   1a=   6a=j 00=   04=   48=H
20=   3f=? 42=B c0=ᴸ 0c=   00=   02=   00=
01=   00=   00=   1a=   6a=j 00=   0f=   03=
6e=n 73=s 34=4 08=   7a=z 6f=o 6e=n 65=e
65=e 64=d 69=i 74=t c0=ᴸ 1a=   c0=ᴸ 0c=
00=   02=   00=   01=   00=   00=   1a=   6a=j
00=   06=   03=   6c=n 73=s 31=1 c0=ᴸ 43=C
c0=ᴸ 3f=? 00=   01=   00=   01=   00=   00=
a9=┌ 24=$ 00=   04=   d8=┼ 62=b 96=û ec=∞
```

Figure 2.10: Request/response bytes for mcpressonline.com A record

Good. For now, let's focus on the request, so that you can learn how to create it. We'll figure out the response a little bit later. Figure 2.11 shows the request again.

```
192.168.129.214->192.168.0.1:
9c=£ 51=Q 01=   00=   00=   01=   00=   00=
00=   00=   00=   00=   0d=   6d=m 63=c 70=p
72=r 65=e 73=s 73=s 6f=o 6e=n 6c=l 69=i
6e=n 65=e 03=   63=c 6f=o 6d=m 00=   00=
01=   00=   01=
```

Figure 2.11: Request bytes for mcpressonline.com A record

The first thing you should do after generating this result is run the call again to see whether anything changes. Running the same command a second time produces the result shown in Figure 2.12.

```
192.168.129.214->192.168.0.1:
29=) f4=ô 01=   00=   00=   01=   00=   00=
00=   00=   00=   00=   0d=   6d=m 63=c 70=p
72=r 65=e 73=s 73=s 6f=o 6e=n 6c=l 69=i
6e=n 65=e 03=   63=c 6f=o 6d=m 00=   00=
01=   00=   01=
```

Figure 2.12: Request bytes for mcpressonline.com A record – take 2

Note that the first two bytes have changed. There are a couple of options as to what these two bytes might signify. They could be a timestamp or a unique ID. They could also be both. To find the answer, let's take a look at the response (Figure 2.13) and see whether anything matches.

```
192.168.0.1->192.168.129.214:
29=) f4=ô 81= 80= 00= 01= 00= 01=
00= 02= 00= 01= 0d= 6d=m 63=c 70=p
. . .
```

Figure 2.13: First response bytes for mcpressonline.com A record

It turns out that the first two bytes of the response match the first two bytes of the request. Interesting.

Okay, so we know that the first two bytes are related to the response. Nothing else changes. So now let's do the same request, but do it for a different domain name.

```
kayhost -t A php.net 192.168.129.1
```

This call produces the request bytes shown in Figure 2.14.

```
192.168.129.214->192.168.0.1:
36=6 de=Þ 01= 00= 00= 01= 00= 00=
00= 00= 00= 00= 03= 70=p 68=h 70=p
03= 6e=n 65=e 74=t 00= 00= 01= 00=
01=
```

Figure 2.14: Request bytes for php.net A record

To make this a little easier, let's compare the two (Figure 2.15).

php.net A record:
```
192.168.129.214->192.168.0.1:
36=6 de=Þ 01= 00= 00= 01= 00= 00=
00= 00= 00= 00= 03= 70=p 68=h 70=p
03= 6e=n 65=e 74=t 00= 00= 01= 00=
01=
```

```
mcpressonline.com A record:
192.168.129.214->192.168.0.1:
9c=£ 51=Q 01=  00=  00=  01=  00=  00=
00=  00=  00=  00=  0d=  6d=m 63=c 70=p
72=r 65=e 73=s 73=s 6f=o 6e=n 6c=l 69=i
6e=n 65=e 03=  63=c 6f=o 6d=m 00=  00=
01=  00=  01=
```

Figure 2.15: Comparison of php.net and mcpressonline.com A records

The first thing this output tells you is that the protocol is a variable-length protocol. That is an important thing to know. Why? Because it means that there will be either bytes stating the length of individual fields or field markers stating the beginning and end of the fields.

One of the first similarities I see is that of the footer. For both requests, the last bytes are **0x00 0x00 0x01 0x00 0x01**. I also see that bytes 3 through 12 are **0x01 0x00 0x00 0x01 0x00 0x00 0x00 0x00 0x00 0x00** in both requests.

So let's review what we know so far. Bytes 1 and 2 are likely some kind of message identifier. Bytes 3–12 seem to be some kind of header, and the last five bytes seem to be some kind of footer. Whatever is in between would seem to be the payload. So let's look at that payload (Figure 2.16).

```
php.net payload:
03=  70=p 68=h 70=p 03=  6e=n 65=e 74=t

mcpressonline.com payload:
0d=  6d=m 63=c 70=p 72=r 65=e 73=s 73=s
6f=o 6e=n 6c=l 69=i 6e=n 65=e 03=  63=c
6f=o 6d=m
```

Figure 2.16: Comparison of php.net and mcpressonline.com payloads

Take a little bit of time to examine this figure before reading to the next paragraph. Look for similarities, and look for differences.

The first difference is relatively obvious. Check out the first byte. It's different in each example. So, clearly, its meaning is significant. But what is that meaning? Let's look throughout the payloads and see whether the value is repeated.

In the php.net example, we see **0x03** repeated once more. So, this value occurs before both "php" and "net". It could be an indicator of separated DNS entries, but that wouldn't explain the **0x0D** in the mcpressonline.com example.

However, if you look carefully at the mcpressonline.com example, you will notice that **0x03** is there as well, before "com". So **0x03** is significant to this example, too. But what about the **0x0D**? What is **0x0D** in decimal? The answer is 13. How many characters are in "mcpressonline"? 13.

Because we know that DNS is a read-only protocol, we should now be able to write a simple script that mimics the earlier DNS request without worrying about changing any data. Figure 2.17 shows such a request.

```
$hostname = 'mcpressonline.com';

$message = pack('CCCCCCCCCCCC',
                0xd6, 0xf2, 0x01, 0x00,
                0x00, 0x01, 0x00, 0x00,
                0x00, 0x00, 0x00, 0x00
);

$parts = explode('.', $hostname);

foreach ($parts as $part) {
        $message .= pack('C', strlen($part));
        $message .= $part;
}

$message .= pack('CCCCC',
                0x00, 0x00,0x01,
                0x00,0x01
);

printBytes($message);
```

Figure 2.17: Mimicked DNS request

When we print out the bytes (using a slightly modified **printBytes()** function call) do
we get the same result as we did before? As Figure 2.18 verifies, the answer is yes.

```
d6=Ö f2=ò 01=  00=  00=  01=  00=  00=
00=  00=  00=  00=  0d=  6d=m 63=c 70=p
72=r 65=e 73=s 73=s 6f=o 6e=n 6c=l 69=i
6e=n 65=e 03=  63=c 6f=o 6d=m 00=  00=
01=  00=  01=
```

Figure 2.18: Mimicked output bytes for mcpressonline.com

What if we change **$hostname** to "php.net"? Figure 2.19 shows the result.

```
d6=Ö f2=ò 01=  00=  00=  01=  00=  00=
00=  00=  00=  00=  03=  70=p 68=h 70=p
03=  6e=n 65=e 74=t 00=  00=  01=  00=
01=
```

Figure 2.19: Mimicked output bytes for php.net

Now that we've confirmed that our very simple protocol code mimics what our
DNS client created, we can try sending it to our DNS server. Figure 2.20 shows the
code for doing that.

```
$dnsServer = '192.168.0.1';
$sock = socket_create(AF_INET, SOCK_DGRAM, SOL_UDP);
socket_connect($sock, $dnsServer, 53);
socket_getsockname($sock, $addr, $port);

echo "Sending ...\n";
printBytes($message);
socket_send($sock, $message, strlen($message), 0);

$port = 0;
socket_recvfrom($sock, $buf, 1024, 0, $dnsServer,
                $port);
echo "\nReceived:\n";
printBytes($buf);
```

Figure 2.20: Sending the mimicked DNS bytes

If all is good, our DNS server should return a similar message to the one we got before (Figure 2.21).

```
Sending ...

d6=Ö f2=ò 01=  00=  00=  01=  00=  00=
00=  00=  00=  00=  0d=  6d=m 63=c 70=p
72=r 65=e 73=s 73=s 6f=o 6e=n 6c=l 69=i
6e=n 65=e 03=  63=c 6f=o 6d=m 00=  00=
01=  00=  01=

Received:

d6=Ö f2=ò 81=  80=  00=  01=  00=  01=
00=  02=  00=  00=  0d=  6d=m 63=c 70=p
72=r 65=e 73=s 73=s 6f=o 6e=n 6c=l 69=i
6e=n 65=e 03=  63=c 6f=o 6d=m 00=  00=
01=  00=  01=  c0=À 0c=  00=  01=  00=
01=  00=  00=  1c=  20=  00=  04=  48=H
...
```

Figure 2.21: Sending and receiving our DNS request

With the exception of the first two bytes, which are probably our message identifier, the response appears to be the same. This means that we were able to create our packet properly. So, now we have a choice. Do we start working on parsing the response, or do we work on additional client communication?

Because DNS is a simple protocol, I am going to opt for the additional client communication. As you may be aware, several different types of DNS records can be made. The A record is one. The MX, or mail exchanger, record is another. Let's try the MX record and see what changes in the protocol request and response:

```
host -t MX mcpressonline.com 192.168.129.1
```

This call produces the result shown in Figure 2.22.

```
192.168.129.214->192.168.0.1:
bb=»  6d=m 01=   00=   01=   00=   00=
00=   00=   00=   00=   0d=   6d=m 63=c 70=p
72=r 65=e 73=s 73=s 6f=o 6e=n 6c=l 69=i
6e=n 65=e 03=   63=c 6f=o 6d=m 00=   00=
0f=   00=   01=
```

Figure 2.22: MX record query

How does this compare with our earlier request packet (which is reproduced in Figure 2.23)?

```
d6=Ö f2=ò 01=   00=   00=   01=   00=   00=
00=   00=   00=   00=   0d=   6d=m 63=c 70=p
72=r 65=e 73=s 73=s 6f=o 6e=n 6c=l 69=i
6e=n 65=e 03=   63=c 6f=o 6d=m 00=   00=
01=   00=   01=
```

Figure 2.23: Earlier A record

Ignoring the first two bytes, the only thing that has changed is the third-to-last byte.

Next, let's try doing a CNAME (canonical name) query:

```
host -t CNAME mcpressonline.com 192.168.129.1
```

Figure 2.24 shows the results.

```
192.168.129.214->192.168.0.1:
c6=Æ 50=P 01=   00=   00=   01=   00=   00=
00=   00=   00=   00=   0d=   6d=m 63=c 70=p
72=r 65=e 73=s 73=s 6f=o 6e=n 6c=l 69=i
6e=n 65=e 03=   63=c 6f=o 6d=m 00=   00=
05=   00=   01=
```

Figure 2.24: CNAME query bytes

Again, the third-to-last byte is the only thing that has changed. Given that we don't know whether the record type is an octet, short, or long value, we can't be completely sure that our assumption is correct without going into the documentation or doing some more extensive testing. But for our short, quick example, we will make that assumption.

So let's define some constants (Figure 2.25).

```
define('DNS_RECORD_A', 0x01);
define('DNS_RECORD_MX', 0x0F);
define('DNS_RECORD_CNAME', 0x05);

$queryType = DNS_RECORD_A;
```

Figure 2.25: Query constants

Now, we'll modify our packet to use the constants (Figure 2.26).

```
$message .= pack('CCCCC',
                 0x00, 0x00,$queryType,
                 0x00,0x01
);
```

Figure 2.26: Packet modified to handle the query type

With that, we can start moving to our response packet. Let's first add some code to give us a somewhat random packet ID at the top of our script (Figure 2.27).

```
$packetId = mt_rand(0, 65535);

$message = pack('sCCCCCCCCCC',
                $packetId, 0x01, 0x00,
                0x00, 0x01, 0x00, 0x00,
                0x00, 0x00, 0x00, 0x00
);
```

Figure 2.27: Creating a packet ID

Then, we'll look at how the response packet compares with the request packet (Figure 2.28).

```
3b=;  d9=Ù 81=   80=   00=   01=   00=   01=
00=   02=   00=   00=   0d=   6d=m 63=c 70=p
72=r 65=e 73=s 73=s 6f=o 6e=n 6c=l 69=i
6e=n 65=e 03=   63=c 6f=o 6d=m 00=   00=
01=   00=   01=   c0=À 0c=   00=   01=   00=
01=   00=   00=   1a=   04=   00=   04=   48=H
20=   3f=? 42=B c0=À 0c=   00=   02=   00=
01=   00=   00=   1a=   04=   00=   0f=   03=
6e=n 73=s 34=4 08=   7a=z 6f=o 6e=n 65=e
65=e 64=d 69=i 74=t c0=À 1a=   c0=À 0c=
00=   02=   00=   01=   00=   00=   1a=   04=
00=   06=   03=   6e=n 73=s 31=1 c0=À 43=C
```

Figure 2.28: Response packet

There are a few changes here, but the interesting thing is that the basic structure is the same. In bytes 3 and 4, we have some different values, as well as in byte 10. However, at byte 12, just like in the request, we see the data being repeated. This indicates that the packet structure is quite similar. Not exact, but similar. To see what is variable, let's again do a query against php.net. Figure 2.29 shows the first part of the result.

```
1e=   bd=½ 81=   80=   00=   01=   00=   01=
00=   04=   00=   04=   03=   70=p 68=h 70=p
03=   6e=n 65=e 74=t 00=   00=   01=   00=
01=   c0=À 0c=   00=   01=   00=   01=   00=
00=   d3=Ó 20=   00=   04=   45=E 93=   53=S
c5=Å c0=À 0c=   00=   02=   00=   01=   00=
01=   4d=M a8=" 00=   11=   03=   6e=n 73=s
31=1 07=   65=e 61=a 73=s 79=y 64=d 6e=n
73=s 03=   63=c 6f=o 6d=m 00=   c0=À 0c=
. . .
```

Figure 2.29: Query for php.net

The actual output is quite long, partly because there is a fair amount of data that can be stored in a DNS record. Because the purpose of this exercise is to give you a basic understanding of how to read a packet, we will proceed with finding the IP address and building the code to discover that. If you would like to go further, I would definitely encourage it.

Because we know that an IP address is just a 32-bit integer, finding it in the packet is actually pretty easy. The first thing to do would be to find out the IP address and convert it to an integer to enable extracting the hex values for it. Finding that is actually very easy. Take the IP address that we had from the mcpressonline.com query before — 72.32.63.66 — and print the hex value for each element. Because an IP address is already separated into octets (8-bit ranges), we don't need to do any number conversion. Figure 2.30 shows the hex values for the sample IP address.

```
$parts = explode('.', '72.32.63.66');

echo dechex($parts[0]). ' ';
echo dechex($parts[1]). ' ';
echo dechex($parts[2]). ' ';
echo dechex($parts[3]). "\n";
```

Figure 2.30: Printing the hexadecimal values for an IP address

This prints out:

```
48 20 3f 42
```

Let's compare this with the packet we retrieved earlier (Figure 2.31).

```
84=    89=    81=    80=    00=    01=    00=    01=
00=    02=    00=    00=    0d=    6d=m  63=c  70=p
72=r  65=e  73=s  73=s  6f=o  6e=n  6c=l  69=i
6e=n  65=e  03=    63=c  6f=o  6d=m  00=    00=
01=    00=    01=    c0=À  0c=    00=    01=    00=
01=    00=    00=    0c=    89=    00=    04=    48=H
20=    3f=?  42=B  c0=À  0c=    00=    02=    00=
01=    00=    00=    0c=    89=    00=    0f=    03=
6e=n  73=s  34=4  08=    7a=z  6f=o  6e=n  65=e
65=e  64=d  69=i  74=t  c0=À  1a=    c0=À  0c=
00=    02=    00=    01=    00=    00=    0c=    89=
00=    06=    03=    6e=n  73=s  31=1  c0=À  43=C
```

Figure 2.31: Finding the hexadecimal values

You can see that we have the IP address in the hex format we were expecting. Notice the byte in front of the hex data? Given what we know about the protocol, it is likely that this byte is a data length field. Having found it, let's write some quick code we can use to retrieve that information (Figure 2.32).

```
$data = unpack('Sid', $buf);

if ($data['id'] == $packetId) {
        echo "Packet verified\n";
} else {
        die('Invalid packet');
}

$partCounter = 0;
$byteCounter = 12;
$name = '';

while ($name !== $hostname &&
        $byteCounter <= strlen($buf)) {
            $dataLength = unpack(
                'Clen',
                substr($buf, $byteCounter++, 1)
        );
        if ($name) $name .= '.';
        $name .= substr($buf, $byteCounter,
                        $dataLength['len']);
        $byteCounter += $dataLength['len'];
}

// Ignoring a bunch of bytes
$byteCounter += 15;

$dataLength = unpack('Slen', substr($buf,
                        $byteCounter, 2));

if ($dataLength['len'] != 2)
    die('Unsupported IP protocol');

$ipAddr = unpack(
    'Nip',
    substr(
        $buf,
        $byteCounter + 2,
        $dataLength['len']
    )
);

echo "{$name} = ".long2ip($ipAddr['ip'])."\n";
```

Figure 2.32: Verifying the packet

This code will echo:

```
Packet verified
mcpressonline.com = 72.32.63.66
```

This code would be inserted toward the end of the script after the data has been received back from the server. As with the request, the first 12 bytes of the DNS packet seems to be header data, with the first two bytes being the packet ID. So the first thing we do is read the packet ID from the buffer and compare it with the ID we had beforehand. If it matches, then we're good to read the rest of the packet.

After we have verified the packet, we need to read in the domain name. That is what we have the loop there for. We basically read in each part, based on the length byte prior to each part, until the domain name matches what we searched for, increasing the byte counter by the length of the name. Having read the name, we increase the byte counter by 15 bytes. This is not because that data isn't important, but because we don't need it right now. The next piece of relevant data is the length field. While our network proxy found only one pertinent byte, the length field is, in fact, a 16-bit field, and so we would unpack it with an **'n'**, which is an unsigned short with big-endian byte order.

Endianness is the order of bits or bytes in a bit, or byte, sequence. Most of the time, you will be working with big endianness. That is, the most significant bit or byte (i.e., the biggest) will be first. You usually will end up using big-endian–based values. Any IP-level data is big-endian.

Once we know how long the IP address is, we can read the IP address itself and call the **long2ip()** function, which will return the IP address in its dotted decimal format. The code we're looking at here does not support IPv6.

If you want to examine the DNS packets in more detail, I would suggest using a tool such as Wireshark to read the packets off your network interface. Wireshark has a plethora of protocols defined, and it shows where in the packet the data it parses belongs, which makes it quite useful for debugging packets.

So what are some of the things we've learned so far?

1. Become familiar with byte-level data.

2. Compare and contrast the results of like data.

3. Look for data you know.

4. Try to make the protocol fail.

5. Worry only about immediately important details. Figure out the less important details later on.

Telnet

We just finished looking at a UDP protocol, so now we're going to look at a TCP-based protocol. There are several options we could look at, but not many that are simple enough to demonstrate in a partial chapter in a book. For that reason, I have chosen Telnet as the example. There are two reasons for this. First, Telnet is not a simple request/response protocol, such as HTTP is. Second, Telnet is more difficult to examine than HTTP, Internet Message Access Protocol (IMAP), Simple Mail Transfer Protocol (SMTP), or some other text-based protocol.

Telnet listens on port 23. So, we need to set up our replay script to listen on port 23 and to connect to a remote Telnet server. For my testing, the Telnet client and server were on the same machine, whereas the replay script was running remotely. Either way, the effect is the same.

Once our replay script is running, the first thing to do is test it (Figure 2.33).

```
kschroeder@desktop:~$ telnet 192.168.129.1
Trying 192.168.129.1...
Connected to 192.168.129.1.
Escape character is '^]'.
Ubuntu 9.04
desktop login:
```

Figure 2.33: Telnet output

Figure 2.34 shows the response that the replay script displays.

```
192.168.129.214:54193->192.168.129.214:23:
ff=ÿ fd=ý 03=  ff=ÿ fb=û 18=  ff=ÿ fb=û
1f=  ff=ÿ fb=û 20=  ff=ÿ fb=û 21=! ff=ÿ
fb=û 22=" ff=ÿ fb=û 27=' ff=ÿ fd=ý 05=

192.168.129.214:23->192.168.129.214:54193:
ff=ÿ fd=ý 18=  ff=ÿ fd=ý 20=  ff=ÿ fd=ý
23=# ff=ÿ fd=ý 27='

192.168.129.214:54193->192.168.129.214:23:
ff=ÿ fc=ü 23=#
192.168.129.214:23->192.168.129.214:54193:
ff=ÿ fb=û 03=  ff=ÿ fd=ý 1f=  ff=ÿ fd=ý
21=! ff=ÿ fe=þ 22=" ff=ÿ fb=û 05=

192.168.129.214:54193->192.168.129.214:23:
ff=ÿ fa=ú 1f=  00=  50=P 00=  18=  ff=ÿ
f0=ð

192.168.129.214:23->192.168.129.214:54193:
ff=ÿ fa=ú 20=  01=  ff=ÿ f0=ð ff=ÿ fa=ú
27=' 01=  ff=ÿ f0=ð ff=ÿ fa=ú 18=  01=
ff=ÿ f0=ð

192.168.129.214:54193->192.168.129.214:23:
ff=ÿ fa=ú 20=  00=  33=3 38=8 34=4 30=0
30=0 2c=, 33=3 38=8 34=4 30=0 30=0 ff=ÿ
f0=ð ff=ÿ fa=ú 27=' 00=  ff=ÿ f0=ð ff=ÿ
fa=ú 18=  00=  78=x 74=t 65=e 72=r 6d=m
ff=ÿ f0=ð

192.168.129.214:23->192.168.129.214:54193:
ff=ÿ fd=ý 01=

192.168.129.214:54193->192.168.129.214:23:
ff=ÿ fc=ü 01=

192.168.129.214:23->192.168.129.214:54193:
ff=ÿ fb=û 01=

192.168.129.214:54193->192.168.129.214:23:
ff=ÿ fd=ý 01=
```

```
192.168.129.214:23->192.168.129.214:54193:
55=U 62=b 75=u 6e=n 74=t 75=u 20=  39=9
2e=. 30=0 34=4 0d=  0a=

192.168.129.214:23->192.168.129.214:54193:
64=d 65=e 73=s 6b=k 74=t 6f=o 70=p 20=
6c=l 6f=o 67=g 69=i 6e=n 3a=: 20=
```

Figure 2.34: Telnet handshake

Take some time to read over that. Look for patterns. Look for data you know. Run the request again and look for data that changes.

The first several packets are clearly part of a handshake process. There are 11 packets exchanged before any printed data is displayed. The printed data is interesting, too. Check out the first byte of a packet that contains printed data. Compare that to the other packets. The packet that contains printed data starts with printed data. The handshake packets start with **0xFF**. **0xFF** would seem to be the indicator of a control packet.

If a packet starting with **0xFF** is a control packet, what could the second byte mean? Because the value of the second byte is generally around the same range as the first byte, the second byte seems to have some request/reply properties (look at **ff=ÿ fd=ý 01=**). If this part of the overall session is a handshake, it is reasonable to conclude that the second byte is the *type* of control packet.

For the sake of time, paper, and sanity, we can consult the RFC for the Telnet protocol to find out what those control packets actually mean. That's not to say that you need to do this, but the Telnet protocol can actually be somewhat complex.

The first Telnet RFC was written in 1969 as RFC 15, and several RFC documents describe additions and extensions to it. We are going to be building according to RFC 854. This example will not be complete, but we are going to implement enough of it so you can see a negotiated TCP-based protocol in action.

The first byte of the packet is **0xFF**, which is called the "Interpret as Command," or IAC, byte. According to the RFC, the client or server is supposed to check the first byte of the packet to see whether the packet contains the IAC byte. This requirement actually harkens back to the original Telnet protocol, where if the high bit was set, the packet was assumed to be a control packet. This step was necessary because Telnet used an 8-bit packet to pass 7-bit ASCII data. So if the high bit was set, it clearly could not be a printable packet.

The control byte, defined as a Telnet command in the RFC, has several different values that can be used. Table 2.2 reproduces the table from the RFC that describes those values.

Table 2.2: Telnet command bytes		
Name	Code	Meaning
End of Sub-Negotiation	240 (0xF0)	End of sub-negotiation parameters
NOP	241 (0xF1)	No Operation
Data Mark	242 (0xF2)	The data stream portion of a Synch. This should always be accompanied by a TCP Urgent notification.
Break	243 (0xF3)	NVT character BRK*
Interrupt Process	244 (0xF4)	The function IP*
Abort Output	245 (0xF5)	The function AO*
Are You There	246 (0xF6)	The function AYT*
Erase Character	247 (0xF7)	The function EC*
Erase Line	248 (0xF8)	The function EL*
Go Ahead	249 (0xF9)	The GA signal*
Sub-Negotiation	250 (0xFA)	Indicates that what follows is sub-negotiation of the indicated option.
Will	251 (0xFB)	Indicates the desire to begin performing, or confirmation that you are now performing, the indicated option.
Won't	252 (0xFC)	Indicates the refusal to perform, or continue performing, the indicated option.
Do	253 (0xFD)	Indicates the request that the other party perform, or confirmation that you are expecting the other party to perform, the indicated option.
Don't	254 (0xFE)	Indicates the demand that the other party stop performing, or confirmation that you are no longer expecting the other party to perform, the indicated option.
* Examine RFC 854 for implementation details on these functions. Source: *http://www.faqs.org/rfcs/rfc854.html.*		

The protocol is starting to make a little more sense now. With this information, we can define some constants as well as some data to help us make sense of the commands (Figure 2.35).

```php
define('TELNET_ESUBNEGO'    , 0xF0);
define('TELNET_NOP'         , 0xF1);
define('TELNET_DM'          , 0xF2);
define('TELNET_BRK'         , 0xF3);
define('TELNET_IP'          , 0xF4);
define('TELNET_AO'          , 0xF5);
define('TELNET_AYT'         , 0xF6);
define('TELNET_EC'          , 0xF7);
define('TELNET_EL'          , 0xF8);
define('TELNET_GA'          , 0xF9);
define('TELNET_SSUBNEGO'    , 0xFA);
define('TELNET_WILL'        , 0xFB);
define('TELNET_WONT'        , 0xFC);
define('TELNET_DO'          , 0xFD);
define('TELNET_DONT'        , 0xFE);
define('TELNET_IAC'         , 0xFF);

$commands = array(
      TELNET_ESUBNEGO       => 'End Sub-Nego',
      TELNET_NOP            => 'No-Op',
      TELNET_DM             => 'Data Mark',
      TELNET_BRK            => 'Break',
      TELNET_IP             => 'Interrupt Process',
      TELNET_AO             => 'Abort Output',
      TELNET_AYT            => 'Are You There',
      TELNET_EC             => 'Erase Character',
      TELNET_EL             => 'Erase Line',
      TELNET_GA             => 'Go Ahead',
      TELNET_SSUBNEGO       => 'Start Sub-Nego',
      TELNET_WILL           => 'Will',
      TELNET_WONT           => 'Won\'t',
      TELNET_DO             => 'Do',
      TELNET_DONT           => 'Don\'t'
);
```

Figure 2.35: PHP constants for Telnet command bytes

Now that we have our commands defined, let's define a function that can parse the commands and add that function call to the **handleTcp()** function (Figure 2.36).

```
// Insert immediately after call to printBytes()
interpretPacket($buf);

// Snip. . .

// Define the function at the bottom of the script
function interpretPacket($packet)
{
    global $commands;
    $data = array_values(unpack('C*', $packet));

    if ($data[0] !== TELNET_IAC) {
        echo $packet;
        return;
    }

    if (isset($commands[$data[1]])) {
        echo "Command: ".$commands[$data[1]]."\n";
    } else {
        echo "Unknown Command\n";
    }
}
```

Figure 2.36: Start of interpretPacket function definition

What this code does is first create an array of bytes that we can check. If the first byte in the array is not the IAC byte, we have a simple string to be output to the screen. If it does match, we have a command to interpret. Figure 2.37 shows the output for my handshake. I have removed the hexadecimal output from the figure to make it more readable.

```
192.168.129.214:59701->192.168.129.214:23: Command: Do

192.168.129.214:23->192.168.129.214:59701: Command: Do

192.168.129.214:59701->192.168.129.214:23: Command: Won't

192.168.129.214:23->192.168.129.214:59701: Command: Will
```

```
192.168.129.214:59701->192.168.129.214:23: Command: Start Sub-Nego

192.168.129.214:23->192.168.129.214:59701: Command: Start Sub-Nego

192.168.129.214:59701->192.168.129.214:23: Command: Start Sub-Nego

192.168.129.214:23->192.168.129.214:59701: Command: Do

192.168.129.214:59701->192.168.129.214:23: Command: Won't

192.168.129.214:23->192.168.129.214:59701: Command: Will

192.168.129.214:59701->192.168.129.214:23: Command: Do

192.168.129.214:23->192.168.129.214:59701: Ubuntu 9.04
desktop login:
```

Figure 2.37: Telnet bytes interpreted

We can now see what the process of logging in is like. But to make some reasonable progress, we need to have a minimal amount of functionality working. So, the next step is to find out what we can do without to initiate the connection ourselves.

If you have worked with Telnet, or Secure Shell (SSH) for that matter, you know that the width and height of the terminal can change. There must be a way to specify it. Let's see whether we can figure out what that is. I'll do the same thing I did before, but before logging in I will adjust the screen with **printBytes()**, printing all the bytes so we can compare the results. Snipping from the last of the bytes we see the transaction shown in Figure 2.38 occurring.

```
192.168.129.214:23->192.168.129.214:38849:
64=d 65=e 73=s 6b=k 74=t 6f=o 70=p 20=
6c=l 6f=o 67=g 69=i 6e=n 3a=: 20=
desktop login:
192.168.129.214:38849->192.168.129.214:23:
ff=ÿ fa=ú 1f=  00=  50=P 00=  19=  ff=ÿ
f0=ð
Command: Start Sub-Nego
```

Figure 2.38: Bytes resulting from a screen resize

We can see the IAC byte, and we see **0xFA**, or Start Sub-Negotiation. This is followed by a **0x1F**, several numbers, a **0xFF** (IAC), and then **0xF0**, or End Sub-Negotiation. What happens if we resize the screen back to its original size? Figure 2.39 shows the result.

```
192.168.129.214:50889->192.168.129.214:23:
ff=ÿ fa=ú 1f=  00=  50=P 00=  18=  ff=ÿ
f0=ð
Command: Start Sub-Neg
```

Figure 2.39: Bytes resulting from another screen resize

One change. **0x18** in the seventh byte. What do **0x50** and **0x18** equate to? 80 x 24. The **0x00** in front of these two numbers implies that the width is a 2-byte number — a short integer.

But the question is, do we need that information to make the Telnet connection work? The **0x1F** is the byte telling the server that the sub-negotiation occurring is for window size. This option is actually defined in RFC 1073, not RFC 854. So it would imply that we do not need it for basic functionality.

This brings us to an important question: What would happen if we just connected? Let's write a simple script that does that. We already know from our replay application what some of the bytes are. Let's connect and see whether we can understand the response (Figure 2.40).

```
$host = '192.168.129.214';
$port = 23;

$sock = socket_create(AF_INET, SOCK_STREAM, SOL_TCP);
socket_connect($sock, $host, $port);
socket_getsockname($sock, $selfAddr, $selfPort);

$data = socket_read($sock, 1024);
printBytes($data, $host, $selfAddr);
interpretPacket($data);
```

Figure 2.40: Attempting to connect with minimal negotiation

Figure 2.41 shows the resulting output.

```
192.168.129.214->192.168.129.1:
ff=ÿ fd=ý 18=   ff=ÿ fd=ý 20=   ff=ÿ fd=ý
23=# ff=ÿ fd=ý 27='
Command: Do
```

Figure 2.41: Output of simple negotiation

We understand it! We see the IAC byte, and we see **0xFD**, or the **DO** command. What's next is finding out what **0x18** stands for. Looking through the RFCs, we see that **0x18** stands for "Terminal Type." In other words, the server is stating that it is willing to receive terminal information. This option is documented in RFC 1091.

So because we want to try to find out what is minimally needed, let's connect to the server and tell it that we do not want to provide anything back. To do that, we write another function to handle the functionality that we do support (Figure 2.42).

```
function handleCommand(array $data, $sock)
{
     switch($data[2]) {
          default:
               $packet =
                    pack(
                         'CCC',
                         TELNET_IAC,
                         TELNET_WONT,
                         $data[2]
                    );
               break;
     }
     printBytes($packet);
     socket_write($sock,$packet);
}
```

Figure 2.42: Starting code to handle known functionality

And in our **interpretPacket** function, we'll modify a line (Figure 2.43).

```
function interpretPacket($packet, $sock)
{
     global $commands;
     $data = array_values(unpack('C*', $packet));

     if ($data[0] !== TELNET_IAC) {
          echo $packet;
          return;
     }

     if (isset($commands[$data[1]])) {
          echo "Command: ".$commands[$data[1]]."\n";
          handleCommand($data, $sock);
     } else {
          echo "Unknown Command\n";
     }

}
```

Figure 2.43: adding a few lines to interpretPacket()

Now when a command comes in that we don't understand, we say we won't do it because that is the default operation for the **switch** statement in **handleCommand()**.

The last change is to the main part of the program, where we check for a response (Figure 2.44).

```
$data = socket_read($sock, 1024);
printBytes($data);
interpretPacket($data, $sock);

$data = socket_read($sock, 1024);
printBytes($data);
interpretPacket($data, $sock);
```

Figure 2.44: Code for reading some data off the connection

When we run the code now, we get the response shown in Figure 2.45.

```
ff=ÿ fd=ý 18=  ff=ÿ fd=ý 20=  ff=ÿ fd=ý
23=# ff=ÿ fd=ý 27='
Command: Do


ff=ÿ fc=ü 18=
```

Figure 2.45: Response packets from reading the code

The last packet is our "won't" packet. So what happens? Nothing. No response back from the server. Apparently, we are missing something. That means we need to take a closer look. What else do we see in the first packet? Several more IAC bytes. There are actually a total of four IAC bytes, which may mean that there are several other commands we may need to process.

So, let's take our **interpretPacket()** function and make some further changes to it (Figure 2.46).

```
function interpretPacket($packet, $sock)
{
     global $commands;
     $data = array_values(unpack('C*', $packet));
     $iacPacket = 0;
     printBytes($packet);
     if ($data[$iacPacket] !== TELNET_IAC) {

          echo $packet;
          return;
     }
     while (($iacPacket
             = array_search(
                  TELNET_IAC,
                  $data
                  )) !== false) {

          $data = array_slice($data, $iacPacket);

          if (isset($commands[$data[1]])) {
```

```
                echo "Command: "
                        . $commands[$data[1]]."\n";

                handleCommand($data, $sock);
        } else {
                echo "Unknown Command\n";
        }
        $data[0] = NULL;
    }
}
```

Figure 2.46: Adding functionality to iterate over IAC bytes

What this function now does is use iteration when it finds an IAC byte. If an IAC byte is found, the function creates a new array with the next IAC byte being found. That IAC snippet is then passed to the **handleCommand()** function, which basically says, "No, I won't."

The script now will run and exit, presumably because the last **socket_read()** command is not blocking but is actually returning data. How do we get that data? Call **socket_read()** again. Remember, we're still discovering the protocol, and we want to see what it takes to get a login prompt, so we don't want to get into too many details. From the original code, I had to add two calls to **socket_read()**. After I did, I received the output shown in Figure 2.47.

```
. . .
ff=ÿ fb=û 01=
Command: Will

Writing:
ff=ÿ fc=ü 01=


55=U 62=b 75=u 6e=n 74=t 75=u 20=  39=9
2e=. 30=0 34=4 0d=  0a=  64=d 65=e 73=s
6b=k 74=t 6f=o 70=p 20=  6c=l 6f=o 67=g
69=i 6e=n 3a=: 20=
Ubuntu 9.04
desktop login:
```

Figure 2.47: Output with IAC byte iteration

We have now successfully negotiated a Telnet session, with no real options set, and it is time to start thinking about interaction. For this purpose, we need to go back to our replay program and see how communication is handled (Figure 2.48).

```
kschroeder@desktop:~$ telnet 192.168.129.1
Trying 192.168.129.1...
Connected to 192.168.129.1.
Escape character is '^]'.
Ubuntu 9.04
desktop login: book
```

Figure 2.48: Interacting with the Telnet terminal: sending the user name

This interaction produces the (snipped) output shown in Figure 2.49.

```
192.168.129.214:23->192.168.129.214:60965:
64=d 65=e 73=s 6b=k 74=t 6f=o 70=p 20=
6c=l 6f=o 67=g 69=i 6e=n 3a=: 20=
desktop login:
192.168.129.214:60965->192.168.129.214:23:
62=b
b
192.168.129.214:23->192.168.129.214:60965:
62=b
b
192.168.129.214:60965->192.168.129.214:23:
6f=o
o
192.168.129.214:23->192.168.129.214:60965:
6f=o
o
. . .
```

Figure 2.49: Interacting with the Telnet terminal: reading interaction bytes

What we notice here is that for the word **book**, the data is being sent one byte at a time, and for each byte sent, a corresponding reply byte is sent back. The first thing that's interesting about this is that it seems to separate what is sent from what is printed. In other words, for something to be printed, it must be received from the server. Given that you don't want a password to appear as clear text on a Telnet window, this fact makes complete sense.

Another thing we notice is the lack of an IAC byte. Because there is no IAC byte, the packet is to be treated as normal. The only outstanding question is whether input can be sent in strings instead of single characters. Given that output can be received in strings, it is logical to presume that input can be given that way as well, and we will test that now.

The first thing we do is create a few constants (Figure 2.50). These constants will be used to note where in the process we are as well as provide our login information.

```
define('TELNET_STATE_NEGO'        , 1);
define('TELNET_STATE_LOGIN_USER' , 2);
define('TELNET_STATE_LOGIN_PW'    , 3);
define('TELNET_STATE_AUTHED'      , 4);

define('TELNET_USERNAME'          , 'book');
define('TELNET_PASSWORD'          , 'password');
```

Figure 2.50: Defining some Telnet constants

A little later on, rather than simply call the **socket_read()** function, we will iterate over it until the connection is closed (Figure 2.51).

```
while (($data = socket_read($sock, 1024)) != false) {
        interpretPacket($data, $sock);
}
```

Figure 2.51: Iterating over socket operations

The biggest change will be in the **interpretPacket()** function definition, where we now are also going to handle the handshake, the login, and sending an arbitrary command. In this case, **df -h** will be the command, so we can get a list of all the mount points on the system and their usage. Figure 2.52 shows the additional code for **interpretPacket()**.

```php
function interpretPacket($packet, $sock)
{
  global $commands;
  static $state    = TELNET_STATE_NEGO;
  $prompt          = '$';
  $data = array_values(unpack('C*', $packet));
  $iacPacket = 0;

  if ($data[$iacPacket] !== TELNET_IAC) {
      echo $packet;
      switch ($state) {
        case TELNET_STATE_NEGO:
            if (strpos(
                    $packet,
                    'login') !== FALSE) {
                socket_write(
                    $sock,
                    TELNET_USERNAME . "\n"
            );

                $state
                    = TELNET_STATE_LOGIN_USER;
            }
            break;
        case TELNET_STATE_LOGIN_USER:
            if (strpos(
                    $packet,
                    'Password') !== FALSE) {

                socket_write(
                        $sock,
                        TELNET_PASSWORD
                        . "\n"
                );

                $state
                    = TELNET_STATE_LOGIN_PW;
            }

            break;
        case TELNET_STATE_LOGIN_PW:
            // First remove \n
```

```
       $packet = trim($packet);
       if (strpos(
              $packet,
              'Login incorrect') !== false) {

              die('Unable to log in');
       }

       $reply = explode("\n", $packet);
       if (trim(array_pop($reply))
              === $prompt) {

              $state = TELNET_STATE_AUTHED;
              socket_write(
                     $sock,
                     "df -h\n"
                     );
       }
       break;
case TELNET_STATE_AUTHED;
       $lines = explode("\n", $packet);
       $cmdPrompt = trim(
                            array_pop(
                                   $lines
                                   )
                            );

       if (strpos(
              $cmdPrompt,
              $prompt) === 0) {
              // 0x04 is
                // End of Transmission
              // Will cause the server
                // to close the connection
              socket_write(
                     $sock,
                     pack(
                            'C',
                            0x04
                     )
              );
              global $mounts;

       }
```

```
        break;
        }

        return;
    }

    //IAC-handling code omitted in example
}
```

Figure 2.52: Full code to handle authentication and df –h command

The last function is incomplete. There is the call to **global $mounts**, but no additional functionality to read the command output. We will get into that in a bit.

The preceding code produces the output shown in Figure 2.53.

```
Ubuntu 9.04
desktop login: book
Password:
Last login: Tue Sep 15 08:44:05 CDT 2009
            from lap-kevin.local on pts/2
$ df -h
Filesystem          Size  Used Avail Use% Mounted on
/dev/sda1           7.5G  5.1G  2.1G  72% /
tmpfs               505M     0  505M   0% /lib/init/rw
varrun              505M  320K  505M   1% /var/run
varlock             505M     0  505M   0% /var/lock
udev                505M  124K  505M   1% /dev
tmpfs               505M     0  505M   0% /dev/shm
/dev/sdb1           4.0G  1.6G  2.3G  41% /opt
/dev/sdc1           7.9G  4.4G  3.2G  59% /srv
$
```

Figure 2.53: Fully implemented output

Our code implements a four-step negotiation process to connect to the Telnet server. The first step is the negotiation phase, where we say, "We're only doing the basics." We note that fact with the constant **TELNET_STATE_NEGO**. This means that the request is currently in the negotiation state. Then, if we're in the negotiation state and we see the text "login" in the stream, we assume we're being prompted for a user name and we enter it. At that point, we change the state to **TELNET_STATE_LOGIN_USER**, indicating that we've sent the password.

Once the password has been entered, we change the state to **TELNET_STATE_LOGIN_PWD**. The next time through the loop, we check the return value for the **'Login incorrect'** string. If we see this in the string, our password is incorrect and we **die()**. The last part of this state is to see whether we have a login prompt. The login prompt is defined beforehand at the start of the function. If the login prompt is different, or more complex, you would need to add code to handle that. But on this system, for this user, the login prompt is **'$'**. Once we see the prompt, we can change the state to **TELNET_STATE_AUTHED** and start processing the output data stream.

We start by reading in the lines from the Telnet stream and **explode()**ing them. The purpose of this step is not to get the individual lines but to find out whether the prompt is there. If the prompt is there, the output has finished and we can close the connection. We do that by sending **0x04** to the terminal. **0x04** is an End of Transmission byte and is the same as pressing **Ctrl-D** on your keyboard.

However, we have a bit of a problem here. That problem is that Telnet may not send all the bytes at once. We saw, when we were testing for the login procedure, that sometimes bytes can be sent one at a time. Therefore, we need to modify some code in the function before we can start extracting the data.

To do that, we're going to rewrite the **TELNET_STATE_AUTHED** portion of the code (Figure 2.54).

```
case TELNET_STATE_AUTHED;
    static $streamData = '';
    $streamData .= $packet;

    $lastCR = strrpos($streamData, "\n");
    $cmdPrompt = trim(substr($streamData, $lastCR));
```

```
    if (strpos(
        $cmdPrompt,
        $prompt) === 0) {
        // 0x04 is End of Transmission
        // Will cause the server to close the connection
        socket_write(
            $sock,
            pack(
                'C',
                0x04
            )
        );
        global $mounts;
        $lines = explode("\n", $streamData);
        array_shift($lines);
        $header = array_shift($lines);
        $headerData = preg_split('/\s+/', $header);

        foreach ($lines as $line) {
            if (strpos($line, $prompt) === 0) continue;
            $rowData = preg_split('/\s+/', $line);
            $row = array();
            foreach ($rowData as $key => $value) {
                $row[$headerData[$key]] = $value;
            }
            $mounts[] = $row;
        }

        $streamData = '';
    }

break;
```

Figure 2.54: Interpreting the df –h bytes

The first thing we do differently here is change how we find the prompt. Rather than simply **explode()**ing the packet, we look for the last line-feed character. We then check the substring from the last line-feed to the end of the string, trim it, and see whether it matches our prompt. If it does, we've reached the end of our response, and we can close the connection and extract the results.

Most of the code that follows that should be very readable to any PHP developer. The only thing to really note is that the reason why we have a single **array_shift()** before reading the header is because the command that was entered is echoed to the stream. Because we don't care about that here, we simply ignore it.

After processing the results of the command, we need to print it out. We do that outside the **interpretPacket()** function in the main body of the script (Figure 2.55).

```
while (($data = socket_read($sock, 1024)) != false) {
        interpretPacket($data, $sock);
}

foreach ($mounts as $mount) {

        echo "Mount Point "
                . $mount['Mounted']
                . " is at "
                . $mount['Use%']
                . "\n";
}
```

Figure 2.55: Code for printing the interpreted df –h bytes

This code prints the output shown in Figure 2.56.

```
Mount Point / is at 72%
Mount Point /lib/init/rw is at 0%
Mount Point /var/run is at 1%
Mount Point /var/lock is at 0%
Mount Point /dev is at 1%
Mount Point /dev/shm is at 0%
Mount Point /opt is at 41%
Mount Point /srv is at 59%
```

Figure 2.56: Output of the interpreted df –h bytes

We have now built a Telnet script that can negotiate, authenticate, execute a command on the server, and read the response. The next step is to take what we've learned here and turn it into a useful API rather than a hacked script. That job, however, I will leave to you.

Building Your Own

We have looked at using other people's protocols; now we're going to look at building our own. The key to building your own protocol is simply structure. Define what you're going to do, and then make sure you do it.

The example we're going to build is a simple client/server application that lets you perform basic Create, Read, Update, Delete (CRUD) operations on an address. The actual CRUD operations are not important to this exercise, so I'll be using the Zend Framework **Zend_Db** classes to handle those. For your reference, the code will be in a file called **Db.php**, and it is defined as shown in Figure 2.57. Note that activity such as this is usually best done using existing standards. This, however, is being shown as an example of the approach that you *could* take if you absolutely *needed* to implement a binary protocol, and CRUD operations should be familiar enough that the binary aspect of what we're doing here is the only really new concept.

```
require_once 'Zend/Db/Table/Abstract.php';
require_once 'Zend/Db/Table/Row/Abstract.php';

class AddressTable extends Zend_Db_Table_Abstract
{
        protected $_name = 'addresses';
        protected $_primary = 'address_key';
        protected $_rowClass = 'AddressRow';
}

class AddressRow extends Zend_Db_Table_Row_Abstract
{
        protected $_data = array(
            'address_key' => NULL,
            'first_name' => NULL,
            'last_name' => NULL,
            'address1' => NULL,
            'address2' => NULL,
            'city' => NULL,
            'state' => NULL,
            'zip' => NULL,
            'country' => NULL,
            'phone' => NULL,
            'fax' => NULL,
            'email' => NULL,
            'notes' => NULL
        );
}
```

```
Zend_Db_Table_Abstract::setDefaultAdapter(
    Zend_Db::factory(
            'PDO_MYSQL',
        array(
                'dbname'      => 'book',
                'username'    => 'root',
                'password'    => ''
        )
    )
);
```

Figure 2.57: Helper models

The protocol will be a request/response protocol with four types of requests, corresponding to the individual CRUD operations. Each request will start with a 1-byte header that denotes the packet options followed by a serialized object that notes the type of data, the overall length of the serialized object, and the payload. If the type of data is **0x00**, the data type is a regular string and not an object. The packet option byte contains all the options for stating the type of request (CRUD) and stating that it is a request. The data type will note the type of data we want to work on from the server. In this example, it will be only the address.

The response packet will contain a 4-byte header that mimics the request but turns the request bit off and the response bit on, specifies the type of data, and notes whether the response was a success. If the result is a failure, the payload will be a string containing the error message.

The payload, if it is not an error, will be a structured format of individual fields. Each field will be preceded by a 3-byte header. The first byte will note the type as an integer and a 2-byte length field. The content will be a UTF-8 encoded string whose length corresponds exactly to the length specified in the field header.

When the payload is part of the request, the type of operation will determine the meaning behind the packet type. For example, for create and update operations, the packet data will need to correspond to the data you want to insert into the database. If you are executing a read or delete request, the payload data is that according to which you want to search.

Let's start by defining our table (Figure 2.58).

```
CREATE TABLE 'addresses' (
 'address_key' int(10) unsigned NOT NULL AUTO_INCREMENT,
 'first_name' varchar(255) NOT NULL,
 'last_name' varchar(255) NOT NULL,
 'address1' varchar(255) NOT NULL,
 'address2' varchar(255) NOT NULL,
 'city' varchar(255) NOT NULL,
 'state' varchar(255) NOT NULL,
 'zip' varchar(255) NOT NULL,
 'country' varchar(255) NOT NULL,
 'phone' varchar(255) NOT NULL,
 'fax' varchar(255) NOT NULL,
 'email' varchar(255) NOT NULL,
 'notes' text NOT NULL,
 PRIMARY KEY ('address_key')
) ENGINE=InnoDB AUTO_INCREMENT=5 DEFAULT CHARSET=utf8
```

Figure 2.58: Table definition

Because we're not hacking another's protocol, we're going to be building our example more like an application. In other words, there will be more structure than what we had before. The structure demonstrated here is not required, and it may not be the absolute best way, but it will illustrate how you can build an application based on binary principles.

The first thing we're going to do is build a model class. In the Model-View-Controller (MVC) architecture, the model is basically an object that represents data and the functionality that pertains directly to that data. Because we are going to lock ourselves in to our own protocol here, we'll begin with an abstract model class that we'll use to facilitate our requests. We'll start with the data and build out the functionality as we go along. Figure 2.59 shows the **BinaryModel** class definition.

```
abstract class BinaryModel
{

    const REQ_CREATE    = 0x01;
    const REQ_READ      = 0x02;
    const REQ_UPDATE    = 0x04;
    const REQ_DELETE    = 0x08;
    const REQ_SUCCESS   = 0x10;
    const REQ_FAILED    = 0x20;
    const REQ_RESPONSE  = 0x40;
    const REQ_REQUEST   = 0x80;


    protected $_type = null;

}
```

Figure 2.59: Abstract binary model class

This abstract class contains all the basic functionality that is common among all the model classes. The parts of the model classes that directly interact with this class are the type and the individual fields. In addition, because the packet option data is important to all models, the bit-based options will be stored in the abstract class.

There will be two ways to identify data. One way is from the binary stream to the object; the other is from the object to the binary stream. The binary field representation will be in the form of class constants, and the object representation will simply be public class properties. However, to map between each representation, they will need to follow a similar naming convention.

Figure 2.60 shows the code for the **Address** model class.

```
class Address extends BinaryModel
{
        public $address_key;
        public $first_name;
        public $last_name;
        public $address1;
        public $address2;
        public $city;
        public $state;
```

```
        public $zip;
        public $country;
        public $phone;
        public $fax;
        public $email;
        public $notes;

        const FLD_ADDRESS_KEY       = 0x01;
        const FLD_FIRST_NAME        = 0x02;
        const FLD_LAST_NAME         = 0x03;
        const FLD_ADDRESS1          = 0x04;
        const FLD_ADDRESS2          = 0x05;
        const FLD_CITY              = 0x06;
        const FLD_STATE             = 0x07;
        const FLD_ZIP               = 0x08;
        const FLD_COUNTRY           = 0x09;
        const FLD_PHONE             = 0x0A;
        const FLD_FAX               = 0x0B;
        const FLD_EMAIL             = 0x0C;
        const FLD_NOTES             = 0x0D;


        const BINARY_TYPE = 0x01;
        protected $_type = self::BINARY_TYPE;
}
```

Figure 2.60: Sample address model class

Each object can have a maximum of 255 individual properties. The code also specifies the binary type representation for this object.

Now, let's go back to our **BinaryModel** class and build out some of the stubs (Figure 2.61).

```
abstract class BinaryModel
{

. . .

        public static function fetch(BinaryModel $obj)
        {
                return false;
        }
```

```
        public function save()
        {

        }

        public function delete()
        {

        }
}
```

Figure 2.61: Stubbed BinaryModel class

You will note that only one of the functions is defined as static, and that is the **fetch()** method. **fetch()** is also the only method that accepts a parameter. The reason for this is that every other function is used within the context of data that already exists. When you call the **fetch()** method, you do not know whether the data exists. But you still need to be able to query based on properties for the object, so we provide the properties there.

The code defines the **fetch()** method to allow only one result being retrieved. A more real-life application would need to be able to retrieve multiple objects, but that's an exercise I will leave to you. There should be enough information for you to be able to build in that functionality yourself should you choose to.

To perform any operations, the first thing we need to be able to do is convert the object to its binary representation. That basically means iterating over the public properties and converting them. So let's add that function to the **BinaryModel** class (Figure 2.62).

```
public static function serialize(BinaryModel $obj)
{
  $class = get_class($obj);
  $packet = '';
  foreach (get_object_vars($obj) as $key => $value) {
        // Make sure we can have a string representation
        if (!$value && $value == (string)$value) {
                continue;
        }
```

```
        $value = utf8_encode($value);
        $fldConst = $class . '::FLD_' . strtoupper($key);
        if (defined($fldConst)) {
                $fldType = constant($fldConst);
                $packet .= pack('CnA*',
                                    $fldType,
                                    strlen($value),
                                    $value
                );
        }
    }
    $packet = pack('CnA*',
                        $obj->getType(),
                        strlen($packet),
                        $packet
    );

    return $packet;
}
```

Figure 2.62: Serialization function

What this code does is get the class name of the object so that we can retrieve the proper binary field representation. Then, we iterate over the properties of the class to encode all the ones that are set. To qualify to be added to the binary stream, the data needs both to be set and to have a constant representation in the class. The constant representation is **FLD_** followed by the name of the property in all uppercase letters. If the property has a corresponding class constant, we then pack it according to the rules we set earlier. The first byte is the name of the field, as determined by the class; the next two bytes are a 16-bit short stating the length of the field followed by the UTF-8 encoded field value. Each individual field will be encoded this way.

If we create an **Address** object, assign it the first name **'James'**, and execute our code, we produce the output shown in Figure 2.63.

```
01=  00=  08=  02=  00=  05=  4a=J 61=a
6d=m 65=e 73=s
```

Figure 2.63: Output of serialization function

The **0x01** byte is the byte stating that this is an **Address** object. The next two bytes indicate the remaining number of bytes in the string. The **0x02** is the field value stating that this is the field for **first_name**. The **0x00 0x05** states that the field is five characters long. The rest of the field is the value.

If I were to provide an **Address** object with the first name **'James'** and the last name **'Madison'**, the output would be as shown in Figure 2.64.

```
01=   00=   12=   02=   00=   05=   4a=J 61=a
6d=m 65=e 73=s 03=   00=   07=   4d=M 61=a
64=d 69=i 73=s 6f=o 6e=n
```

Figure 2.64: Output of serialization function with data included

The type is an 8-bit value, so with this structure you could have up to 255 individual models defined. If you will have more than that (which is somewhat unlikely although not outside the realm of possibility for a larger project), you could make it a 16-bit short. If you have more than 65,000 models in your application, you're doing it wrong.

So, in our abstract class, let's define the function for getting the type (Figure 2.65).

```
abstract class BinaryModel
{
. . .

    public function getType()
    {
        if ($this->_type === null) {
            throw new Exception(
                'Type for object cannot be null'
            );
        }
        return $this->_type;
    }
}
```

Figure 2.65: Retrieving the type for the model

We need to define **$this->_type** in the class extending **BinaryModel** so that **BinaryModel** knows the type of the rendered object. In our example, we have only **Address**, but any real-life application could include several types. So we need a way to determine the type.

Because this is a relatively simple packet structure, our code to build the packet is relatively simple as well (Figure 2.66).

```
public static function createPacket(
        $options,
        $data
        )
{

        return pack('CnA*',
               $options,
               strlen($data),
               $data
        );
}
```

Figure 2.66: Creating the packet

The **$data** parameter is fairly easy to understand, but what about **$options**? **$options** is where we put the commands we're going to send to the server. To illustrate how we set that value, let's look at a revised **fetch()** function (Figure 2.67).

```
abstract class BinaryModel
{
. . .

        public static function fetch(BinaryModel $obj)
        {
                $packet = self::createPacket(
                        self::REQ_READ | self::REQ_REQUEST,
                        self::serialize($obj)
                );

                printBytes($packet);
        }
}
```

Figure 2.67: Binary fetch method

The "magic" is done with the **self::REQ_READ | self::REQ_REQUEST** evaluation. You might be looking at that and saying to yourself, "But don't you want to set read *and* request?" Yes. That's what we're doing. We're not using Boolean operations here; we're using bitwise. So to get both options into single value, we use a bitwise OR.

To test this, let's write a simple test script (Figure 2.68).

```
$a = new Address();
$a->first_name = 'James';
$a->last_name = 'Madison';
BinaryModel::fetch($a);
```

Figure 2.68: Fetching James Madison

Figure 2.69 shows the output of the **printBytes()** function.

```
82=  01=  00=  12=  02=  00=  05=  4a=J
61=a 6d=m 65=e 73=s 03=  00=  07=  4d=M
61=a 64=d 69=i 73=s 6f=o 6e=n
```

Figure 2.69: Bytes for fetching James Madison

The first byte is the option byte, which is set to "request" and "read." The second byte is the "type" byte, which states what type of data we are asking to read (in this case, "Address"). The next two bytes, the 16-bit short, state the length of the payload (in this case, 12 bytes). After that come the individual fields of the object.

Now that we have the packet serialization process completed, we have a decision to make. Do we finish up the model, or do we work on the server for handling the requests? If there were multiple people working on the project, I would say to complete the model classes first. But because we're the only ones working on this, I am going to opt to build a working server first. The reason for this is that I simply prefer to work with real, or properly simulated, data.

So let's change gears a bit and look at a server component. We're going to make it a simple TCP server — no non-blocking I/O or anything like that. For this reason, the solution will not be able to handle multiple simultaneous requests and thus will not scale well. But don't worry about that. We'll cover that concern in a later chapter.

The first thing we're going to do is build a quick test to make sure the basic functionality is there. That basic functionality is to check whether the stream contains a request or a response. If neither is found, we need to send an error packet. Figure 2.70 shows the code.

```
require_once 'Db.php';
require_once 'addrClasses.php';

$sock = socket_create(AF_INET, SOCK_STREAM, SOL_TCP);
socket_bind($sock, 0, 10000);
socket_listen($sock);

while
  (($client = socket_accept($sock)) !== false) {

    $header = socket_read($client, 1);
    $hdrData = unpack(
                'Coptions',
                $header
    );

    if ($hdrData['options'] &
        BinaryModel::REQ_REQUEST) {

        $data = BinaryModel::createPacket(
                BinaryModel::REQ_RESPONSE
                    | BinaryModel::REQ_SUCCESS,
                0x00,
                'Received a request'
        );

    } else if ($hdrData['options'] &
            BinaryModel::REQ_RESPONSE){

        $data = BinaryModel::createPacket(
                BinaryModel::REQ_RESPONSE
                    | BinaryModel::REQ_FAILED,
                0x00,
                'Functionality not implemented yet'
        );
    } else {
```

```
                $data = BinaryModel::createPacket(
                    BinaryModel::REQ_RESPONSE
                        | BinaryModel::REQ_FAILED,
                    0x00,
                    'Unknown packet type'
            );

        }
        socket_write($client, $data, strlen($data));
        socket_close($client);
}
```

Figure 2.70: Server code to receive binary model objects

This code creates the socket, binds it, and receives new connections. Upon receipt of a new connection, the code reads the first byte from the stream. It does this so it can check to see what type of packet it is and call the appropriate function.

Our if-else statement makes the check to see what kind of stream we have received. We use a bitwise check to see whether the request or response bit has been set.

Because this is a test, we're going to just return a string to the client stating whether the request was successful. This technically breaks the protocol, but we're just testing at this point. Figure 2.71 shows the code for the test.

```
$sock = fsockopen('localhost', 10000);
fwrite($sock, pack('C', 0x00 ));
$data = fread($sock, 1024);
printBytes($data);
fclose($sock);

$sock = fsockopen('localhost', 10000);
fwrite($sock, pack('C', BinaryModel::REQ_REQUEST));
$data = fread($sock, 1024);
printBytes($data);
fclose($sock);

$sock = fsockopen('localhost', 10000);
fwrite($sock, pack('C', BinaryModel::REQ_RESPONSE ));
$data = fread($sock, 1024);
printBytes($data);
fclose($sock);
```

Figure 2.71: Client code to send and receive binary model data

The first step is to test to make sure that the unknown packet type is found. The second is to test the request, and the third is to test for the response. Figure 2.72 shows the results.

```
60=' 00=  00=  13=  55=U 6e=n 6b=k 6e=n
6f=o 77=w 6e=n 20=  70=p 61=a 63=c 6b=k
65=e 74=t 20=  74=t 79=y 70=p 65=e

50=P 00=  00=  12=  52=R 65=e 63=c 65=e
69=i 76=v 65=e 64=d 20=  61=a 20=  72=r
65=e 71=q 75=u 65=e 73=s 74=t

50=P 00=  00=  13=  52=R 65=e 63=c 65=e
69=i 76=v 65=e 64=d 20=  61=a 20=  72=r
65=e 73=s 70=p 6f=o 6e=n 73=s 65=e
```

Figure 2.72: Output of test code

If you read slowly through that, you can see that the test was successful.

The next thing to do is to write the function that handles the requests. To do that, we need to pass the options byte to the function and then the socket. The function will return the serialized result of the operation. Our loop will be changed to include the error-handling code shown in Figure 2.73.

```php
if ($hdrData['options'] & BinaryModel::REQ_REQUEST) {

    try {
        $data = handleRequest(
                    $hdrData['options'],
                    $client
        );
    } catch (Exception $e) {
        $data = generateError(
                BinaryModel::REQ_RESPONSE
                    | BinaryModel::REQ_FAILED,
                $e->getMessage()
        );
    }
}
```

Figure 2.73: Handling errors

We will also add a generic error helper function that creates the packet for when an error occurs (Figure 2.74).

```
function generateError($options, $error)
{
        return BinaryModel::createPacket(
                $options,
                pack(
                        'CnA*',
                        0x00,
                        strlen($error),
                        $error
                )
        );
}
```

Figure 2.74: Error helper function

For us to be able work on this data, we need to be able to work with an object that represents the data we have transmitted. To do that, we will need to be able to unserialize that data. For that purpose, we will add an **unserialize()** function to the **BinaryModel** class (Figure 2.75).

```
abstract class BinaryModel

{
. . .


  public static function unserialize($string)
  {
    if (strlen($string) < 3) return NULL;
    $hdr = unpack('Ctype/nlen', substr($string, 0, 3));

    if (strlen($string) != $hdr['len'] + 3) return NULL;

    if ($hdr['type'] === 0x00) {
        return substr($string, 3, $hdr['len']);
    }
```

```
    switch ($hdr['type']) {
        case Address::BINARY_TYPE:
            $obj = new Address();
            break;
        default:
            return NULL;
            break;

    }

  $class = get_class($obj);
  $properties = array_keys(
                        get_object_vars(
                            $obj
                        )
  );

  $strpos = 3; // Start of the payload
  while ($strpos < $hdr['len'] + 3) {
      $fld = unpack('Ctype/nlen',
                  substr($string, $strpos, 3)
      );
      foreach ($properties as $p) {
          $fldConst = $class
                      . '::FLD_'
                      . strtoupper($p);

          if (defined($fldConst)) {
              $fldType = constant($fldConst);
              if ($fldType === $fld['type']) {
                  $obj->$p = substr(
                              $string,
                              $strpos + 3,
                              $fld['len']
                  );
                  unset($properties[$i]);
                  break;
              }
          }
      }
      $strpos += 3 + $fld['len'];
  }

  return $obj;
  }
}
```

Figure 2.75: Binary unserialize method

What the **unserialize()** function does is interpret the string that the **serialize()** function has created. So, the first thing it does is get the type of object that was serialized and the total length of the payload. If the type is less than 3, the payload is an invalid serialized string and we return **NULL**. If the type is **0x00**, or string as we had mentioned earlier, we simply return the raw string after checking to make sure that its length matches the declared length.

With that work accomplished, we go on to creating and populating the correct object. The first thing we do is switch on the type and create the **Address** object if that is the type that is requested. If we do not recognize the type, we return **NULL**.

Next, we set up for iterating over the payload. We start by getting the name of the class, so we can build the correct class constant to query as we iterate over the fields, and the names of all the properties in the class. That done, we define the start position as 3. This is because bytes 0, 1, and 2 were used to denote the object type and the length.

At that point, we start looping over the individual fields. For each field, we get the type and length and then compare the type value to the constant defined for the individual class. If we find a match, we set the object's property to the value, remove the property from the **$properties** variable so we don't test it again, and break so we don't iterate over the rest of that loop. At the end of the loop, we increase the position by the length of the field plus 3 to account for the field's header.

Once that is all done, we return the object that we created. It seems a little complicated, but the best way to see whether this works is to simply test it. Figure 2.76 shows some simple test code that serializes an object and then unserializes the string.

```
$addr = new Address();
$addr->first_name = 'James';
$addr->last_name = 'Madison';

$addr = BinaryModel::serialize($addr);
printBytes($addr);

$addr = BinaryModel::unserialize($addr);
var_dump($addr);
```

Figure 2.76: Serializing and unserializing objects

This code prints out the results shown in Figure 2.77.

```
01=  00=  12=  02=  00=  05=  4a=J 61=a
6d=m 65=e 73=s 03=  00=  07=  4d=M 61=a
64=d 69=i 73=s 6f=o 6e=n

object(Address)#1 (14) {
  ["address_key"]=>
  NULL
  ["first_name"]=>
  string(5) "James"
  ["last_name"]=>
  string(7) "Madison"
  ["address1"]=>
  NULL
  ["address2"]=>
  NULL
  ["city"]=>
  NULL
  ["state"]=>
  NULL
  ["zip"]=>
  NULL
  ["country"]=>
  NULL
  ["phone"]=>
  NULL
  ["fax"]=>
  NULL
  ["email"]=>
  NULL
  ["notes"]=>
  NULL
  ["_type:protected"]=>
  int(1)
}
```

Figure 2.77: Output of serialize/unserialize functionality

It would seem that it has worked.

Now, what we need to do is put it all together so we can send a request from a client, read the response, create the object, query the database from the object, retrieve the results, convert it to the binary model, send it, receive it, check for errors, and then print the errors or print the object, depending on the result of the transaction.

Because we're starting at the client, let's look at some of the functions we need to add to handle it (Figure 2.78).

```php
abstract class BinaryModel
{
. . .
    public static function fetch(BinaryModel $obj)
    {
      $packet = self::createPacket(
            self::REQ_READ | self::REQ_REQUEST,
            self::serialize($obj)
      );

      printBytes($packet);

      return self::_handle($packet);

    }

    protected static function _handle($packet)
    {
      $sock = fsockopen('localhost', 10000);
      fwrite($sock, $packet);
      $data = unpack('Coptions/nlen', fread($sock, 3));
      if ($data['options'] & self::REQ_RESPONSE
            && $data['options'] & self::REQ_SUCCESS) {

            if ($data['len'] > 0) {
                  return self::unserialize(
                        fread($sock, $data['len']));
            } else {
                  return true;
            }


      } else if ($data['options'] & self::REQ_FAILED) {
            $msg  = self::unserialize(
                        fread($sock, $data['len']));

            throw new Exception($msg);
      } else {
            throw new Exception(
                  'An unknown error has occurred');
      }

      fclose($sock);
    }
}
```

Figure 2.78: Adding the fetching and retrieval functionality to the client class

The **fetch()** function is now completed in that it will take a binary model object, create a packet to request the object, pass the packet to the **_handle()** function (which will create the connection), send the packet, and read the result. If the result is unknown, the code will throw an exception stating that it couldn't understand the response. If the result is a failure, it will throw an exception with the message that was returned. If the result was a success, it will return the unserialized result.

On the server side, we have one new function in the server and then two new functions in the **BinaryModel** class.

The function is the one for actually handling the request (Figure 2.79).

```
function handleRequest($options, $socket)
{

    $len = unpack('n', socket_read($socket, 2));
    $obj = BinaryModel::unserialize(
        socket_read(
            $socket,
            array_shift($len)
        )
    );

    $table = BinaryModel::getTableObj($obj);
    if ($options & BinaryModel::REQ_READ) {

        $select = $table->select();
        foreach ($obj as $key => $value) {
            if ($value === NULL) {
                continue;
            }
            $select->where($key . ' = ?', $value);
        }

        $obj = $select->query()->fetchObject(
            $table->getRowClass()
        );
        if ($obj === false) {
            return generateError(
                BinaryModel::REQ_RESPONSE
                    | BinaryModel::REQ_FAILED
                    | BinaryModel::REQ_READ,
                'Unable to find record'
            );
        }
```

```
            if ($obj instanceof Zend_Db_Table_Rowset) {
                    $obj = $obj->current();
            }

            $obj = BinaryModel::dbObj2BinObj($obj);

            return BinaryModel::createPacket(
                    BinaryModel::REQ_RESPONSE
                            | BinaryModel::REQ_SUCCESS
                            | BinaryModel::REQ_READ,
                    BinaryModel::serialize($obj)
            );
        } else {
                // Handle write operations
        }

        return NULL;
}
```

Figure 2.79: Handling the request on the server side

Because we have already read the option byte, we read in the next two bytes, which contain the length. We then read and unserialize the result. This operation should return an instance of **BinaryModel**. If it returns an instance of **Zend_Db_Table_Rowset**, it means that more than one row matched the criteria; in that case, we return only the first instance. Next, we check to see which action we are going to perform. At present, we have only the read option built. We will work on the write functionality once we have the read functionality working.

What we need to do next is to use that object to query the database based on the parameters supplied. We do this by retrieving the **Zend_Db_Table** object that corresponds to the **BinaryModel** object. That code is in the **BinaryModel** class and is relatively simple (Figure 2.80).

```
public static function getTableObj($obj)
{
    if ($obj instanceof BinaryModel) {
            $class = get_class($obj);
            $tableClass = $class.'Table';
            return new $tableClass();
```

```
    } else if ($obj instanceof Zend_Db_Table_Row) {
          return $obj->getTable();
    }
    return NULL;

}
```

Figure 2.80: Retrieving the table object

Once we have the table class, we can create a select statement that we will then iterate over for each of the properties, creating an SQL **AND** statement for as many properties as have been provided.

After we have created the statement, we query the database, stating that we want to retrieve an instance of the row object for this table — in this case, **AddressRow**, which is an instance of **Zend_Db_Table_Row_Abstract**. If we cannot find any corresponding data, we create an error message and return from the function.

If we do find an object, we convert it to its corresponding **BinaryModel** object via the **BinaryModel::dbObj2BinObj()** method (Figure 2.81).

```
public static function dbObj2BinObj(
      Zend_Db_Table_Row_Abstract $obj)
{
      $className = get_class($obj);
      $className = substr($className,
                          0,
                          strlen($className)-3);
      $binObj = new $className();
      foreach ($obj->toArray() as $key => $value) {
            $binObj->$key = $value;
      }
      return $binObj;
}
```

Figure 2.81: Converting the database object to its binary representation

Once we have the proper **BinaryModel** instance, we serialize it, stating that it is a response and a success for a read operation, appending the serialized object to the result.

Does it all work? Again, the only way to test is to run it. Figure 2.82 shows a simple test script.

```php
$addr = new Address();
$addr->first_name = 'James';
$addr->last_name = 'Madison';

try {
        $addr = BinaryModel::fetch($addr);
        var_dump($addr);
} catch (Exception $e) {
        echo "Error: " . $e->getMessage() . "\n";
}
```

Figure 2.82: Test code

This code echoes the output shown in Figure 2.83.

```
object(Address)#2 (14) {
  ["address_key"]=>
  string(1) "4"
  ["first_name"]=>
  string(5) "James"
  ["last_name"]=>
  string(7) "Madison"
  ["address1"]=>
  string(16) "1209 Madison Ave"
  ["address2"]=>
  NULL
  ["city"]=>
  string(11) "Port Conway"
  ["state"]=>
  string(2) "VA"
  ["zip"]=>
  string(5) "22535"
  ["country"]=>
  string(3) "USA"
  ["phone"]=>
  string(12) "540-555-7243"
  ["fax"]=>
  NULL
  ["email"]=>
  string(18) "jmadison@constconv"
```

```
["notes"]=>
  string(205) "James Madison was a political philosopher
                and the fourth President of the United
                States. He is also commonly considered
                to be the father of the United States
                Constitution since he was the principal
                author."
  ["_type:protected"]=>
  int(1)
}
```

Figure 2.83: Output of test code

Clearly, it was populated from the results that the server sent back from it. If you are typing out this code and this is not the result you get, it is advisable to use a debugger on the code.

Testing for success is one thing. How about testing for failure? The code in Figure 2.84 deliberately checks for an error.

```
$addr = new Address();
$addr->first_name = 'John';
$addr->last_name = 'Madison';

try {
        $addr = BinaryModel::fetch($addr);
        var_dump($addr);
} catch (Exception $e) {
        echo "Error: " . $e->getMessage() . "\n";
}
```

Figure 2.84: Code to test for an error

This test echoes:

```
Error: Unable to find record
```

It would seem like it works as well.

The last thing we need to do is handle the CRUD operations now. Thankfully, because we're using Zend Framework's database abstraction layer, much of that work is already done for us. As before, let's start on the client side in the **BinaryModel** class. Because we've already built out most of the protocol code, the rest is actually really easy (Figure 2.85).

```
abstract class BinaryModel
{
. . .
    public function save()
    {
            $packet = self::createPacket(
                    self::REQ_UPDATE | self::REQ_REQUEST,
                    self::serialize($this)
            );
            $obj = self::_handle($packet);
            foreach ($obj as $key => $value) {
                    $this->$key = $value;
            }
    }

    public function delete()
    {
            $packet = self::createPacket(
                    self::REQ_DELETE | self::REQ_REQUEST,
                    self::serialize($this)
            );
            return self::_handle($packet);
    }
}
```

Figure 2.85: Handing Create, Update, and Delete functionality

Because Zend Framework takes care of determining whether we're going to do an update or an insert, we need to worry only about doing the save. The save operation is sent to the server to insert into the database. That is done simply by sending the packet to the server and letting it handle the database operations. On a create or update, the only thing we need to worry about is making sure our binary object has been updated with any changes from the database. One example of this would be the primary key from an initial save operation. Another would be if a trigger modifies a value for one of the fields.

With the delete operation, we have even less to do. Just send the request with a delete option, and if **_handle()** doesn't throw an exception, the request has been executed.

On the server side there's more code, but not too much (Figure 2.86).

```
function handleRequest($options, $socket)
{

  $len = unpack('n', socket_read($socket, 2));
  $obj = BinaryModel::unserialize(
        socket_read(
              $socket,
              array_shift($len)
        )
  );

  $table = BinaryModel::getTableObj($obj);

  if ($options & BinaryModel::REQ_READ)

. . .

  } else {
     $primaryKey = $table->info(
                      Zend_Db_Table_Abstract::PRIMARY);

     $primaryKey = array_shift($primaryKey);

     if (isset($obj->$primaryKey)) {

            $dbObj = $table->find($obj->$primaryKey);
            if (!$dbObj) {
                  throw new Exception(
                            'Could not find record');
            }
            if ($dbObj instanceof Zend_Db_Table_Rowset) {
                  $dbObj = $dbObj->current();
            }

     } else {
            $dbObj = $table->fetchNew();
     }
     foreach ($obj as $key => $value) {
            if ($key == $primaryKey) continue;
            $dbObj->$key = $value;
     }
```

```
  if ($options & BinaryModel::REQ_DELETE) {
      $dbObj->delete();

      return BinaryModel::createPacket(
          BinaryModel::REQ_RESPONSE
                  | BinaryModel::REQ_SUCCESS
                  | BinaryModel::REQ_DELETE,
          ''
      );

  } else if ($action
        = ($options & BinaryModel::REQ_CREATE)
          || $action
        = ($options & BinaryModel::REQ_UPDATE)) {

          $dbObj->save();
          $obj = BinaryModel::dbObj2BinObj($dbObj);
          return BinaryModel::createPacket(
              BinaryModel::REQ_RESPONSE
                  | BinaryModel::REQ_SUCCESS
                  | $action,
              BinaryModel::serialize($obj)
          );
      }
  }

  return NULL;
}
```

Figure 2.86: Handling delete functionality on the server side

The first thing we need to do is find out which property is the primary key and whether or not it's set. To do that, we get the meta information from our **AddressTable** class. If the primary key is set, we do a query on the database and get the corresponding **Zend_Db_Table_Row_Abstract** class. If a non-object is returned, we throw an exception to state that we did not find a row matching it. If a result set is returned instead of a row, we get the first item, although because we're querying based on the primary key, this shouldn't be an issue.

After that, we check the option we're trying to execute. If it's the delete option, we simply call **delete()** on the object and return, saying that the operation was successful. If it's the update or create option, we save the object and then immediately convert it to its **BinaryModel** representation. That representation is then returned, and the success flag is set.

Conclusion

That brings us to the end of our discussion of binary protocols. There are many more topics we could cover here, but this material is enough to get you started on working with binary protocols. Because PHP is typically used for Web development, a lot of these concepts might seem somewhat foreign to you. But once you start getting an understanding of some lower-level programming, there is a pretty large world for you to explore.

As a side note, one question you may have is why we are doing all this over our own server instead of over HTTP. The reason for that is that we're trying to make the solution as efficient as possible. If efficiency is not overly important, there are a wealth of other protocols you could use to transfer data. Here, we're talking binary. However, if you wanted to implement this protocol over HTTP, you could. Simply send the data as POST data and read from **php://stdin**.

CHAPTER 3

Character Encoding

Many developers understand what the purpose of a character set is. With internationalization becoming a more important feature, the nature of the character set is even more significant. And while many people know how to use a character set, understanding of the underlying mechanism is not as great. In this chapter, we look at what a character set is, how to use one, and what happens behind the scenes to make it work.

The Basics

Computers know nothing about language. Actually, when you get right down to it, they know nothing of numbers either. All that computers know is on and off. They can change the ons and offs based on other ons and offs. If certain ons are on, the processor will do one thing; if they are off, it will do another. A computer is perfectly happy with this arrangement.

However, the purpose of a computer is to do work for a human. A computer is a machine whose purpose is to make a human's job easier (or enable a human to blow up zombies, for that matter). That means that the computer has a problem: it doesn't know how to talk to the human in its own language. For this reason, humans needed to teach computers how to talk with them.

In the early days, this task was quite simple. Given that computers were basically created in the English-speaking part of the world, English was a natural choice to provide the interface so that humans and computers could talk. However, if you were to read through some of the mainframe program calls, it would be apparent that some give and take took place in both directions; the commands that the humans gave the system are actually quite cryptic, unless you know the language.

The reason for this is the limitation of resources. In the early days of computing, every bit was sacred. Every bit was great. And so we started with what is called the American Standard Code for Information Interchange, or ASCII as we now know it. ASCII is a 7-bit code that gave developers more than enough room to handle the 26 characters of the English alphabet plus some punctuation, special characters, and control characters. All told, 127 options for managing data.

At its most basic level, a character set is a translation for the computer. It translates the numbers that the computer stores into graphical characters. A computer cannot store a letter, but it can store a numeric representation of that letter. The character set defines the standard of translation between the number and the graphical character.

For example, you cannot store the letter "A" on a computer. A computer doesn't really know numbers, and it *really* doesn't know letters. But numbers can have binary representations. You could also have a binary representation of a letter, but it would conflict with the binary representation of a number. Say you had the number **12** and you wanted to add **4** to it. Would that be the number 4 or the letter "d"?

So, a computer's primary method of communication is via numbers, and the character set is the mapping between the numbers, which the computer *is* able to work with, and the human. And thus the communication problem between computer and human is solved, right? Not exactly.

In the early days of computing, ASCII was not as prevalent as it is today. A competitor was Extended Binary Coded Decimal Interchange Code, or EBCDIC. Written on the IBM System/360, EBCDIC became quite common due to the popularity of that system.

With that (and other situations like it), character encoding issues arose. Why? Remember that a letter is just a certain number. In ASCII, the number for the letter A is **65**. In EBCDIC, the number for the letter A is **193**. Why the difference? I have heard from some IBM i (the IBM midrange integrated system) people that

EBCDIC was good for punch cards because the way the bits were laid out made for more durable cards.

Before the Web-based whippersnappers (I count myself part of this crowd) go off on this, remember that modern computer science is a very new endeavor. The problems that people in the 1950s and 1960s had to solve were basically the same, but different limitations applied. The first commercially available microprocessor, the Intel 4004, was a 4-bit machine that debuted in 1971. Both ASCII and EBCDIC were available in 1963, eight years earlier. In other words, punch cards were a necessary step for us to get to the point where we are today.

But the problem of how to represent characters remains, and that is where character set conversion comes into play. Imagine that you have one system, an IBM mainframe, that started its life in the 1960s and has been upgraded through the years, first to a System/390 and then to a System i or System z. You may have some applications that continue to use EBCDIC, but you run on a computer that uses ASCII as its default character set, and you need to read from the older computer.

To illustrate the problem, let's take a look at what an EBCDIC encoded "hello world" looks like. Figure 3.1 shows this PHP code.

```
$str = pack( 'CCCCCCCCCCC',
        0x88, 0x85, 0x93, 0x93, 0x96, 0x40, 0xa6, 0x96,
        0x99, 0x93, 0x84
);

echo $str;
```

Figure 3.1: EBCDIC-encoded character string

Remember that a character encoding is just a sequence of numbers, but each individual number represents an individual character. When we run the preceding code, we get something a little different from what we intended:

```
^ ...""‐@¦‐™"„
```

The reason for this is simple. My browser understands ASCII, and according to ASCII, those are the characters I asked it to print out. To show this, let's change the code to its ASCII representation (Figure 3.2).

```
$str = pack( 'CCCCCCCCCCC',
        0x68, 0x65, 0x6c, 0x6c, 0x6f, 0x20, 0x77,0x6f,
        0x72, 0x6c, 0x64
);
echo $str;
```

Figure 3.2: ASCII-encoded character string

The code looks the same, except with different numbers. But when we print it out in the browser, we get a different result:

```
hello world
```

The question, then, is how do we get something that was returned to us in EBCDIC to display properly on a browser that does not support it? You typically do this with some kind of character set conversion. All the character set conversion does is change the numbers in a string of one character set to the numbers in the string of the other character set that matches the letter. This is usually done using a *conversion table*.

A conversion table is a very simple concept. In PHP, it's also very simple to implement. You basically have a numerical array of all characters that are convertible, starting at zero. Then, for each numerical key of the array, you have the corresponding value in the other character set that represents the same letter. So, for example, in ASCII the ordinal for the letter "h" is **0x68**, or **104**. In EBCDIC, the letter "h" is **0x88** or **136**. So, basically, the conversion table for EBCDIC to ASCII will have, at key number **136**, the number **104**.

Figure 3.3 shows an EBCDIC-to-ASCII character converter.

```
$table = array(
        0x00, 0x10, 0x20, 0x30, 0x00, 0x90, 0x00, 0x7f,
        0x00, 0x00, 0x00, 0xb0, 0xc0, 0xd0, 0xe0, 0xf0,
```

```
        0x10, 0x11, 0x12, 0x00, 0x00, 0x00, 0x80, 0x17,
        0x18, 0x19, 0x00, 0x00, 0x1c, 0x1d, 0x1e, 0x1f,
        0x00, 0x00, 0x00, 0x00, 0x00, 0xa0, 0x16, 0x1b,
        0x00, 0x00, 0x00, 0x00, 0x00, 0x50, 0x60, 0x70,
        0x00, 0x00, 0x15, 0x00, 0x00, 0x00, 0x00, 0x40,
        0x00, 0x00, 0x00, 0x00, 0x13, 0x14, 0x00, 0x1a,
        0x20, 0x00, 0x00, 0x00, 0x00, 0x00, 0x00, 0x00,
        0x00, 0x00, 0x5b, 0x2e, 0x3c, 0x28, 0x2b, 0x21,
        0x26, 0x00, 0x00, 0x00, 0x00, 0x00, 0x00, 0x00,
        0x00, 0x00, 0x5d, 0x24, 0x2a, 0x29, 0x3b, 0x5e,
        0x2d, 0x2f, 0x00, 0x00, 0x00, 0x00, 0x00, 0x00,
        0x00, 0x00, 0x7c, 0x2c, 0x25, 0x5f, 0x3e, 0x3f,
        0x00, 0x00, 0x00, 0x00, 0x00, 0x00, 0x00, 0x00,
        0x00, 0x60, 0x3a, 0x23, 0x40, 0x27, 0x3d, 0x22,
        0x00, 0x61, 0x62, 0x63, 0x64, 0x65, 0x66, 0x67,
        0x68, 0x69, 0x00, 0x00, 0x00, 0x00, 0x00, 0x00,
        0x00, 0x6a, 0x6b, 0x6c, 0x6d, 0x6e, 0x6f, 0x70,
        0x71, 0x72, 0x00, 0x00, 0x00, 0x00, 0x00, 0x00,
        0x00, 0x7e, 0x73, 0x74, 0x75, 0x76, 0x77, 0x78,
        0x79, 0x7a, 0x00, 0x00, 0x00, 0x00, 0x00, 0x00,
        0x00, 0x00, 0x00, 0x00, 0x00, 0x00, 0x00, 0x00,
        0x00, 0x00, 0x00, 0x00, 0x00, 0x00, 0x00, 0x00,
        0x7b, 0x41, 0x42, 0x43, 0x44, 0x45, 0x46, 0x47,
        0x48, 0x49, 0x00, 0x00, 0x00, 0x00, 0x00, 0x00,
        0x7d, 0x4a, 0x4b, 0x4c, 0x4d, 0x4e, 0x4f, 0x50,
        0x51, 0x52, 0x00, 0x00, 0x00, 0x00, 0x00, 0x00,
        0x5c, 0x00, 0x53, 0x54, 0x55, 0x56, 0x57, 0x58,
        0x59, 0x5a, 0x00, 0x00, 0x00, 0x00, 0x00, 0x00,
        0x30, 0x31, 0x32, 0x33, 0x34, 0x35, 0x36, 0x37,
        0x38, 0x39, 0x00, 0x00, 0x00, 0x00, 0x00, 0x00
);

// EBCDIC "hello world"
$str = pack( 'CCCCCCCCCCC',
        0x88, 0x85, 0x93, 0x93, 0x96, 0x40, 0xa6, 0x96,
        0x99, 0x93, 0x84

);

$len = strlen($str);
$strBytes = array_values(
                   unpack(
                            'C*',
                            $str
                   )
);
```

```
for ($c = 0; $c < $len; $c++) {
        $str[$c] = pack(
                      'C',
                      $table[
                             $strBytes[$c]
                      ]
        );
}

echo $str;
```

Figure 3.3: EBCDIC-to-ASCII character converter

The first part of this code is the conversion table. It may look like just a series of bytes, but it is actually the numerically indexed array we noted earlier that matches the characters from one character set to another.

The first stage of the process is to extract the numerical values of the string. You could achieve this with repeated calls to the **ord()** function, but, in general, if you can do something in one call, you should. The **$strBytes** constant will contain all the individual byte values in our EBCDIC-encoded string.

The next step is just value replacement. Replace the value of **$str[$c]** with the table-corrected value. That's it. Now, when we run our code we get the output we expect:

```
hello world
```

Our code is now complete. We have the mechanism for converting between any character set in the English language. So, we're all done, right? Nope. Clearly, there are other languages in the world. So, how do we handle many of them? Enter the eighth bit.

Most "Latin" character encodings support ASCII as part of their encoding. This is simply because large parts of most Western language alphabets using English characters, and the people who use these character sets will have a fair amount of contact with English-speaking people. For those two reasons, many of the Western world's character sets include the English ASCII component for the lower bits and then the language-specific characters in the upper values — those above character 127.

To see this in action, consider the script shown in Figure 3.4.

```php
header(
        'Content-Type: text/plain; charset="'
        . $_GET['charset']
        . '"'
);
for ($c = 0; $c < 255; $c++) {

        if ($c % 16 == 1) echo "\n";

        $char = pack('C', $c);
        if (ctype_print($c)) {
            echo $char . ' ';
        } else {
            echo '  ';
        }
}
```

Figure 3.4: Demonstrating high-bit characters

What this code does is print the byte of each character from 0 to 254. However, you can tweak the character set via the query string. So, if we enter the URL **print.php?charset=ISO-8859-1**, we get the output shown in Figure 3.5.

```
! " # $ % & ' ( ) * + , - . / 0
1 2 3 4 5 6 7 8 9 : ; < = > ? @
A B C D E F G H I J K L M N O P
Q R S T U V W X Y Z [ \ ] ^ _ `
a b c d e f g h i j k l m n o p
q r s t u v w x y z { | } ~
, ƒ „ … † ‡  ‰ Š ‹ Œ   Ž
` ' " " • – — ˜   š › œ   ž Ÿ
  ¡ ¢ £ ¤ ¥ ¦ § ¨ © ª « ¬ ® ¯ °
± ² ³ ´ µ ¶ · ¸ ¹ º » ¼ ½ ¾ ¿ À
Á Â Ã Ä Å Æ Ç È É Ê Ë Ì Í Î Ï Ð
Ñ Ò Ó Ô Õ Ö × Ø Ù Ú Û Ü Ý Þ ß à
á â ã ä å æ ç è é ê ë ì í î ï ð
ñ ò ó ô õ ö ÷ ø ù ú û ü ý þ
```

Figure 3.5 Output of high-bit characters with ISO-8859-1 encoding

If we enter the URL **print.php?charset=ISO-8859-7**, the same bytes are being printed, but we're telling the browser to use the ISO Greek character set to render those bytes (Figure 3.6).

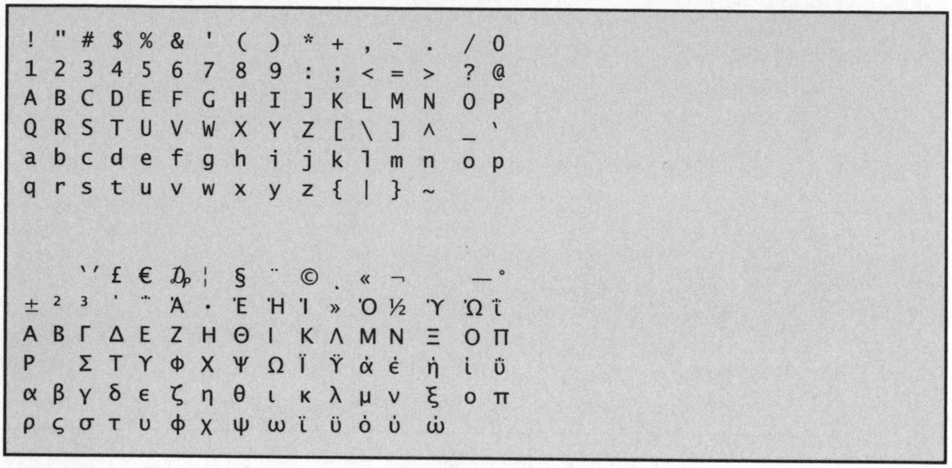

Figure 3.6: Output of high-bit characters with ISO-8859-7 encoding

If we enter **print.php?charset=Windows-1255**, we get the Hebrew characters (Figure 3.7).

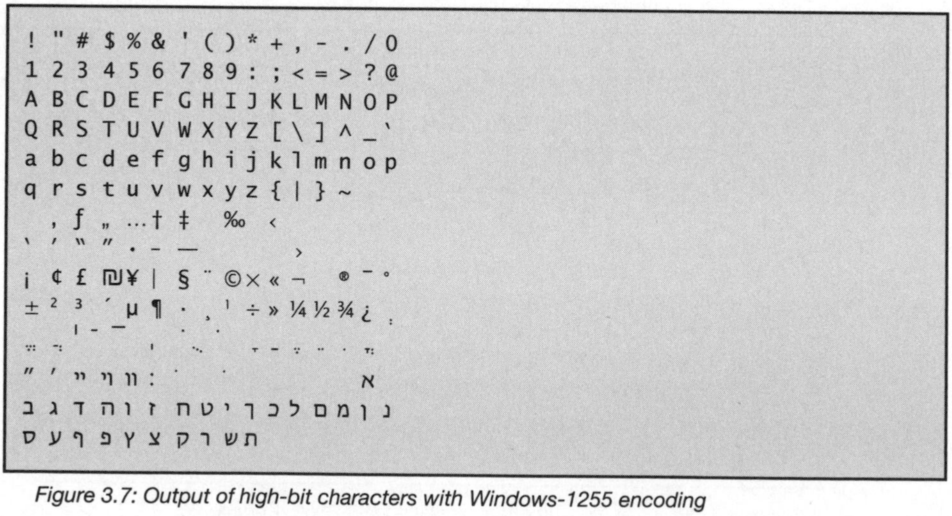

Figure 3.7: Output of high-bit characters with Windows-1255 encoding

Again, nothing has changed in terms of the output between the individual URLs. Only the charset variable, as part of the header, has changed.

Multi-Byte Character Sets

What if you have a language that has more than 255 characters in it? Many non-Western languages fit this description. The solution in this case is what is called a *multi-byte* or, often, a *variable-width* character set. What a multi-byte character set means is that using a combination of bytes, the correct character will be displayed.

However, you run into a bit of a problem. That problem is the Western world. Just because your content will be multi-byte does not mean your markup will be. Consider Hypertext Markup Language (HTML). HTML uses tags, such as **div**, **span**, and so on. These are English words, and for an individual Web page to work, these English characters need to work.

Take, for example, the code shown in Figure 3.8, which prints out "hello world" (or so I'm told) using the EUC-JP character set.

```
header(
        'Content-Type: text/html; charset="EUC-JP"'
);
?>
<div>
<?php
$data = pack('CCCCCCCCCCCC',
        0xBA, 0xA3, 0xC6, 0xFC, 0xA4, 0xCF, 0xA1, 0xA2,
        0xC0, 0xA4, 0xB3, 0xA6
);

echo $data;

?>
</div>
```

Figure 3.8: Printing "hello world" using EUC-JP

The **div** tags need to work, but the problem is that EUC-JP is a multi-byte character set and HTML is single-byte. The solution for any implementation that is valid for HTML is to retain the ASCII character set. What this means, from a practical standpoint, is that most (if not all) character sets that are multi-byte exercise their multi-byte tendencies with the high bit on — in other words, in values above 127. This solution preserves compatibility with Latin characters and, thus, with most markup languages.

But you still have a problem. Simply turning the high bit on is fine if you know you're going to have only two bytes used to represent the character. But this situation is seldom the case. In the case of EUC-JP, there are actually four different ways to interpret the bytes, with three specific Japanese character sets being represented.

The first is JIS-X-0201 between **0x21** (!) and **0x7E** (-), and it is implemented as single-byte encoding. JIS-X-0201 could be considered ASCII-ish in that it contains most of the ASCII character equivalents.

The next is JIS-X-0201 between **0xA1** (.) and **0xDF** ('). However, any character byte in this set must be preceded by **0x8E**. Figure 3.9 shows an example that demonstrates this point.

```
header(
        'Content-Type: text/plain; charset="EUC-JP"'
);

$data = pack('C', 0xA1);

echo $data;
```

Figure 3.9: Printing a character without the leading byte

Here, **0xA1** is the . character, but if we try to print this on our browser, we get a blank screen. However, by placing the **0x8E** ahead of **0xA1**, we get a properly rendered character (Figure 3.10).

```
header(
        'Content-Type: text/plain; charset="EUC-JP"'
);

$data = pack('CC', 0x8E, 0xA1);

echo $data;
```

Figure 3.10: Printing a character with the lead byte

This code prints out the following:

```
。
```

That marker byte is an important piece of information for this character set.

The third way to render EUC-JP is with two bytes, but only if those bytes are between **0xA1** and **0xFE**. It is the combination of the two bytes, which are between those two values, that determines which character is going to be used. Figure 3.11 shows (hopefully) our Japanese "hello world" code.

```
header(
        'Content-Type: text/plain; charset="EUC-JP"'
);

$data = pack('CCCCCCCCCCCC',
        0xBA, 0xA3, 0xC6, 0xFC, 0xA4, 0xCF, 0xA1, 0xA2,
        0xC0, 0xA4, 0xB3, 0xA6
);

echo $data;
```

Figure 3.11: Printing characters in EUC-JP

This code prints out

```
今日は、世界
```

Notice the values that we pack into the string. All of them are between **0xA1** and **0xFE**, and there are exactly double the numbers of bytes, showing that this is a two-byte interpretation of EUC-JP.

The last way to interpret EUC-JP is using a three-byte method, interpreting the JIS-X-0212 character set. Remember how JIS-X-0201 would be interpreted only if it was preceded by **0x8E**? JIS-X-0212 will be interpreted only if it is preceded by **0x8F**. Say we want to print the character 卢. The byte values for this character are

0xBBA4. However, if we echo the raw characters, we get a different value (Figure 3.12).

```
header(
        'Content-Type: text/plain; charset="EUC-JP"'
);

$data = pack('CC', 0xBB, 0xA4);

echo $data;
```

Figure 3.12: Printing 3-byte JIS-X-0212 characters

This code prints out:

擦

Clearly, 尸 and 擦 are different characters. But the reason 擦 is printed is because **0xBBA4** is using JIS-X-0201 instead of JIS-X-0212. To use JIS-X-0212, we need to prepend **0xBBA4** with the **0x8F** byte (Figure 3.13). This tells the browser to use a different code page to render the character.

```
header(
        'Content-Type: text/plain; charset="EUC-JP"'
);

$data = pack('CCC', 0x8F, 0xBB, 0xA4);

echo $data;
```

Figure 3.13: Adding 0x8F to force the use of JIS-X-0212

When we do this, we get the proper character:

尸

I show this not so you can understand EUC-JP but so you can see how a multi-byte character set works. The problem is, however, that there are many incompatibilities between local character sets, as well as other consistency issues.

That is where Unicode comes in.

Unicode and UTF-8

Unicode was built with the goal of unifying as many of the world's languages as possible into one standard implementation. How well that goal has been implemented is a minor point of debate, but, by and large, it does the job. Unicode contains 90 scripts (character sets) and more than 100,000 individual characters. In terms of limits, there are just over one million possible code points, which means that the standard is currently under 10 percent utilized.

Unicode Transformation Format (UTF) is most likely the closest contact you will have with Unicode on the Web. UTF-8 is probably the format you will end up using the most because it is designed to be compatible with ASCII, which is, of course, what HTML pages are marked up in.

Like EUC-JP, UTF-8 is a variable-width encoding, but unlike EUC-JP, its method of encoding is completely compatible with other languages because it is all part of the Unicode standard. You don't need to understand how the coding works to make your Web page UTF-8 compatible, but understanding how it works does help you to build a complete, end-to-end, internationalized application.

To gain an understanding of how UTF-8's variable-length encoding works, we need to look at the bit level. With that goal in mind, Figure 3.14 shows an example that does just that.

```php
header('Content-Type: text/html; charset="UTF-8"');

if (isset($_POST['text'])) {
        echo $_POST['text'] . '<br/>';
        $bytes = array_values(
                        unpack(
                                'C*',
                                $_POST['text']
                        )
        );
        $len = count($bytes);
        for ($c = 0; $c < $len; $c++) {
```

```
            echo str_pad(
                    decbin(
                            $bytes[$c]
                    ),
                    8,
                    0,
                    STR_PAD_LEFT
                )
                . ' ';
            echo '0x' . str_pad(strtoupper(
                    dechex(
                            $bytes[$c]
                    )
                ), 2, 0) . ' ';
            echo $bytes[$c];
            echo '<br />';
        }
    }

?>
<form method="post">
Text: <input type="text" name="text" /><br />
<input type="submit" />
</form>
```

Figure 3.14: Code to look at the bits of a character encoding

What this code does is quite basic. It simply takes input, extracts each byte, and then prints the binary and hexadecimal representation of it with the numeric value thrown in. (And, yes, there is a massive security vulnerability there so don't write me.) Let's start with a simple **'ABCDEF'**. Figure 3.15 shows how this string will be printed out. No surprises here.

```
ABCDEF
01000001 0x41 65
01000010 0x42 66
01000011 0x43 67
01000100 0x44 68
01000101 0x45 69
01000110 0x46 70
```

Figure 3.15: Output of bits and bytes for ASCII characters

How about some characters with the high bit set? If you remember back to our byte-printing example, there were several characters we could use in standard ASCII encoding that had the high bit set. Figure 3.16 shows the full character set.

```
! " # $ % & ' ( ) * + , - . / 0
1 2 3 4 5 6 7 8 9 : ; < = > ? @
A B C D E F G H I J K L M N O P
Q R S T U V W X Y Z [ \ ] ^ _ `
a b c d e f g h i j k l m n o p
q r s t u v w x y z { | } ~
    , ƒ „ … † ‡    ‰ Š ' Œ    ž
 ` ' " " . – —    š ' œ    ž Ÿ
¡ ¢ £ ¤ ¥ | § ¨ © ª « ¬    ® ¯ °
± ² ³ ´ µ ¶ · ¸ ¹ º » ¼ ½ ¾ ¿ À
Á Â Ã Ä Å Æ Ç È É Ê Ë Ì Í Î Ï Ð
Ñ Ò Ó Ô Õ Ö × Ø Ù Ú Û Ü Ý Þ ß à
á â ã ä å æ ç è é ê ë ì í î ï ð
ñ ò ó ô õ ö ÷ ø ù ú û ü ý þ
```

Figure 3.16: High-bit on ASCII encoding

Remember that these are all single-byte encodings. They are all full ASCII, or rather ISO-8859-1 because ASCII is technically only 7-bit. So, let's copy some of the single-byte characters from this group. The characters "¢£¤¥" are some good examples because they are currency marks. We'll copy these symbols, paste them into the text box, and hit submit. Figure 3.17 shows the result of the conversion.

```
¢£¤¥
11000010 0xC2 194
10100010 0xA2 162
11000010 0xC2 194
10100011 0xA3 163
11000010 0xC2 194
10100100 0xA4 164
11000010 0xC2 194
10100101 0xA5 165
```

Figure 3.17: Converting high-bit single-byte text to UTF-8

What? What happened to the single-byte stuff? UTF-8, that's what happened. Because we set the content type character encoding to UTF-8, the browser automatically sends all data in a UTF-8 compatible format. Why not just send the 8-bit ISO-8859-1 that we had asked for? Because UTF-8 has a certain encoding mechanism that lets it do multi-byte character encoding that is compatible with 7-bit ASCII. Table 3.1 presents the rules. The **x**'s are the character data, and the **1**s and **0**s are static bits.

Table 3.1: Bit mapping for UTF-8 encoded characters		
Bytes	Usable bits	Character representation
1	7	0xxxxxxx
2	11	110xxxxx 10xxxxxx
3	16	1110xxxx 10xxxxxx 10xxxxxx
4	21	11110xxx 10xxxxxx 10xxxxxx 10xxxxxx

There are three types of bytes in a UTF-8 representation. The first is the standard ASCII byte. This type starts with the high bit off. The second type is a *lead byte*. The lead byte informs the UTF-8 mechanism how long the multi-byte string is. A lead byte always has a bitmask of **11000000**; additional bits can be set, but those first two bits will always be on in a lead byte. The third type is a *fill byte*. It generally will contain most of the data for the character. Getting to a point where we can do bit-level operations requires a few steps, but it's not overly difficult.

One of the nice things about UTF-8 using bit-level data is that this type of data is very friendly to processors. Processors can twiddle bits faster than they can perform almost any other operation, so these types of checks, and subsequently matching characters from multiple bytes, can occur extremely quickly.

Let's change up our earlier code so that it can do some of the bit-level work. In Figure 3.18, the added code appears in bold.

```
if (isset($_POST['text'])) {
        echo $_POST['text'] . '<br/>';
        $bytes = array_values(
                        unpack(
                                'C*',
                                $_POST['text']
                        )
        );
        $len = count($bytes);
```

```
        for ($c = 0; $c < $len; $c++) {
            echo str_pad(
                      decbin(
                            $bytes[$c]
                      ),
                      8,
                      0,
                      STR_PAD_LEFT
                )
                . ' ';
            echo '0x' . str_pad(strtoupper(
                        dechex(
                                $bytes[$c]
                        )
                ), 2, 0) . ' ';

            if (($bytes[$c] & 0xC0) === 0xC0) {
                echo 'L';
            }
            if ((($bytes[$c] ^ 0xC0) & 0x40) === 0x40) {
                echo 'F';
            }
            if ((~$bytes[$c] & 0x80) === 0x80) {
                echo 'A';
            }
            echo ' ' . $bytes[$c];
            echo '<br />';
        }
}
```

Figure 3.18: Code to determine lead, fill, and ASCII bytes

When we submit our "¢£¤¥" sequence again, the letter **L** in the resulting output (Figure 3.19) indicates a lead byte, **F** signals a fill, and A is for ASCII.

```
¢£¤¥
11000010 0xC2 L 194
10100010 0xA2 F 162
11000010 0xC2 L 194
10100011 0xA3 F 163
11000010 0xC2 L 194
10100100 0xA4 F 164
11000010 0xC2 L 194
10100101 0xA5 F 165
```

Figure 3.19: Output of determining lead, fill, and ASCII bytes

The first bit check is quite simple. If the bits **11000000** are on, the byte is a lead byte. The second check is a little more difficult. We could do a simple else statement and check at this point to see whether the value is above 127; if it is, we could assume that the byte is a fill byte, since we've already tested for the lead byte. But for the example, it is beneficial to make sure that the exact bits that are meant to be set actually are. For that reason, we'll do a bit of bit-twiddling.

The first thing we do is turn off all the bits that are not in the first two positions. **0xC0** is **11000000**. A fill byte technically has only six bits of data, so what we're doing is discarding any data bits. If the byte is a fill byte, the result of this operation should be **01000000** because the seventh bit should be turned off and the eighth bit turned on. A fill bit is **10xxxxxx**, so the result of the **NOT** operation will be **01000000**. **01000000** is also **0x40**. So if the **NOT** operation against **0xC0** equals **0x40**, we have a fill byte.

Checking for ASCII is relatively simple. Because ASCII is 7-bit, only the eighth bit should be zero. So we do a **NOT** against it to flip the eighth bit to its inverse and then do a bitwise **AND** against the value **0x80**, or **10000000**. If the two values match, the value is ASCII.

To test out this solution, let's throw an ASCII character into the middle of our string of characters. We'll test the string "¢£A¤¥"; note the letter "A" in the third position. Figure 3.20 shows the program's output.

```
¢£A¤¥
11000010 0xC2 L 194
10100010 0xA2 F 162
11000010 0xC2 L 194
10100011 0xA3 F 163
01000001 0x41 A 65
11000010 0xC2 L 194
10100100 0xA4 F 164
11000010 0xC2 L 194
10100101 0xA5 F 165
```

Figure 3.20: Output with an ASCII character added

This result correctly identifies the letter A as an ASCII character in the stream of Unicode characters.

Okay, so we've been able to read and understand how Unicode characters are transferred to PHP, but how about if we wanted to *write* Unicode characters? Not only that, but say we wanted to write Unicode characters that are interspersed between various multilingual planes and have them encoded using UTF-8 for full browser compatibility? Now that would be fun.

For our test, we'll take the defined ranges from ASCII to Domino Tiles (the final Unicode code page) for all Unicode language blocks and print the middle character. The first and last characters of a block are often unprintable, so for that reason we'll find the middle and print that. Figure 3.21 shows the code to print the middle character of all current Unicode blocks. (*Hint:* Copy the bytes from somewhere else. Don't type them out.)

```
header('Content-Type: text/plain; charset="UTF-8"');

$data = array(
    array(0x0000, 0x007F),      array(0x0080, 0x00FF),
    array(0x0100, 0x017F),      array(0x0180, 0x024F),
    array(0x0250, 0x02AF),      array(0x02B0, 0x02FF),
    array(0x0300, 0x036F),      array(0x0370, 0x03FF),
    array(0x0400, 0x04FF),      array(0x0500, 0x052F),
    array(0x0530, 0x058F),      array(0x0590, 0x05FF),
    array(0x0600, 0x06FF),      array(0x0700, 0x074F),
    array(0x0750, 0x077F),      array(0x0780, 0x07BF),
    array(0x07C0, 0x07FF),      array(0x0900, 0x097F),
    array(0x0980, 0x09FF),      array(0x0A00, 0x0A7F),
    array(0x0A80, 0x0AFF),      array(0x0B00, 0x0B7F),
    array(0x0B80, 0x0BFF),      array(0x0C00, 0x0C7F),
    array(0x0C80, 0x0CFF),      array(0x0D00, 0x0D7F),
    array(0x0D80, 0x0DFF),      array(0x0E00, 0x0E7F),
    array(0x0E80, 0x0EFF),      array(0x0F00, 0x0FFF),
    array(0x1000, 0x109F),      array(0x10A0, 0x10FF),
    array(0x1100, 0x11FF),      array(0x1200, 0x137F),
    array(0x1380, 0x139F),      array(0x13A0, 0x13FF),
    array(0x1400, 0x167F),      array(0x1680, 0x169F),
    array(0x16A0, 0x16FF),      array(0x1700, 0x171F),
    array(0x1720, 0x173F),      array(0x1740, 0x175F),
    array(0x1760, 0x177F),      array(0x1780, 0x17FF),
    array(0x1800, 0x18AF),      array(0x1900, 0x194F),
    array(0x1950, 0x197F),      array(0x1980, 0x19DF),
    array(0x19E0, 0x19FF),      array(0x1A00, 0x1A1F),
    array(0x1B00, 0x1B7F),      array(0x1B80, 0x1BBF),
    array(0x1C00, 0x1C4F),      array(0x1C50, 0x1C7F),
```

```
array(0x1D00, 0x1D7F),      array(0x1D80, 0x1DBF),
array(0x1DC0, 0x1DFF),      array(0x1E00, 0x1EFF),
array(0x1F00, 0x1FFF),      array(0x2000, 0x206F),
array(0x2070, 0x209F),      array(0x20A0, 0x20CF),
array(0x20D0, 0x20FF),      array(0x2100, 0x214F),
array(0x2150, 0x218F),      array(0x2190, 0x21FF),
array(0x2200, 0x22FF),      array(0x2300, 0x23FF),
array(0x2400, 0x243F),      array(0x2440, 0x245F),
array(0x2460, 0x24FF),      array(0x2500, 0x257F),
array(0x2580, 0x259F),      array(0x25A0, 0x25FF),
array(0x2600, 0x26FF),      array(0x2700, 0x27BF),
array(0x27C0, 0x27EF),      array(0x27F0, 0x27FF),
array(0x2800, 0x28FF),      array(0x2900, 0x297F),
array(0x2980, 0x29FF),      array(0x2A00, 0x2AFF),
array(0x2B00, 0x2BFF),      array(0x2C00, 0x2C5F),
array(0x2C60, 0x2C7F),      array(0x2C80, 0x2CFF),
array(0x2D00, 0x2D2F),      array(0x2D30, 0x2D7F),
array(0x2D80, 0x2DDF),      array(0x2DE0, 0x2DFF),
array(0x2E00, 0x2E7F),      array(0x2E80, 0x2EFF),
array(0x2F00, 0x2FDF),      array(0x2FF0, 0x2FFF),
array(0x3000, 0x303F),      array(0x3040, 0x309F),
array(0x30A0, 0x30FF),      array(0x3100, 0x312F),
array(0x3130, 0x318F),      array(0x3190, 0x319F),
array(0x31A0, 0x31BF),      array(0x31C0, 0x31EF),
array(0x31F0, 0x31FF),      array(0x3200, 0x32FF),
array(0x3300, 0x33FF),      array(0x3400, 0x4DBF),
array(0x4DC0, 0x4DFF),      array(0x4E00, 0x9FFF),
array(0xA000, 0xA48F),      array(0xA490, 0xA4CF),
array(0xA500, 0xA63F),      array(0xA640, 0xA69F),
array(0xA700, 0xA71F),      array(0xA720, 0xA7FF),
array(0xA800, 0xA82F),      array(0xA840, 0xA87F),
array(0xA880, 0xA8DF),      array(0xA900, 0xA92F),
array(0xA930, 0xA95F),      array(0xAA00, 0xAA5F),
array(0xAC00, 0xD7AF),      array(0xD800, 0xDB7F),
array(0xDB80, 0xDBFF),      array(0xDC00, 0xDFFF),
array(0xE000, 0xF8FF),      array(0xF900, 0xFAFF),
array(0xFB00, 0xFB4F),      array(0xFB50, 0xFDFF),
array(0xFE00, 0xFE0F),      array(0xFE10, 0xFE1F),
array(0xFE20, 0xFE2F),      array(0xFE30, 0xFE4F),
array(0xFE50, 0xFE6F),      array(0xFE70, 0xFEFF),
array(0xFF00, 0xFFEF),      array(0xFFF0, 0xFFFF),
array(0x10000, 0x1007F),    array(0x10080, 0x100FF),
array(0x10100, 0x1013F),    array(0x10140, 0x1018F),
array(0x10190, 0x101CF),    array(0x101D0, 0x101FF),
array(0x10280, 0x1029F),    array(0x102A0, 0x102DF),
```

```
        array(0x10300, 0x1032F),    array(0x10330, 0x1034F),
        array(0x10380, 0x1039F),    array(0x103A0, 0x103DF),
        array(0x10400, 0x1044F),    array(0x10450, 0x1047F),
        array(0x10480, 0x104AF),    array(0x10800, 0x1083F),
        array(0x10900, 0x1091F),    array(0x10920, 0x1093F),
        array(0x10A00, 0x10A5F),    array(0x12000, 0x123FF),
        array(0x12400, 0x1247F),    array(0x1D000, 0x1D0FF),
        array(0x1D100, 0x1D1FF),    array(0x1D200, 0x1D24F),
        array(0x1D300, 0x1D35F),    array(0x1D360, 0x1D37F),
        array(0x1D400, 0x1D7FF),    array(0x1F000, 0x1F02F),
        array(0x1F030, 0x1F09F)
);
$count = 0;
foreach ($data as $set) {
        // Use the average to calculate middle char
        $c = (int)(($set[0] + $set[1])/2);

        echo '0x'
         . strtoupper(dechex($c))
         . ' = ';

        $uc = array();
        if ($c < 0x80) {
                $uc[0] = $c;
        }
        else if ($c < 0x800) {
                $uc[0] = 0xC0 | $c>>6;
                $uc[1] = (0x80 | $c & 0x3F);
        }
        else if ($c < 0x10000) {
                $uc[0] = (0xE0 | $c>>12);
                $uc[1] = (0x80 | $c>>6 & 0x3F);
                $uc[2] = (0x80 | $c & 0x3F);
        }
        else if ($c < 0x200000) {
                $uc[0] = (0xF0 | $c>>18);
                $uc[1] = (0x80 | $c>>12 & 0x3F);
                $uc[2] = (0x80 | $c>>6 & 0x3F);
                $uc[3] = (0x80 | $c & 0x3F);
        }
        foreach ($uc as $u) {
                echo pack('C', $u);
        }
```

```
        // for formatting
        if ($count / 3 === 1) {
                echo "\n";
                $count = 0;
        } else {
                echo "\t";
                $count++;
        }
}
```

Figure 3.21: Printing the middle character of all current Unicode blocks

What this code does is check to see which byte range (which I had copied from a Unicode Web site) the individual character is in (the **if** statements). Next, it shifts the bits the proper amount for that byte range. Then, it **OR**s the individual lead bytes to the proper value to arrive at the number of bytes that are needed to display the individual character.

Remember the chart that showed which bits in the lead byte were turned on? That's where the **0xC0**, **0xE0**, and **0xF0** come in to play. Those each represent the proper lead byte for each number of additional bytes. But, you may also remember that the lead byte can carry some payload as well. That's why we see the bits being shifted 6, 12, and 18 places instead of 8 or 16. In other words, every bit is sacred, every bit is great.

Let's take a look at what this code prints out (Figure 3.22).

0x3F = ?	0xBF = ¿	0x13F = Ŀ	0x1E7 = ǧ
0x27F = ɿ	0x2D7 = ˗	0x337 = ̷	0x3B7 = η
0x47F = ѿ	0x517 = ԗ	0x55F = ՟	0x5C7 = ☒
0x67F = 0	☒x727 = 0	☒67 = 0	☒x79F = ☒
0x7DF = 0	☒x93F = ☒	0x9BF = ☒	0xA3F = ☒
0xABF = ☒	0xB3F = ̑	0xBBF = ☒	0xC3F = ☒
0xCBF = ☒	0xD3F = ☒	0xDBF = ☒	0xE3F = ฿
0xEBF =	0xF7F = ☒	0x104F = ☒	0x10CF =
0x117F = ☒	0x12BF =	0x138F = ☒	0x13CF = ☒
0x153F = ☒	0x168F = ☒	0x16CF = ☒	0x170F = ☒
0x172F = ☒	0x174F = ☒	0x176F = ☒	0x17BF = ☒
0x1857 = ☒	0x1927 = ☒	0x1967 = ☒	0x19AF =
0x19EF = ☒	0x1A0F = ☒	0x1B3F = ☒	0x1B9F =
0x1C27 =	0x1C67 =	0x1D3F = R	0x1D9F = ³

```
0x1DDF =            0x1E7F = v         0x1F7F =           0x2037 = ‴
0x2087 = 7          0x20B7 = Ş        0x20E7 = ¬         0x2127 = Ƕ
0x216F = M          0x21C7 = ⇇        0x227F = ≿         0x237F = ⎬
0x241F = ▼          0x244F = ▨        0x24AF = (t)       0x253F = ┿
0x258F = ▏          0x25CF = ●        0x267F = ♿        0x275F = ❟
0x27D7 = ⟗          0x27F7 = ⟷        0x287F = ⡿        0x293F = ⤿
0x29BF = ⦿          0x2A7F = ⩿        0x2B7F = ▨         0x2C2F =
0x2C6F =            0x2CBF = ⲿ        0x2D17 = ⴗ         0x2D57 = ⵗ
0x2DAF =            0x2DEF =           0x2E3F = ⸿         0x2EBF = ⺿
0x2F6F = 田         0x2FF7 = ⿷        0x301F = 〟        0x306F = は
0x30CF = ハ         0x3117 = ㄗ        0x315F = ㅟ        0x3197 = ㆗
0x31AF = ㆯ         0x31D7 =           0x31F7 = ㇷ        0x327F = ㉿
0x337F = ㍿         0x40DF = 䃟        0x4DDF = ䷟         0x76FF = 盿
0xA247 = ꉇ         0xA4AF = ꒯        0xA59F =           0xA66F = ꙯
0xA70F = ꜏         0xA78F = ꞏ        0xA817 = ꠗ         0xA85F = ꡟ
0xA8AF =            0xA917 =           0xA947 =           0xAA2F =
0xC1D7 = 쇗         0xD9BF = ﬡ        0xDBBF = ﬡ         0xDDFF = ﬡ
0xEC7F =            0xF9FF = 刺        0xFB27 = 0         ﬁxFCA7 = ﭧ
0xFE07 = ︇         0xFE17 = ︗        0xFE27 = ▨         0xFE3F = ⌢
0xFE5F = #          0xFEB7 = 0        ᱷxFF77 = ≢        0xFFF7 =
0x1003F = �𐀿        0x100BF = 𐂿       0x1011F = 𐄟        0x10167 = 𐅧
0x101AF = 𐆯        0x101E7 = 𐇧       0x1028F = 𐊏        0x102BF = 𐊿
0x10317 = X        0x1033F = 𐌿       0x1038F = ⟨        0x103BF = 𐎿
0x10427 = 𐐧        0x10467 = 𐑧       0x10497 = ᴕ        0x1081F = ᴕ
0x1090F = 0        °x1092F = 0       𐨏x10A2F = 0        𐇳x121FF = ⚑
0x1243F = 𒐿        0x1D07F = ·       0x1D17F = ˬ        0x1D227 = 𝈧
0x1D32F = ⠿        0x1D36F = 𝍯       0x1D5FF = r        0x1F017 = 🀗
0x1F067 = ⚃
```

Figure 3.22: Unicode page output

For all the Unicode characters we have fonts for, you can see that we have properly created UTF-8 encoded Unicode characters. So this example indicates that we have properly formatted UTF-8 encoding for generated (not inputted) Unicode characters.

At this point, you might start seeing the beginning of an interesting problem. We have all these characters that we're working with that are represented by more than one byte. Let's take a look at our previous output again (Figure 3.23).

```
¢£A¤¥
11000010 0xC2 L 194
10100010 0xA2 F 162
11000010 0xC2 L 194
```

```
10100011 0xA3 F 163
01000001 0x41 A 65
11000010 0xC2 L 194
10100100 0xA4 F 164
11000010 0xC2 L 194
10100101 0xA5 F 165
```

Figure 3.23: Multi-byte output

We had entered five characters, but the output produced nine bytes. What does that mean for a string-based operation? Let's return to the previous example and add some code to the top to include a string length check (Figure 3.24).

```
echo $_POST['text']
       . ' Length: '
       . strlen($_POST['text'])
       . '<br/>';
```

Figure 3.24: Adding length check

Figure 3.25 shows the output that results when we run the modified code.

```
¢£A¤¥ Length: 9
11000010 0xC2 L 194
10100010 0xA2 F 162
11000010 0xC2 L 194
10100011 0xA3 F 163
01000001 0x41 A 65
11000010 0xC2 L 194
10100100 0xA4 F 164
11000010 0xC2 L 194
10100101 0xA5 F 165
```

Figure 3.25: Output with length check added

What? Nine characters? No. Nine bytes. This is a perfect example of the internationalization problem in PHP. That problem is set to be solved as of PHP 6, which adds native support for Unicode.

But does that mean that PHP cannot do internationalization? Absolutely not. All it means is that you have to use a different set of functions for string-based operations that need to understand multi-byte character sets — things such as string length, substrings, or character positions in a string. In other words, it really affects only text *manipulation*. As I noted earlier, a computer doesn't think in terms of language; it thinks in terms of bits, or numbers. So unless you have to do string manipulation, such as replacing a Chinese character with a Latin character, most of what PHP is really doing is transferring bits from the browser to the database, and vice versa. Because of that, the issues with Unicode that PHP has are not as insurmountable as they sometimes sound.

But to transfer those bits correctly, we need to have them transferred properly and stored properly. The easiest way to do that is simply to explicitly state that you are going to be using UTF-8. In other words, you tell the database that you're going to be providing UTF-8, and you tell the browser that it needs to supply UTF-8.

The easiest way to do this is to change one setting in **php.ini**:

```
default_charset = "UTF-8"
```

That's it? From the browser side, yes. If I run a test script and print out the headers, you will see that the charset is now being specified, even if I set a Content-Type header that does not specify it. Figure 3.26 shows the test code I ran; note that it does not specify the charset in the Content-Type header call.

```
header('Content-Type: text/plain');
echo 'hello world';
```

Figure 3.26: Test script to verify that the charset has been specified

Figure 3.27 shows the headers printed out from this test.

```
HTTP/1.1 200 OK
Date: Mon, 09 Nov 2009 00:46:57 GMT
Server: Apache/2.2.12 (Win32) mod_ssl/2.2.12
        OpenSSL/0.9.8k
X-Powered-By: PHP/5.2.10 ZendServer/4.0
```

```
Set-Cookie: ZDEDebuggerPresent=php,phtml,php3; path=/
Connection: close
Content-Type: text/plain;charset=UTF-8

hello world
```

Figure 3.27: Headers verifying the UTF-8 charset

Even though we did not explicitly state that our content type was UTF-8, PHP appended the charset. However, if we add it manually:

```
header('Content-Type: text/plain; charset="ASCII"');
echo 'hello world';
```

our explicit declaration is honored (Figure 3.28).

```
HTTP/1.1 200 OK
Date: Mon, 09 Nov 2009 00:49:23 GMT
Server: Apache/2.2.12 (Win32) mod_ssl/2.2.12
        OpenSSL/0.9.8k
X-Powered-By: PHP/5.2.10 ZendServer/4.0
Set-Cookie: ZDEDebuggerPresent=php,phtml,php3; path=/
Connection: close
Content-Type: text/plain; charset="ASCII"

hello world
```

Figure 3.28: Result of explicitly specifying the charset

We've now got our browser working in UTF-8, so how about PHP? Because PHP does not understand UTF-8 internally, we need the help of some additional functions. To test those functions, we'll use a string made up of a couple of different single and multi-byte Unicode characters: "Aﾟは株式会社ｷ".

What we're going to do is submit these characters to a couple different functions available in PHP and see what happens.

You might be tempted to think that the **utf8_encode()** and **utf8_decode()** functions will solve your problems. But just because they have the word "UTF-8" in there does not mean that is the case. These two functions work only on single-byte characters. They can decode and encode multi-byte characters, but depending on your operation, one side of the equation needs to be a single-byte character. To illustrate this limitation, let's use some test code (Figure 3.29).

```
<pre><?php
if (isset($_POST['text'])) {

        $data = $_POST['text'];
        var_dump($data);
        echo strlen($data) . "\n";

        $data = utf8_decode($data);
        var_dump($data);
        echo strlen($data) . "\n";
}

?>
<form method="post">
Text: <input type="text" name="text" /><br />
<input type="submit" />
</form>
```

Figure 3.29: Code to test utf8_* functions

This code takes the UTF-8 encoded data "Aℤは株式会社キ" and translates it to ISO-8859-1. Let's look at "キ". Figure 3.30 shows the results of the sample code.

```
string(3) "キ"
3
string(1) "?"
1
```

Figure 3.30: Output of utf8* test

As you can see, decoding it makes it unprintable. This example demonstrates how the purpose of the **utf8_*** functions is not to provide true multi-byte functionality but rather to handle the translation of ISO-8859-1 to UTF-8, and vice versa.

Two primary extensions enable PHP to handle multi-byte character sets: **iconv** and **mbstring**. Both have the ability to handle multi-byte encodings, as you can see in the following test. Starting with the same code we were using earlier, we'll test out both extensions (Figure 3.31).

```
<pre><?php
if (isset($_POST['text'])) {
        echo 'IConv: '
                . iconv_strlen($_POST['text'], 'UTF-8')
                . "\n";
        echo 'MBString: '
                . mb_strlen($_POST['text'], 'UTF-8')
                . "\n";
}

?>
<form method="post">
Text: <input type="text" name="text" /><br />
<input type="submit" />
</form>
```

Figure 3.31: Code for iconv and mbstring test

Putting our test string into the form produces the result shown in Figure 3.32.

```
IConv: 5
MBString: 5
```

Figure 3.32: Output for iconv test

Both extensions correctly understood the UTF-8 encoding. But which one to use? The answer is based on what you are trying to do. **iconv** is not a string function replacement. In other words, it is not designed to replace some of the functionality within PHP to handle the intricacies of string manipulation. In fact, **iconv** is a utility available on many open-source operating systems and is used to convert text between different character sets. Although it does perform some string manipulation, its primary purpose is to handle the conversion of text from one encoding to another.

The **mbstring** extension, on the other hand, is designed to be a replacement for internal PHP functions. In fact, for most of the functions available in PHP for handling string manipulation, **mbstring** has a corresponding function. Not all, such as Perl Compatible Regular Expressions (PCRE), but many.

In our previous example, we had to explicitly set the encoding that was going to be set. However, you can set the default internal encoding in **mbstring** to UTF-8 in the **php.ini** file:

```
mbstring.internal_encoding = UTF-8
```

If we set that and remove the **UTF-8** in our code, it comes out fine.

So, we are now able to do a lot of the string functionality in our application, but we have a massive refactoring that we need to do, right? Actually, no. **mbstring** has another trick up its sleeve. Although you cannot replace a function once it's been defined, an extension can. Once again, we go to **php.ini** (Figure 3.33).

```
; overload(replace) single byte functions by mbstring
; functions. mail(), ereg(), etc are overloaded by
; mb_send_mail(), mb_ereg(), etc. Possible values are
; 0,1,2,4 or combination of them. For example, 7 for
; overload everything.
; 0: No overload
; 1: Overload mail() function
; 2: Overload str*() functions
; 4: Overload ereg*() functions
mbstring.func_overload = 2
```

Figure 3.33: php.ini setting to overload internal string functions

To test this, let's go back to the earlier code where we first saw this issue and test again with the string "Aとは株式キ". Figure 3.34 shows how the output now reads.

```
Aとは株式キ Length: 5
01000001 0x41 A 65
11100010 0xE2 L 226
10001001 0x89 F 137
10111111 0xBF F 191
11100011 0xE3 L 227
10000001 0x81 F 129
```

```
10101111 0xAF F 175
11100011 0xE3 L 227
10001101 0x8D F 141
10111111 0xBF F 191
11101111 0xEF L 239
10111101 0xBD F 189
10110111 0xB7 F 183
```

Figure 3.34: Output with overloaded PHP functions

Even though we did not change anything, and we are using **strlen()** in this code, it worked. We get the proper length value for the string, while our **unpack()** call clearly gives us all the bytes. But even though this test worked, you should not assume that it will work everywhere. Just because it works as you expect in one place doesn't mean that it will work as expected in another.

PCRE, on the other hand, requires a little bit of work. Figure 3.35 shows a bit of test code on which we can demonstrate our test string.

```php
if (isset($_POST['text'])) {
    $matches = array();
    preg_match('/.(.).+/', $_POST['text'], $matches);
    echo '<pre>';
    var_dump($matches);
    echo '</pre>';
}

?>
<form method="post">
Text: <input type="text" name="text" /><br />
<input type="submit" />
</form>
```

Figure 3.35: Code to test PCRE without UTF-8 flag

As you can see from the code, we're going to skip over the first character, and that's because it's the letter A. While the string is a UTF-8 encoded string, the pattern is not. When we run our test string against this code, we get the output shown in Figure 3.36.

```
array(2) {
  [0]=>
  string(13) "A≳は株式会社キ"
  [1]=>
  string(1) "◆"
}
```

Figure 3.36: Output of PCRE without UTF-8 flag

We see our matched string, which is the entire string that we passed in. It is the same as we entered it. This is because the page is set up as being UTF-8 encoded, so multi-byte characters will be interpreted properly. In the **preg_match()** call, we state that we want to match the second character. But because **preg_match()** doesn't intrinsically know about UTF-8, it matches the **0xE2** character, which is the second byte. But in this case, that's not what we're trying to do; we're trying to get the second character. With PCRE, however, that distinction is easy to make. We pass the **u** pattern modifier to the pattern. The **u** tells it that we want this string operated on as if it were UTF-8 encoded (Figure 3.37).

```
if (isset($_POST['text'])) {
    $matches = array();
    preg_match('/.(.).+/u', $_POST['text'], $matches);
    echo '<pre>';
    var_dump($matches);
    echo '</pre>';
}
```

Figure 3.37: PCRE code with UTF-8 flag

Now when we pass our test string in, we get very different results (Figure 3.38).

```
array(2) {
  [0]=>
  string(13) "A≳は株式会社キ"
  [1]=>
  string(3) "≳"
}
```

Figure 3.38: Output of PCRE code with UTF-8 flag

As you can see, we now match the full three bytes of that individual string.

The next stage of the process is the database. In this example, we'll use MySQL with the table defined in Figure 3.39.

```
CREATE TABLE 'book'.'utf8text' (
  'text_key' INTEGER UNSIGNED NOT NULL AUTO_INCREMENT,
  'text1' varchar(64) CHARACTER SET ascii NOT NULL,
  'text2' VARCHAR(64) CHARACTER SET utf8 COLLATE
      utf8_unicode_ci NOT NULL,
  PRIMARY KEY ('text_key')
)
ENGINE = InnoDB
CHARACTER SET utf8 COLLATE utf8_unicode_ci;
```

Figure 3.39: Table definition including UTF-8

In this table, there are a couple of things to note. The second column, or **'text1'**, is set to use the ASCII charset. The third column is our UTF-8 based column.

So let's write some code to insert some data into the database (Figure 3.40).

```
$pdo = new PDO('mysql:dbname=book', 'root', '');

$pdo->exec('DELETE FROM utf8text');

$stmt = $pdo->prepare(
    'INSERT INTO utf8text (text1, text2) VALUES (?, ?)'
);

$stmt->execute(
    array(
        'Ĉĥêŵßą©čå™',
        'Ĉĥêŵßą©čå™'
    )
);

$stmt = $pdo->prepare('SELECT * FROM utf8text');
$stmt->execute();
while (($row = $stmt->fetch(PDO::FETCH_ASSOC))
        !== false) {
    var_dump($row);
}
```

Figure 3.40: Code inserting UTF-8 encoded strings into a database

Running this code produces the output shown in Figure 3.41.

```
array(3) {
  ["text_key"]=>
  string(2) "1"
  ["text1"]=>
  string(21) "?????????????????????"
  ["text2"]=>
  string(21) "Ĉĥêŵßą©čå™"
}
```

Figure 3.41: Output of inserted code

When we get back our data, we see all 21 bytes that we had inserted into the database. With that our job is done. Right?

No. Actually, these results are indicative of a problem. What we're actually seeing in this example, from a practical standpoint, is ISO-8859-1 characters printed to a browser that's expecting UTF-8. So, what we're really doing is printing "Ä^" to a browser expecting UTF-8. Ä is the lead byte for "Ĉ". In the database, as in PHP, unless we're working with raw bytes, such as getting the length of a file, we don't really want to work with bytes so much as we want to work with characters. This point is equally, if not more, important in the database. This is because while we can do sorting and various collation activities in PHP, in practice the database is often a better place to do that than in code.

And why would we? When working with open-source software, we tend to rely on other programs more than what you might find elsewhere. That's because with open source a lot of programs are written by volunteers, and if you can use what someone else has written, that means you can get more done.

This type of mentality should also, in general, be used in the development of a Web-based application. If the database does something and can do it in a more efficient way, closer to the data, use it and not PHP.

So what we can do is harness the ability of the database to handle collation. To show that the database thinks we're sending ISO-8859-1 instead of UTF-8, we can simply take a look at what the MySQL Query Browser shows us. The Query Browser's internal encoding is UTF-8, and so it will be representative of the content that the database thinks it has. Figure 3.42 shows what we see when we look at it.

Figure 3.42: Test data displayed in the MySQL Query Browser

It would seem that the database doesn't think it has UTF-8 encoded data. So how do we make certain that the database knows for sure what the encoding is for our database connection? We do that by telling it (Figure 3.43).

```
$pdo = new PDO('mysql:dbname=book', 'root', '');
$pdo->exec('SET CHARACTER SET utf8');
```

Figure 3.43: Setting the connection to use UTF-8

After running these statements and then re-running our sample code, the MySQL Query Browser displays the results shown in Figure 3.44.

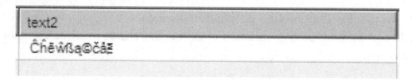

Figure 3.44: Output with UTF-8 set database connection

With that, we have been able to store our UTF-8 encoded data properly in the database.

Conclusion

Although there definitely may be things that you run into when building out an application that needs to have some level of internationalization, the things you've learned about in this chapter will take you a good chunk of the way toward doing it and give you enough information to demystify character encoding to some extent.

CHAPTER 4

Streams

Streams, alongside the Standard PHP Library (SPL), are probably one of the features in PHP that go most unused by many PHP developers. We often think of streams simply as a way to easily obtain data from an external source, such as a text file or a Hypertext Transfer Protocol (HTTP) Uniform Resource Locator (URL). However, there are many practical applications for streams that go beyond simple retrieval of data.

We usually use streams by calling **fopen()**, **file_get_contents()**, or some other URL-aware function. For example, if we wanted to open a connection to the PHP Web site to read it, we could simply call:

```
$fh = fopen('http://www.php.net', 'r');
```

The **fopen()** function would call the stream opener for the specified protocol, and the appropriate wrapper would be "registered" with that resource. The wrapper would handle all the functionality, such as opening, reading, or closing, that is required for the stream.

You generally make stream functionality available by including an individual module in your **php.ini** configuration, and most of the streams you would end up using are registered in the standard extension. These do not require any external modules to be included to be available. These streams are:

- **php://**
- **file://**

- **data://**

- **http://**

- **ftp://**

If for some reason these wrappers are not available, the Curl wrapper may register itself to handle **ftp://**, **http(s)://**, and **ldap://**.

Several additional stream wrappers are available via several optional modules:

- **compress.bzip2://** (provided by BZip2)

- **https://** (provided by OpenSSL)

- **ftps://** (provided by OpenSSL)

- **zip://** (provided by Zip)

- **compress.zlib://** (provided by zlib)

- **ldap://** (provided by Curl)

Configuration

The first thing to look at with PHP streams is which ones you have compiled into PHP. In general, you don't need to do any configuration to use a stream because the stream is often included in tandem with an existing extension. For example **ssl** is included with the **openssl** extension. To see what functionality is available, you can simply consult **phpinfo()**. Figure 4.1 shows sample stream information reported by this function.

Registered PHP Streams	https, ftps, php, file, data, http, ftp, compress.zlib, compress.bzip2, zip
Registered Stream Socket Transports	tcp, udp, ssl, sslv3, sslv2, tls
Registered Stream Filters	convert.iconv.*, string.rot13, string.toupper, string.tolower, string.strip_tags, convert.*, consumed, zlib.*, bzip2.*

Figure 4.1: phpinfo() information showing streams, sockets, and filters

Here, you can see what stream wrappers, stream transports, and stream filters are available. Understanding how streams and transports differ from filters might be easy, but there is a significant difference between a stream wrapper and a stream transport. You cannot use the two interchangeably. Wrappers and transports use the same Uniform Resource Identifier (URI) naming, but they are handled in a completely different way internally.

For example, the sample **phpinfo()** information lists "tcp" as a stream transport that is available. Without knowing the underlying implementation, we might reasonably therefore conclude that we could simply do an **fopen()** on a Transmission Control Protocol (TCP) connection. Let's test that out:

```
$a = fopen('tcp://localhost:10000', 'r');
```

The resulting output:

```
Notice: fopen(): Unable to find the wrapper "tcp" - did
    you forget to enable it when you configured PHP?
```

To have direct access to a TCP stream, we must either create a new socket or use the **fsockopen()** function:

```
$a = fsockopen('tcp://localhost:10000');
var_dump($a);
```

This prints out:

```
resource(4) of type (stream)
```

As you can see, it's important to note which functionality you are using. Are you using a wrapper, or are you using a transport? The two are not the same.

Besides simply restricting what can be used by which functions, there is another difference. You can write your own wrapper in PHP code, but you cannot write your own transport. To write your own transport, you would need to do so in C and then compile it into PHP. However, given the available transports, it is unlikely you will need to write your own, unless you want to build a Doom server for Internetwork Packet Exchange (IPX) in PHP (which, admittedly, would be pretty cool, but not very useful).

You can produce lists of the streams, wrappers, and filters programmatically from PHP. To get a list of the available wrappers, call the **stream_get_wrappers()** function, as Figure 4.2 demonstrates. Figure 4.3 shows the resulting output.

```php
foreach (stream_get_wrappers() as $stream) {

        echo "{$stream}: registered\n";
}
```

Figure 4.2: Code to print registered stream wrappers

```
https: registered
ftps: registered
php: registered
file: registered
data: registered
http: registered
ftp: registered
compress.zlib: registered
compress.bzip2: registered
zip: registered
```

Figure 4.3: Output of printing registered stream handlers

To produce a list of transports, call the **stream_get_transports()** function (Figure 4.4). Figure 4.5 shows the results.

```php
foreach (stream_get_transports() as $stream) {

        echo "{$stream}: registered\n";
}
```

Figure 4.4: Code to print registered stream transports

```
tcp: registered
udp: registered
ssl: registered
sslv3: registered
sslv2: registered
tls: registered
```

Figure 4.5: Output of printing registered stream transports

To list the filters available on a stream, call the **stream_get_filters()** function (Figure 4.6). Figure 4.7 shows the results.

```
foreach (stream_get_filters() as $stream) {

        echo "{$stream}: registered\n";
}
```

Figure 4.6: Code to print registered stream filters

```
convert.iconv.*: registered
string.rot13: registered
string.toupper: registered
string.tolower: registered
string.strip_tags: registered
convert.*: registered
consumed: registered
zlib.*: registered
bzip2.*: registered
```

Figure 4.7: Output of registered stream filters

The practicality of the string filters may be debatable, but the wrappers and transports can be quite useful. You can use the **iconv.*** filters to convert between character sets, and you would use **zlib.*** and **bzip2.*** for compression/ decompression. The asterisk (*) indicates that there are different types of filters. For example, **bzip2.*** includes **bzip2.compress** and **bzip2.decompress**. For a full list of stream filters, go to *http://www.php.net/filters*.

Stream Contexts

A stream *context* is simply a method for adding options to a wrapper either before it initiates its connection or during the course of the stream's lifetime. Depending on the stream and the option, either alternative may be available to you. Some options can be set only upon creation; others can be added once a connection has been initiated. In general, however, you will add options upon creation, using the **stream_context_create()** function instead of **stream_context_set_option()**. To underscore this point, consider that the **stream_context_create()** documentation includes several pages worth of options, while **stream_context_set_option()** has none.

Example: HTTP

The examples we could use for HTTP are many. For our purposes here, we'll just use a simple crawler. The code that contains the stream functionality will act as a proxy. It will retrieve the form from the specified URL, look for the form elements for which it has data, and then post that data to the URL for which the form was originally destined. Figure 4.8 shows some simple HTML that we will make available for this exercise.

```
<!DOCTYPE html PUBLIC "-//W3C//DTD XHTML 1.0 Strict//EN"
 "http://www.w3.org/TR/xhtml1/DTD/xhtml1-strict.dtd">
<html xmlns="http://www.w3.org/1999/xhtml">
<head>
<meta http-equiv="Content-Type"
      content="text/html; charset=UTF-8" />
<title>Simple Form</title>
</head>
<body>
<form method="post" action="/handle.post.php">
 <div>First Name: <input type="text" name="first.name" />
 </div>
 <div>Last Name: <input type="text" name="last.name" />
 </div>
 <div><input type="submit" /></div>
</form>
</body>
</html>
```

Figure 4.8: Sample HTML form to be submitted

The next step is to load the form as a **DOMDocument** object. The **DOMDocument** class, via the **loadHTMLfile()** function, can handle HTML files better than the **SimpleXML** extension. To retrieve the data from the form, we'll use an XML Path Language (XPath) query.

To test the logic of our script, we're going to just output the **$_POST** variables. We'll take the format that was defined in the previously defined form (which is saved as **form.html**) and post it to the form URL that was defined there as well. Figure 4.9 shows the code at the endpoint that we are going to use. This code is defined as the file **handle.post.php** in the preceding form.

```
header('Content-Type: text/plain');
var_dump($_POST);
```

Figure 4.9: handle.post.php, which prints the POST variables

Figure 4.10 shows the code to read the HTML and **POST** the results. It is a little more complicated, although not by much; it's just a little longer.

```
$dom = new DOMDocument();
$dom->loadHTMLFile('http://localhost/form.html');
$xPath = new DOMXPath($dom);
$forms = $xPath->query('//form');

if ($forms->length !== 1) {
        die('This code only handles exactly one form');
}

$form = $forms->item(0);

$method = $form->getAttribute('method');
$action = $form->getAttribute('action');

if (strtolower($method) == 'get') {
        die('No point in doing this on a GET request');
}

$input = array(
        'first.name'  => 'Kevin',
        'last.name'   => 'Schroeder'
);
```

```php
$data = array();

foreach ($xPath->query('//form//input[@type="text"]')
        as $node) {

    if (isset($input[$node->getAttribute('name')])) {
        $data[$node->getAttribute('name')]
                = $input[$node->getAttribute('name')];
    }
}

$data = http_build_query($data);

$ctx = stream_context_create(
  array(
        'http'    => array(
        'method'  => strtoupper($method),
        'content' => $data,
        'header'  => 'Content-Type:
                    application/x-www-form-urlencoded'
        )
  )
);

var_dump(
        file_get_contents(
          'http://localhost'.$action,
          0,
          $ctx
        )
);
```

Figure 4.10: Using XPath to find form elements and submit the code in Figure 4.9

What this script does is read the form by calling the page that contains the HTML file, parse it as an XML document, and apply the XPath query to retrieve the form element. We do this to get the method and the action from the form. After that, we extract the individual text elements in the form using another XPath query and see whether we have input that matches. If we do, we put that input into the data we're going to send to the server in our **POST**, and then we build our **POST** string.

Next, we create our context, via the call to the **stream_context_create()** function. This function returns a resource that has all the options defined in it. We pass in the method and the **POST** data and also specify the content type. (The stream handler would automatically create the proper content type if we omitted the content type, but it would throw a notice, so we define the type explicitly here.)

When we make our request, even though we are pushing data to the server, we call **file_get_contents()**. That is because we are reading the *results* of our **POST**. You cannot write to a URL as you would a file. The first parameter is our URL, the second is bitwised flags, and the third is our context. We put a **0** in the flags because that is equivalent to saying we have no flags set.

Upon running our code, we receive the output shown in Figure 4.11.

```
string(94) "array(2) {
  ["first_name"]=>
  string(5) "Kevin"
  ["last_name"]=>
  string(9) "Schroeder"
}
"
```

Figure 4.11: Output of file_get_contents() on code of Figure 4.9

You can see that while the output is that of a **var_dump()** call, the output is wrapped in a string. What this means is that we were able to make a **POST** call to the remote URL and read the contents, which were generated by doing a **var_dump()** on the **$_POST** variable.

Example: Compression "On the Fly"

On some occasions, it may be necessary to change stream properties on the fly. To demonstrate this technique, we will write a simple echo client/server application. The server will listen on a port, echoing whatever it receives and writing it back to the socket. Let's start with the basics.

Figure 4.12 shows the server code.

```
$sock = stream_socket_server(
                'tcp://0.0.0.0:10000',
                $errno,
                $errstr
);
```

```
if (!$sock) die($errstr);

while
  (($client = stream_socket_accept($sock)) !== false) {
     while (($line = fgets($client)) != null) {
            echo $line;
     }
}
```

Figure 4.12: Simple TCP-based server

Figure 4.13 shows the client.

```
$sock = stream_socket_client(
                  'tcp://localhost:10000',
                  $errno,
                  $errstr
);

if (!$sock) die($errstr);
$in = fopen('php://stdin', 'r');

while (($line = fgets($in)) != null) {
     fwrite($sock, $line, strlen($line));
}
```

Figure 4.13: Simple TCP-based client

We can run both the server and client quite simply from the command line. When we do, we get the following output.

From the client:

```
$ php ./enc.client.php
You want to do WHAT with PHP?
```

The client script reads the data we type in to the console, sends it to the server, and then writes out whatever it is that the server sends back. The server prints out much the same:

```
$ php enc.server.php
You want to do WHAT with PHP?
```

No surprise here. The application is doing exactly what you would expect. But let's add a little code to the client (Figure 4.14).

```
$sock = stream_socket_client(
                'tcp://localhost:10000',
                $errno,
                $errstr
);

if (!$sock) die($errstr);
$in = fopen('php://stdin', 'r');

$filter = null;
while (($line = fgets($in)) != null) {

    if (trim($line) === 'COMPRESS') {
            fwrite($sock, $line, strlen($line));
            $filter = stream_filter_append(
                $sock,
                'bzip2.compress',
                STREAM_FILTER_WRITE
            );

            echo "\nCompression Enabled.\n";
            continue;
    }

    fwrite($sock, $line, strlen($line));
}
```

Figure 4.14: Code to enable compression on the stream

This code reads the input from the input line, just as before, but appends the BZip2 filter if the user types the word **COMPRESS**. When we enable the filter, we call **stream_filter_append()**, take the return value, and store it in a sort of global variable. The return value is a resource that describes the socket and filter combination. Later, when we want to remove the filter, we simply pass the **$filter** variable to **stream_filter_remove()**, and that filter flushes its contents and is removed. The flushing part is the primary reason why we use the remove function here. Compression engines work in blocks and as such may not actually send data to the endpoint when you write to it. Removing the filter causes the stream to flush, thereby sending all data to the client.

When we run the client code, we can simply type these commands, and any other text, on the keyboard (Figure 4.15).

```
$ php ./enc.client.php
You want to do WHAT with PHP?
COMPRESS

Compression Enabled.
You want to do WHAT with PHP?
```

Figure 4.15: Client output of enabled compression

Easy enough. But the output on the server side looks quite different (Figure 4.16).

```
$ php ./enc.server.php
You want to do WHAT with PHP?
COMPRESS
BZh41AY&SYb@ @D $a 1M211HÉ gHñ%,-#aâ±3)Â
                                    öÏÐ
```

Figure 4.16: Server output of enabled compression

We see "You want to do WHAT with PHP?" in clear text once, followed by a bunch of binary data. That is about what we would expect to see because by typing **COMPRESS**, we were instructing the client to start compressing the stream.

To make sure both sides are happy, the next step is to add a read filter on the server side (Figure 4.17).

```
while (($line = fgets($client)) != null) {

        echo $line;
        if (trim($line) === 'COMPRESS') {
```

```
        $filter = stream_filter_append(
            $client,
            'bzip2.decompress',
            STREAM_FILTER_READ
        );

        echo "\nCompression Enabled.\n";
    }
}
```

Figure 4.17: Adding decompression on the server side

It looks like a similar implementation, but rather than prepending the filter we append it, and we specify **'bzip2.decompress'** instead of **'bzip2.compress'**. The reason we prepend the filter instead of appending it, as we did on the client side, is to make sure that the data is processed in the inverse order of that in which it was processed on the client side.

When we run our code now, we get the proper output (Figure 4.18).

```
You want to do WHAT with PHP?
COMPRESS

Compression Enabled.
You want to do WHAT with PHP?
```

Figure 4.18: Server output after added decompression on the server side

You may be trying this example but not getting the same results. In fact, you might not be getting any results at all. That's because BZip2 is a buffered protocol. To maximize the compression of the stream, the filter will retain as much data as it can. To flush the filter, you must either fill up the buffer or close the network connection. For this reason, turning compression on and off at will on a stream may not be practical, so if you are going to implement compression on your own, it would probably make sense to specify it as a handshake parameter when you connect.

Building Your Own Stream Handler

For an example of a stream handler, we're going to build a stream wrapper called **dbfs**, which, based on the name, you can tell will implement a file system in a database. The file system will be limited in terms of its scalability and functionality in that it won't be designed to scale to great heights and it may not be implemented in a perfect way from a database design perspective. The purpose of building this example is to demonstrate how to build a stream wrapper, not how to build a file system. For the 95 percent of you for whom this approach is sufficient, this one's for you.

Figure 4.19 shows the structure of our database.

```
CREATE TABLE 'fs' (
  'fs_key' int(10) unsigned NOT NULL AUTO_INCREMENT,
  'fs_name' varchar(255) NOT NULL,
  'fs_parent_key' int(10) unsigned NOT NULL,
  'fs_type' enum('f','d') NOT NULL,
  'fs_data' blob NOT NULL,
  'fs_created' int(10) unsigned DEFAULT NULL,
  'fs_modified' int(10) unsigned DEFAULT NULL,
  'fs_accessed' int(10) unsigned DEFAULT NULL,
  PRIMARY KEY ('fs_key')
) ENGINE=InnoDB AUTO_INCREMENT=5 DEFAULT CHARSET=utf8
```

Figure 4.19: Table definition for a database-based stream wrapper

Figure 4.20 shows the data we will use.

```
INSERT INTO 'fs' ('fs_key', 'fs_name', 'fs_parent_key',
    'fs_type','fs_data','fs_created','fs_modified',
    'fs_accessed')
VALUES
(3,'home',0,'d','',1254144181,1254144181,1254144181),
(4,'kevin',3,'d','',1254144181,1254144181,1254144181),
(5,'bob',3,'d','',1254144181,1254144181,1254144181),
(6,'david',3,'d','',1254144181,1254144181,1254144181),
(7,'steve',3,'d','',1254144181,1254144181,1254144181),
(8,'peter',3,'d','',1254144181,1254144181,1254144181),
(9,'kevin',7,'d','',1254144181,1254144181,1254144181);
```

Figure 4.20: Data for structure of the file system

We'll look at this example step by step to help you learn how to implement it. To do that, we'll start with a simple class definition, register the stream wrapper with PHP, and see what happens when we run code against it. This code has no functionality and is designed simply to show the names of the method calls that PHP uses rather than implement any kind of functionality. It will test both the file-name functions and the resource-based functions. Figure 4.21 shows the code to register the stream handler.

```
stream_wrapper_register('dbfs', 'DbStream');

file_exists('dbfs://home/kevin');
$fh = fopen('dbfs://home/kevin/test.txt', 'r');

class DbStream
{

    const CTX_THROW_EXCEPTIONS    = 'exceptions';
    const CTX_READONLY            = 'readonly';
    const CTX_USE_ATIME           = 'atime';
    const CTX_USERNAME            = 'username';
    const CTX_PASSWORD            = 'password';
    const CTX_DATABASE            = 'database';
    const CTX_TABLE               = 'table';

    public function __call($funcName, $args)
    {
        echo "Function Name:\n$funcName()\n\n";
        echo "Function Args: \n";
        var_dump($args);
        echo "\n";
        return false;
    }
}
```

Figure 4.21: Registering a stream handler for the database

Figure 4.22 shows the output that results when we run this code.

```
Function Name:
url_stat()

Function Args:
array(2) {
  [0]=>
  string(17) "dbfs://home/kevin"
  [1]=>
  int(2)
}

Function Name:
stream_open()

Function Args:
array(4) {
  [0]=>
  string(26) "dbfs://home/kevin/test.txt"
  [1]=>
  string(1) "r"
  [2]=>
  int(4)
  [3]=>
  &NULL
}
```

Figure 4.22: Output of testing code

The two reported functions represent the two primary types of functions we will need to handle: the "file-based" functions and the "resource-based" functions. File-based functions are generally one-off functions in which you do all the work in one function call, such as **file_get_contents()**. Resource-based functions usually have several steps involved in reading their data, such as calling **fopen()**, followed by **fread()**, followed by **fclose()**.

What you see here is similar to an abstraction layer, which is what the stream wrapper layer is. Some defined functions need to be written to harness the individual integration points.

So, let's take this little bit of knowledge and build the functionality for the **file_exists()** function (Figure 4.23).

```php
stream_wrapper_register('dbfs', 'DbStream');

var_dump(
    file_exists('dbfs:///home/kevin')
);



class DbStream
{

    const CTX_THROW_EXCEPTIONS   = 'exceptions';
    const CTX_READONLY           = 'readonly';
    const CTX_USE_ATIME          = 'atime';
    const CTX_USERNAME           = 'username';
    const CTX_PASSWORD           = 'password';
    const CTX_DATABASE           = 'database';
    const CTX_TABLE              = 'table';

    /**
     * @var PDO
     */

    private $_db = null;

    private function _createDb()
    {
        if ($this->_db instanceof PDO) return;
        $this->_db = new PDO(
            'mysql:dbname=book',
            'root',
            ''
        );
    }

    private function _parseUrl($path)
    {
      if (stripos($path, 'dbfs://') === 0) {
          $path = substr($path, 7);
      }
      return preg_split(
          '/\//',
          $path,
          NULL, PREG_SPLIT_NO_EMPTY
      );
    }
```

```php
public function url_stat($path, $opts)
{
  $this->_createDb();
  $select = '';
  $joins = array();
  $wheres = array();
  $joinCount = 1;
  $paths = $this->_parseUrl($path);
  $pathCount = count($paths);
  foreach ($paths as $node) {

    $ojc = $joinCount - 1;

    if ($joinCount !== $pathCount) {
        $joins[] = "INNER JOIN fs AS fs{$joinCount}
          ON fs{$joinCount}.fs_parent_key
            = fs{$ojc}.fs_key";
    }

    $wheres[] = "fs{$ojc}.fs_name = ?";
    $joinCount++;
  }
  $select = "SELECT
    fs{$ojc}.fs_key,
    fs{$ojc}.fs_created,
    fs{$ojc}.fs_modified,
    fs{$ojc}.fs_parent_key,
    LENGTH(fs{$ojc}.fs_data) as fs_size,
    fs{$ojc}.fs_type
FROM fs AS fs0 ";
  $select .= implode("\n", $joins);
  $select .= ' WHERE ' . implode(' AND ', $wheres);

  // Handle the situation where it is the root
  // and there is no INNER JOIN to provide
  // structure
  if ($pathCount == 1) {
      $select .= ' AND fs_parent_key = 0';
  }

  $stmt = $this->_db->prepare($select);
  if ($stmt->execute($paths)) {
      /* @var $stmt PDOStatement */
      if (($row = $stmt->fetchObject())
              === false) {
```

```
                    return false;
            }
            $return = array(
                    'dev'       => 1,
                    'ino'       => -1,
                    'mode'      => 0,
                    'nlink'     => 1,
                    'uid'       => 0,
                    'gid'       => 0,
                    'rdev'      => 0,
                    'size'      => $row->fs_size,
                    'atime'     => 0,
                    'mtime'     => $row->fs_modified,
                    'ctime'     => $row->fs_created,
                    'blksize'   => -1,
                    'blocks'    => -1,
                    'fs_key'    => $row->fs_key,
                    'fs_parent' => $row->fs_parent_key,
                    'type'      => $row->fs_type
            );
            $return = array_merge(
                    $return,
                    array_values($return)
            );
            return $return;
        }
        return false;
    }
}
```

Figure 4.23: Implementing stat() data collection

The first thing you might wonder is, "What is that massive array we're returning there?" That array is the data that PHP is looking for after a successful **stat()** call. This is the same **stat()** data that is provided by a Unix **stat()** C call. For compatibility's sake, we need to return as much information as we can to implement it properly, and that's why we have so much code there.

The next question you might have is, "What is that massive **JOIN** we're doing here?" As you may be aware, relational databases do not do well with hierarchical data. This is because the data is organized into tables, not hierarchy. So we need to build our hierarchy from a tabular structure. We do that by building a multiple-level self **JOIN** on the table. By iterating over each individual path component and joining against its parent, we can calculate the record that corresponds to a full path.

Say we want to check whether **/home/kevin** exists. The query we build will look like Figure 4.24.

```
SELECT
        fs1.fs_key,
        fs1.fs_created,
        fs1.fs_modified,
        LENGTH(fs1.fs_data) as fs_size,
        fs1.fs_parent_key,
        fs1.fs_type
FROM fs AS fs0 INNER JOIN fs AS fs1
        ON fs1.fs_parent_key = fs0.fs_key
WHERE
        fs0.fs_name = 'home'
        AND fs1.fs_name = 'kevin'
```

Figure 4.24: SQL code to "stat" a directory

The row we get back is the row that contains the data for the individually requested file, supported by the **INNER JOIN** clauses to make sure it's in the correct path. When we execute this query against the data provided earlier, we get the result set shown in Figure 4.25.

```
object(stdClass)#4 (5) {
  ["fs_key"]=>
  string(1) "4"
  ["fs_created"]=>
  string(10) "1254144181"
  ["fs_modified"]=>
  string(10) "1254144181"
  ["fs_size"]=>
  string(1) "0"
  ["fs_parent_key"]=>
  string(1) "3"
  ["fs_type"]=>
  string(1) "d"
}
```

Figure 4.25: Row from "stat" result set

Because our table contains two "kevin" directories, we can check the primary key to be sure we got the right one. The **fs_key** value in the output matches that in the **INSERT** statement we executed earlier.

Figure 4.26 shows the query we would generate if we were to search for **/home/steve/kevin**. Figure 4.27 shows the result set.

```
SELECT
        fs2.fs_key,
        fs2.fs_created,
        fs2.fs_modified,
        LENGTH(fs1.fs_data) as fs_size,
        fs1.fs_parent_key,
        fs2.fs_type
FROM fs AS fs0 INNER JOIN fs AS fs1
        ON fs1.fs_parent_key = fs0.fs_key
INNER JOIN fs AS fs2
        ON fs2.fs_parent_key = fs1.fs_key
WHERE
        fs0.fs_name = 'home'
        AND fs1.fs_name = 'steve'
        AND fs2.fs_name = 'kevin'
```

Figure 4.26: SQL for stat()ing /home/steve/kevin

```
object(stdClass)#4 (5) {
  ["fs_key"]=>
  string(1) "9"
  ["fs_created"]=>
  string(10) "1254144181"
  ["fs_modified"]=>
  string(10) "1254144181"
  ["fs_size"]=>
  string(1) "0"
  ["fs_parent_key"]=>
  string(1) "7"
  ["fs_type"]=>
  string(1) "d"
}
```

Figure 4.27: Result set from stat()ing /home/steve/kevin

From these two tests, we can see that we were able to retrieve the proper row for the requested file name.

Because we need to be able to structure the files that we want to place in the file system, the next step is to create the directory structure. To do this, we need to define a function called **DbStream::mkdir()**, which will handle creating the directories. Because we are not implementing permissions in this system, we will ignore the octal values in the second **mkdir()** parameter, but we'll check whether we are instructed to create the directory structure recursively.

We will define two methods: **DbStream::mkdir()** will handle the logic of the request, and **DbStream::_mkdir()** will handle the inserting of the directory into the database. Figure 4.28 shows the code to handle the **mkdir()** calls.

```php
class DbStream
{

. . .

    public function mkdir($path, $perms, $opts)
    {
      $this->_createDb();

      if ($this->url_stat($path)) {
          trigger_error(
              'Directory exists already',
              E_USER_WARNING
          );
          return false;
      }
      $parts = $this->_parseUrl($path);
      $name = array_pop($parts);

      if (count($parts) > 0) {
          $testParent = 'dbfs://'
                      . implode('/', $parts);
          if (($statData = $this->url_stat(
              $testParent)) === false

              && !($opts & STREAM_MKDIR_RECURSIVE
          )) {
```

```
                return false;
        }
    } else {
        // Create a directory in the root dir
        $this->_mkdir(0, $name);
        return true;
    }

    if ($statData !== false) {
        $this->_mkdir($statData['fs_key'], $name);
    } else {
        $nonExistent = array($name);
        do {
                $nonExistent[] = array_pop($parts);
                $testParent = 'dbfs://'
                                . implode('/', $parts);
        } while (
                ($stat = $this->url_stat($testParent))
                === false);
        $parentKey = $stat['fs_key'];

        foreach(array_reverse($nonExistent) as $name) {
                $parentKey = $this->_mkdir(
                    $parentKey,
                    $name
                );
        }
    }

    return true;
}

private function _mkdir($parent, $name)
{
    $stmt = $this->_db->prepare(
        'INSERT INTO fs
                (
                fs_name, fs_parent_key, fs_type,
                fs_created, fs_modified, fs_accessed
                )
        VALUES
                (
                ?, ?, \'d\', UNIX_TIMESTAMP(),
                UNIX_TIMESTAMP(), UNIX_TIMESTAMP()
                )
    ');
```

```
    /* @var $stmt PDOStatement */
    $stmt->execute(array($name, $parent));
    return $this->_db->lastInsertId();

  }

}
```

Figure 4.28: Code to handle mkdir() calls

The first thing we do is check to see whether the file exists. We do so by calling the **url_stat()** method we defined earlier. If the file exists, we return false. Then, we check to see whether the parent exists. If the parent does not exist and **STREAM_MKDIR_RECURSIVE** is not set in the **$opts** parameter, we return false.

The next thing we do is check to see whether the value for **$statData** is a Boolean false. If it is not false, that means we found the parent, and so we can just do a simple call to **_mkdir()** and be done with it. Otherwise, we need to find out what is the closest existing directory parent and start building the tree from there.

The way we do it is by starting at the highest level that we have not tested and work our way down until we find a parent that exists. For each directory that does not exist, we place it in the **$nonExistent** array. This array will be used to recursively create the directory structure.

Once we find a directory that exists, we leave our do-while loop and iterate over the nonexistent directories, creating each one as we go along. Because **_mkdir()** requires that only the parent key and the name be provided, we simply need to iterate over the list of nonexistent directories, taking the return value, or last insert ID, from the previously called **_mkdir()** method and using it as the parent key for the next directory.

That takes care of creating directories.

The next thing we're going to look at is how to handle **fopen()**, **file_get_contents()**, **fwrite()**, and so on — basically, how do we stream data to and from the database?

Because we have no files in our system, the first operation we should implement is writing files to the system. However, we have a bit of a problem. How do we handle large files? Or, more appropriately, how do we stream content from PHP to the wrapper without consuming inordinate amounts of memory?

The way we do that is through the use of prepared statements and bound parameters. A bound parameter can be a variable of almost any kind, including a resource. Using a bound parameter also means that we can "stream" content into the database. This is how we will minimize the impact of a large file in the file system.

Before we go too far along that route, we need to first build out some of the basic functionality to ensure that everything is working properly with the stream API. After that, we'll worry about the actual database calls to handle the pseudo-file. And because we have no files in the database, the first operation we need to do is a simple write. So let's add some code to the **DbStream** class to implement that operation (Figure 4.29).

```
class DbStream
{

    private $_fopenStatement = null;
    private $_fopenResource = null;
    private $_fopenMode = 0;


. . .


    public function stream_open($path, $mode,
                    $options, &$opened_path)
    {
       $this->_createDb();
       $this->_fopenMode = $this->_parseMode($mode);
       // We are just going to support
       // simple reading and writing
       if (($stat = $this->url_stat($path)) === false
       && !($this->_fopenMode & self::MODE_CANWRITE)){
              trigger_error(
                  'File does not exist',
                  E_USER_WARNING);
              return false;
       }
```

```php
            if ($stat['type'] === 'd') {
                trigger_error(
                    'Requested file is a directory',
                    E_USER_WARNING
                );
                return false;
            }
            if ($options & STREAM_USE_PATH) {
                $opened_path = $path;
            }

            $this->_fopenResource = fopen(
                                        'php://temp',
                                        'r+'
                                    );

            return true;
        }

        public function stream_write($data)
        {
            if(!($this->_fopenMode & self::MODE_CANWRITE)){
                trigger_error(
                    'File is open in read-only mode',
                    E_USER_WARNING
                );
                return false;
            }
            fwrite($this->_fopenResource, $data);

            return strlen($data);
        }
        public function stream_close()
        {
            fseek($this->_fopenResource, 0);
            echo "Received: "
                . fread($this->_fopenResource, 1024);
            fclose($this->_fopenResource);
        }

        private function _parseMode($mode)
        {
            $bitMode= 0;
            switch ($mode[0]) {
                case 'r':
                    $bitMode = self::MODE_CANREAD;
```

```
                        break;
            case 'w':
                        $bitMode = self::MODE_CANWRITE;
                        break;

        }
        return $bitMode;
    }
}
```

Figure 4.29: Code to open a stream on a database row

This code defines four methods: **stream_open()**, **stream_write()**, **stream_close()**, and **_parseMode()**. Method **_parseMode()** is there to examine the second parameter of an **fopen()** call to determine how the file should be opened. For the sake of simplicity, we're going to support only pure read or pure write with this example.

The **stream_open()** method does a couple of things. It first checks to see which mode the file has been opened under. Then it checks to see whether the file exists. If the file does not exist and we are in read-only mode, we return false because we have no file to read. If the file exists but it is a directory, we trigger an error and return false. The option check on **STREAM_USE_PATH** is there for compatibility with the stream API.

Next, we open a temporary resource that we'll use as a temporary storage area until the file handle is closed. The temporary resource will start by storing data in RAM, but once it reaches a certain limit (2 MB by default), it will flush the data to the disk and store it there.

We will actually execute the prepared statement when the file handle is closed, although we will prepare it in the **stream_open()** call (we'll look at that in a bit). We take this approach because we don't have the ability to execute the prepared statement with anything other than a complete file. That's just the nature of SQL. We would need to be able to seek and buffer the data over multiple queries. There is "seek" functionality in the database, but it pertains to seeking a specific row, not a specific byte in a column. Therefore, we need to write to the **DbStream** object and let it store the data in temporary space so it can stream it later on.

Handling the writing functionality is quite simple. Just take the data that was passed to the function and write it to our temporary stream. However, because we're supporting only pure read and pure write, we do a check on the mode to make sure writing is allowed. When **fclose()** is called, we simply echo out the data that was aggregated and close the temporary file. Once we've validated that this works, we will actually implement the statement execution.

Figure 4.30 shows our test code, which is quite simple. Figure 4.31 shows the output that results when we run this test.

```
$fh = fopen('dbfs://home/kevin/test.txt', 'w');
fwrite($fh, 'Test');
fclose($fh);
```

Figure 4.30: Code to test writing to a file

```
Function Name:
stream_flush()

Function Args:
array(0) {
}

Received: Test
```

Figure 4.31: Output of file write test

Notice the **stream_flush()** call. Because we can do only an all-or-nothing operation, we are going to ignore that call. This is so that a developer does not accidentally execute the prepared statement prematurely. Beyond that, however, the test was a success, and so it is time to build the code that writes the file to the database (Figure 4.32).

```
public function stream_open($path, $mode, $options,
                            &$opened_path)
{
  $this->_createDb();
  $this->_fopenMode = $this->_parseMode($mode);
  // We are just going to support simple
  // reading and writing
```

```php
if (($stat = $this->url_stat($path)) === false
    && !($this->_fopenMode & self::MODE_CANWRITE)) {
    trigger_error(
        'File does not exist',
        E_USER_WARNING
    );
    return false;
}

if ($stat['type'] === 'd') {
    trigger_error(
        'Requested file is a directory',
        E_USER_WARNING
    );
    return false;
}
if ($options & STREAM_USE_PATH) {
    $opened_path = $path;
}

if ($stat === false) {
        $this->_fopenResource =
            fopen('php://temp', 'r+');

    $dirname = dirname($path);
    $parent = $this->url_stat($dirname);

    // $dirname, handle special root dir case
    if ($dirname == 'dbfs:') {
        $parent['fs_key'] = 0;
    } else if ($parent === false) {
        trigger_error(
            'Parent directory does not exist',
            E_USER_WARNING
        );
        return false;
    }
    $this->_fopenStatement =
        $this->_db->prepare(
            'INSERT INTO fs
                (
                fs_data, fs_name, fs_type,
                fs_parent_key, fs_created,
                fs_modified, fs_accessed
                )
```

```
                    VALUES
                        (
                        ?, ?, \'f\', ?,
                        UNIX_TIMESTAMP(), UNIX_TIMESTAMP(),
                        UNIX_TIMESTAMP()
                        )'
            );
        $fileName = basename($path);
        $this->_fopenStatement->bindParam(
            1,
            $this->_fopenResource, PDO::PARAM_LOB
        );
        $this->_fopenStatement->bindParam(
            2,
            $fileName
        );
        $this->_fopenStatement->bindParam(
            3,
            $parent['fs_key']
        );
    } else {
        $this->_fopenResource =
            fopen('php://temp', 'r+');

        $this->_fopenStatement =
            $this->_db->prepare(
                'UPDATE fs SET
                    fs_data = ?,
                    fs_modified = UNIX_TIMESTAMP(),
                    fs_modified = UNIX_TIMESTAMP()
                WHERE
                    fs_key = ?'
            );
        $this->_fopenStatement->bindParam(
            1,
            $this->_fopenResource, PDO::PARAM_LOB
        );
        $this->_fopenStatement->bindParam(
            2,
            $stat['fs_key']
        );
    }

    return true;
}
```

```
public function stream_close()
{
    fseek($this->_fopenResource, 0);
    $this->_fopenStatement->execute();


}
```

Figure 4.32: Code to open the stream for a file in the database

Most of the work occurs in **stream_open()**. It is there where we decide whether we are going to be doing an insert or an update. If we are doing an insert, we need to provide some additional data, such as the parent key and the name of the file. But if we are doing an update, all we need is the file's primary key and the resource to which it is being written. To put the data into the database, we bind the parameter as a **PDO::PARAM_LOB**, which tells PHP to use the data parameter as a resource and not a regular variable. This is how we handle the large files.

To test this code, we need to do two calls to the same file, to make sure both the insert and the update work (Figure 4.33).

```
$fh = fopen('dbfs://home/kevin/test.txt', 'w');
fwrite($fh, 'Test');
fclose($fh);

$fh = fopen('dbfs://home/kevin/test.txt', 'w');
fwrite($fh, 'Test Again');
fclose($fh);
```

Figure 4.33: Code to validate inserting different values into the same node

Looking at the database after the second write, we see that the second value is there, but to validate that both worked, we can also look at the query log to see what the actual entered values were (Figure 4.34).

```
376 Query      INSERT INTO fs
               (
               fs_data, fs_name, fs_type, fs_parent_key,
               fs_created, fs_modified,
               fs_accessed
               )
```

```
       VALUES
              (
              'Test', 'test.txt', 'f', '4',
              UNIX_TIMESTAMP(), UNIX_TIMESTAMP(),
              UNIX_TIMESTAMP()
              )

377 Query     UPDATE fs SET
              fs_data = 'Test Again',
              fs_modified = UNIX_TIMESTAMP(),
              fs_accessed = UNIX_TIMESTAMP()
       WHERE
              fs_key = '26'
```

Figure 4.34: Queries demonstrating insert and update functionality

Both calls were executed properly, and the end result is working. That means that our next step is writing the code to handle read operations (Figure 4.35).

```
class DbStream
{

  const MODE_CANWRITE       = 0x01;
  const MODE_CANREAD         = 0x02;


  private $_fopenStatement = null;
  private $_fopenResource = null;
  private $_fopenMode = 0;

  public function stream_open($path, $mode, $options,
                                  &$opened_path)
  {
    $this->_createDb();
    $this->_fopenMode = $this->_parseMode($mode);
. . .


    if ($stat === false) {

. . .

    } else if ($this->_fopenMode & self::MODE_CANREAD) {
```

```
        $stmt = $this->_db->prepare(
            'SELECT fs_data FROM fs WHERE fs_key = ?'
        );
        $stmt->bindColumn(
            1,
            $this->_fopenResource,
            PDO::PARAM_LOB
        );

        $stmt->bindParam(1, $stat['fs_key']);
        if ($stmt->execute()) {
            $stmt->fetch(PDO::FETCH_BOUND);
            if (is_string($this->_fopenResource)) {
                $data = $this->_fopenResource;
                $this->_fopenResource = fopen(
                    'php://temp',
                    'r+'
                );
                fwrite(
                    $this->_fopenResource,
                    $data
                );
                fseek($this->_fopenResource, 0);
            }
            return true;
        }
        return false;

    } else {
. . .
    }

    return true;
}

public function stream_read($count)
{
    return fread($this->_fopenResource, $count);
}

public function stream_eof()
{
    return feof($this->_fopenResource);
}
}
```

Figure 4.35: Handling read operations

What this code does is fairly self-explanatory, although it does require some knowledge of PHP Data Objects (PDO). The **stream_read()** and **stream_eof()** methods do just what they say they will do. They read from the resource created by the **PDOStatement** object and return the result.

As before, most of the heavy lifting is done in **stream_open()**. Earlier, we used prepared statements to stream data into the database, but now we're going to stream data out. We prepare our **SELECT** statement, bind our resource property to the column and our primary key to the primary key in the statement, and execute. The **PDO::bindColumn()** method, with **PDO::PARAM_LOB**, tells PDO that we are expecting the column to be either a binary large object (BLOB) or a character large object (CLOB) and as such we want the column to be returned as a resource.

Unfortunately, at the time of this writing, some databases (*coughmysql*) do not support **bindColumn()** with a LOB. Instead, the function returns a string. To mitigate this limitation, and to standardize it, we create a temporary PHP resource, write the data there, and set the pointer to zero. Why do this as opposed to just taking the string and storing it in the class? My reason for taking this approach is so that the data can go out of scope and the memory can be reclaimed if a large file is being accessed. So, although we still take a hit if the column is returned as a string, that hit will be limited to immediately after the database call and will be scoped to that initial call as well.

Let's look at the result of this code with some test data. When we run the test shown in Figure 4.36, we get the result shown in Figure 4.37.

```
stream_wrapper_register('dbfs', 'DbStream');

$fh = fopen('dbfs://home/kevin/test.txt', 'w');
fwrite($fh, 'Test Again');
fclose($fh);


$fh = fopen('dbfs://home/kevin/test.txt', 'r');
echo fgets($fh);
fclose($fh);
```

Figure 4.36: Code to test read operations

```
Test Again
```

Figure 4.37: Output of read operation test

The last thing we need to do is handle the deletion of files and directories.
Deleting files is done by creating an **unlink()** method in the class (Figure 4.38).
This function simply checks to see whether the file exists, verifies that it is not a
directory, and, if neither of those checks fails, deletes the row.

```php
class DbStream
{
        public function unlink($path)
        {
            $this->_createDb();
            if (($stat = $this->url_stat($path))===false) {
                    trigger_error(
                            'File not found',
                            E_USER_WARNING
                    );
                    return false;
            } else if ($stat['type'] == 'd') {
                    trigger_error(
                            'File is a directory',
                            E_USER_WARNING
                    );
                    return false;
            }
            $stmt = $this->_db->prepare(
                    'DELETE FROM fs WHERE fs_key = ?'
            );
            return $stmt->execute(array($stat['fs_key']));
        }
}
```

Figure 4.38: Code to test deleting nodes

Deleting a directory requires a little bit more logic (Figure 4.39). That's because a
directory itself can hold children, whereas a file cannot. By definition, **rmdir()** is
not recursive, although a new context parameter was added for PHP 5.0. However,
no examples of an actual context setting could be found as of the writing of this
chapter with PHP 5.2.11.

```
class DbStream
{
    public function rmdir($path, $opts)
    {
      if (($stat = $this->url_stat($path))===false) {
            trigger_error(
                    'Directory not found',
                    E_USER_WARNING
            );
            return false;
      } else if ($stat['type'] == 'f') {
            trigger_error(
                    'Path is not a directory',
                    E_USER_WARNING
            );
            return false;
      }
      $stmt = $this->_db->prepare(
            'SELECT fs_key FROM fs
            WHERE fs_parent_key = ? LIMIT 1'
      );
      if ($stmt->execute(array($stat['fs_key']))) {
            if ($stmt->fetch() !== false) {
                  trigger_error(
                          'Directory is not empty',
                          E_USER_WARNING
                  );
                  return false;
            }
      }
      $stmt = $this->_db->prepare(
            'DELETE FROM fs WHERE fs_key = ?'
      );
      return $stmt->execute(array($stat['fs_key']));
    }
}
```

Figure 4.39: Code to remove directories

This code checks whether the directory exists, whether the directory is actually a file, and whether it has any children in it. If there are children, we cannot delete. We could execute the delete, but then there would be orphaned data, which you generally do not want in a relational database.

The last operation we need to do with files is rename them. To do that, our code needs to perform a fair amount of additional checking. We need to verify that the old file exists, make sure the directory of the new file exists, and verify that the new directory is not, itself, a file. And then we need to execute the query to update the file. Figure 4.40 shows the code to rename a file.

```
class DbStream
{
    public function rename($oldName, $newName)
    {
        if (($stat = $this->url_stat($oldName))
                    === false) {
            trigger_error(
                    'File does not exist',
                    E_USER_WARNING
            );
            return false;
        }

        $newDir = dirname($newName);
        $newFilename = basename($newName);
        if ($newDir == 'dbfs:') {
            $parentKey = 0;
        } else {
            if (($dirStat = $this->url_stat($newDir))
                        === false) {

                trigger_error(
                  'New parent directory does not exist',
                  E_USER_WARNING
                );
                return false;
            } else if ($dirStat['type'] == 'f') {
                trigger_error(
                  'New parent directory is a file',
                  E_USER_WARNING
                );
                return false;
            }
            $parentKey = $dirStat['fs_key'];
        }
        $stmt = $this->_db->prepare(
            'UPDATE fs SET
                    fs_parent_key = ?,
                    fs_name = ?
```

```
        WHERE
                fs_key = ?
        '
    );
    return $stmt->execute(
        array(
                $parentKey,
                $newFilename,
                $stat['fs_key']
        )
    );
    }
}
```

Figure 4.40: Code to rename a node

In this case, our test suite is going to be a little more complicated than the other ones. This is mostly because renaming, more so than deleting, introduces the possibility of orphaning nodes in the database (this is one of the risks of the adjacency model). Figure 4.41 shows the code to test our full functionality.

```
echo "\nWriting to dbfs://home/kevin/test.txt : ";
$fh = fopen('dbfs://home/kevin/test.txt', 'w');
fwrite($fh, 'Test Again');
fclose($fh);

echo "\nWriting to dbfs://home/kevin/test2.txt : ";
$fh = fopen('dbfs://home/kevin/test2.txt', 'w');
fwrite($fh, 'Test Again');
fclose($fh);

echo "\nCreating Directory dbfs://test : ";
var_dump(
    mkdir('dbfs://test')
);

echo "\nCreating Directory dbfs://test/test : ";
var_dump(
    mkdir('dbfs://test/test')
);
```

```
echo "\nMoving directory dbfs://test/test
     to /home/david/test : ";
var_dump(
    rename('dbfs://test/test', 'dbfs://home/david/test')
);

echo "\nMoving file dbfs://home/kevin/test.txt
     to dbfs://home/peter/test.txt : ";
var_dump(
    rename(
          'dbfs://home/kevin/test.txt',
          'dbfs://home/peter/test.txt'
    )
);

echo "\nMoving file dbfs://home/peter/test.txt
     to dbfs://home/nobody/test.txt
     (error expected) : ";
var_dump(
    rename(
          'dbfs://home/peter/test.txt',
          'dbfs://home/nobody/test.txt'
    )
);

echo "\nMoving file dbfs://home/peter/test.txt
     to dbfs://test2.txt : ";

var_dump(
    rename(
          'dbfs://home/peter/test.txt',
          'dbfs://test2.txt'
    )
);

echo "\nMoving file dbfs://home/kevin/test2.txt
    to dbfs://test2.txt/test2.txt (expecting error) : ";

var_dump(
     rename(
           'dbfs://home/kevin/test2.txt',
           'dbfs://test2.txt/test2.txt'
     )
);
```

Figure 4.41: Full test of functionality

Figure 4.42 shows the output of our test.

```
Writing to dbfs://home/kevin/test.txt :
Writing to dbfs://home/kevin/test2.txt :
Creating Directory dbfs://test : bool(true)

Creating Directory dbfs://test/test : bool(true)

Moving directory dbfs://test/test
      to /home/david/test : bool(true)

Moving file dbfs://home/kevin/test.txt
      to dbfs://home/peter/test.txt : bool(true)

Moving file dbfs://home/peter/test.txt
      to dbfs://home/nobody/test.txt (error expected) :

Warning:  New parent directory does not exist in
  DbStream.php on line 494

bool(false)

Moving file dbfs://home/peter/test.txt
      to dbfs://test2.txt : bool(true)

Moving file dbfs://home/kevin/test2.txt
      to dbfs://test2.txt/test2.txt (expecting error) :

Warning:  New parent directory is a file in
  DbStream.php on line 500

bool(false)
```

Figure 4.42: Output of full test

Mission accomplished. Almost.

We have been reading data and writing data, but only for known file names. What about searching directories? That is where we now need to go.

The first thing we need to do is handle the **opendir()** function. To do so, we need to add a method called **dir_opendir()** to the class. It will take the directory as its first parameter and options as the second parameter. At present, the only option that is passed is whether Safe Mode should be enforced; this option is passed as the value **0x04**. Figure 4.43 shows the code to open a directory.

```
class DbStream
{
. . .
    public function dir_opendir($dir, $options)
    {
        if (($stat = $this->url_stat($dir))!== false) {
            $this->_fopenStatement
                = $this->_db->prepare(
                'SELECT fs_name FROM fs
                WHERE fs_parent_key = ?'
            );
            if ($stat['type'] !== 'd') {
                trigger_error(
                    'Node is a file',
                    E_USER_WARNING
                );
                return false;
            }
            if ($this->_fopenStatement
                ->execute(array($stat['fs_key']))) {
                return true;
            }
        }
        trigger_error(
            'Directory does not exist',
            E_USER_WARNING
        );
        return false;
    }
}
```

Figure 4.43: Code to open a directory node

We first check to see whether the file exists. If it does, we need to check whether it is a directory. If it is a file, we trigger an error and return false. Otherwise, we prepare a statement, execute it, and place it into the **$this->_fopenStatement** property. We do this so that we can iterate over the results in another method, **dir_readdir()**. This method takes no parameters and returns either a string containing the next directory element's name or a Boolean false if there are no

more items (or no items to begin with). The implementation of the **dir_readdir()**
method is relatively simple (Figure 4.44).

```php
public function dir_readdir()
{
    if (!$this->_fopenStatement) return false;
    return $this->_fopenStatement->fetchColumn();
}
```

Figure 4.44: Return true if a node exists

Closing the directory is a simple operation, too, and probably does not need to be
implemented because PHP will clean up on garbage collection. However, to close
the directory handle, we can simply write a **dir_closedir()** method (Figure 4.45).

```php
public function dir_closedir()
{
    $this->_fopenStatement = null;
}
```

Figure 4.45: Close the prepared statement when a closedir() call is made

We've now written the base functionality, so what's left is to test it (Figure 4.46).

```php
stream_wrapper_register('dbfs', 'DbStream');

var_dump(opendir('dbfs://nodir'));
var_dump(opendir('dbfs://test2.txt'));

$dh = opendir('dbfs:///home');
while (($fname = readdir($dh)) !== false) {
    echo "Found {$fname}<Br>";
}
closedir($dh);
```

Figure 4.46: Code to test opening and reading a directory

What we do here is first test to make sure that we get a false return for a directory
that doesn't exist. Then, we test for a directory that exists but is a file. Then, we test

the **/home** directory to see whether we can retrieve the names for each of the files in there. Figure 4.47 shows the results returned by our testing.

```
Warning:  Directory does not exist in DbStream.dir.php
  on line 52


Warning:  opendir(dbfs://nodir) [function.opendir]:
  failed to open dir: "DbStream::dir_opendir" call
  failed in DbStream.dir.php on line 5

bool(false)


Warning:  Node is a file in C:\Documents and Settings\
  kevin\Desktop\New Book\workspace\Test\Streams\
  DbStream.dir.php on line 45


Warning:  opendir(dbfs://test2.txt) [function.opendir]:
  failed to open dir: "DbStream::dir_opendir" call
  failed in DbStream.dir.php on line 6

bool(false)
Found kevin
Found bob
Found david
Found steve
Found peter
```

Figure 4.47: Output of code test reading from a directory

It appears our testing was successful.

The last feature we will look at is creating your own context. In this example, we will use the context to specify the authentication parameters for our stream handler — in other words, to change the user name, password, and database name.

To examine this functionality, let's first look at the test script (Figure 4.48).

```
$ctx = stream_context_create(
     array(
            'dbfs' => array(
                   DbStream::CTX_USERNAME     => 'root',
                   DbStream::CTX_PASSWORD     => '',
                   DbStream::CTX_DATABASE     => 'book',
            )
     )
);

$fh = fopen('dbfs://home/kevin/writefile.txt',
            'w', false, $ctx);
fwrite($fh, 'test');
fclose($fh);

echo "File was written\n";
```

Figure 4.48: Creating a custom stream context

If you remember back to some earlier code, we defined several class constants for various context options. Here, we are using them. You do not have to define them as class constants, but I find that using class constants to define parameters for an array is quite useful. Rather than hard-coding the key values, you specify the constant name. Then, if your code changes and you need to change the value of the parameter you are using, you simply change the class constant value, and every place in your code that uses that constant will reflect the change. It's very useful for code completion, too.

Creating a new context involves calling the **stream_context_create()** function. The options passed in need to be formatted as an associative array. Numeric arrays will not work; those options need to be added to an array key named after the wrapper.

To test this, we need to change only the **_createDb()** method. As you can see from the options, there are several more that we could do.

When a stream has a context assigned to it, it is set on in the public **$context** property by the Zend Engine. To retrieve the context settings, we need only test this property to see whether it is a resource and then call the **stream_context_get_options()** function (Figure 4.49).

```
private function _createDb()
{
  $db              = 'book';
  $username        = 'root';
  $password        = '';
  if ($this->_db instanceof PDO) return;
  if (is_resource($this->context)) {
      $options = stream_context_get_options(
                      $this->context
      );

      if (isset($options['dbfs'][self::CTX_DATABASE])) {
          $value =
                  $options['dbfs'][self::CTX_DATABASE];
          echo "Changing Database to '{$value}'\n";
          $db = $value;
      }
      if (isset($options['dbfs'][self::CTX_USERNAME])) {
          $value =
                  $options['dbfs'][self::CTX_USERNAME];
          echo "Changing Username to '{$value}'\n";
          $username = $value;
      }
      if (isset($options['dbfs'][self::CTX_PASSWORD])) {
          $value =
                  $options['dbfs'][self::CTX_PASSWORD];
          echo "Changing Password to '{$value}'\n";
          $password = $value;
      }
      if (isset($options['dbfs'][self::CTX_TABLE])) {
          $value =
                  $options['dbfs'][self::CTX_TABLE];
          echo "Changing Table to '{$value}'\n";
          $this->_table = $value;
      }
  }

  $this->_db = new PDO(
      'mysql:dbname=' . $db,
      $username,
      $password
  );
}
```

Figure 4.49: Handling a custom stream context

When we run our test against this code, we receive the output shown in Figure 4.50.

```
Changing Database to 'book'
Changing Username to 'root'
Changing Password to ''
File was written
```

Figure 4.50: Output of handling a custom stream context

This example shows how you can pass in different options to your custom-written stream implementations.

Conclusion

Streams are another one of the features in PHP that tend not to be hooked in to. They're available, they're pluggable, but in my experience streams are a feature that goes unused in many pertinent situations. I hope this example sparks some ideas about how you can go about implementing streams for your own applications.

CHAPTER 5

SPL

Not enough has been said about the Standard PHP Library (SPL). By that, I am referring to how often I see SPL implemented. When you look at the PHP features that are a combination of cool and under-used, SPL is close to, if not *at*, the top. With a lot of the new SPL libraries in PHP 5.3, this assessment will be doubly true. However, even though PHP 5.3 has already been released, I will be sticking to classes found in PHP 5.2. This chapter is an introduction to SPL, not a comprehensive explanation, and my goal is to get you familiar enough with SPL that you can move forward on your own. For that, the SPL components in PHP 5.2 should suffice.

Why SPL?

SPL is a set of classes and interfaces that let you hook in with the internals of the PHP engine automatically, generally on the array level. Because a lot of business logic is often written with arrays in mind, SPL might offer a fair amount of benefit for you.

For example, I once did some work for a company that had a "legacy" application that was experiencing serious performance problems (I put "legacy" in quotes there because I've done a fair amount of work with IBM midrange systems; *those* run real legacy applications). This application was loading up more than a hundred objects at the start of the script, each time, because it needed to know some information up front. The problem was that the application didn't know what it needed to load up front. So it loaded it all.

Fixing a problem such as this one often requires a lot of pain on the developers' part because a lot of refactoring and a lot of testing might need to occur to make the application perform better. However, by using SPL I was able to reduce the amount of time spent in that code from just under 2.5 seconds to under 1/100th of a second. The solution involved the use of lazy loading integrated with SPL.

Beyond simply being able to keep your own code and possibly make it perform better, SPL offers other benefits. For instance, using SPL, you can force an "array" to accept only data of a certain type. How? You'll see in a bit. Another example is the ability to match values in an object simply by doing a **foreach** loop. How? Patience! You'll find out in a bit.

SPL Basics

We've looked at the "why" of SPL, but before we get to the "how," we need to get some of the basics out of the way.

A series of interfaces represent the base functionality of SPL. These interfaces are the basis for virtually all the functionality available in SPL. Several interfaces are made available:

- **Countable**

- **RecursiveIterator**

- **SeekableIterator**

- **Traversable**

- **Iterator**

- **IteratorAggregate**

- **ArrayAccess**

- **Serializable**

I've committed a bit of heresy by including the last five interfaces in this list. These technically are not part of SPL. You can disable SPL in PHP 5.1 and 5.2, although as of PHP 5.3 you cannot. (PHP 5.3 also has significantly more SPL classes and interfaces for you to use.) **Countable**, **RecursiveIterator**, and **SeekableIterator** are defined in SPL, but **Traversable**, **Iterator**, **IteratorAggregate**, **ArrayAccess** and **Serializable** are not. These five are part of the standard engine build. However, from a practical standpoint, all the interfaces all do the same thing, all are implemented in the same way, and all provide the same benefits. And there is no real reason not to have SPL installed. So, from the point of view of practicality and general implementation practice, I will, purposefully and heretically, lump them all under the same SPL umbrella. I hope the PHP community developers can forgive me for that.

The first thing to say about these interfaces is that they all let you harness the engine in unique ways. We can *talk* about how to do this all day long, but I am a believer that code, not bullet points, speaks best. So let's look at some code.

The first example (Figure 5.1) shows how we can use the **Countable** interface to give PHP information other than what it would normally get. It's a simple example, so you'll need to use your imagination a little bit.

```
class UserCollection
{

    public $adapter  = 'LDAP';
    public $binddn   = 'cn=auth, o=Auth Service, c=US';
    public $password = 'password';
}

$col = new UserCollection();
echo count($col);
```

Figure 5.1: Class with no SPL interfaces

Running this code provides no surprises:

```
1
```

But what if we wanted to use **count()** to tell PHP the number of users we had in this directory server? All we'd need to do is implement the **Countable** interface and the method that it requires. Figure 5.2 shows the code to do this.

```
class UserCollection implements Countable
{

    public $adapter  = 'LDAP';
    public $binddn   = 'cn=auth, o=Auth Service, c=US';
    public $password = 'password';

    public function count()
    {
        return 5231;
    }

}

$col = new UserCollection();
echo count($col);
```

Figure 5.2: Class implementing the Countable interface

This code now echoes:

```
5231
```

Clearly, you would want to implement some kind of true logic in that function, but perhaps you can start to see some of the benefits of using this type of functionality in your own applications, if you haven't seen this before. Let's look at another example, iteration.

To implement the **Iterator** interface, we need to implement five methods. Each of these methods has a special purpose. Each takes responsibility for a certain part of the required functionality for iterating over the object in a **foreach** loop. In case you breezed over that last point, let me state it again. Each required method provides part of the required functionality for iterating over the object in a **foreach** loop:

- **current()** — Used to retrieve the currently selected item
- **key()** — Used to retrieve the key of the currently selected item
- **next()** — Used to increase the internal pointer by 1
- **rewind()** — Used to set the internal pointer back to 0
- **valid()** — Used to verify whether if **current()** were called it would return a valid object

For our first test, let's ignore the actual iteration and instead look at the order in which the methods are called (Figure 5.3).

```php
class UserCollection implements Iterator
{

    public function current()
    {
        echo "current()\n";
        return 'string';
    }

    public function key()
    {
        echo "key()\n";
        return 1;
    }

    public function next()
    {
        echo "next()\n";
    }

    public function rewind()
    {
        echo "rewind()\n";
    }

    public function valid()
    {
        echo "valid()\n";
        return true;
    }
}
```

```
$col = new UserCollection();
$die = false;
foreach ($col as $user) {
    if ($die) die();
    echo "Found: {$user}\n";
    $die = !$die;
}
```

Figure 5.3: Class implementing the Iterator interface

This code prints out:

```
rewind()
valid()
current()
Found: string
next()
valid()
current()
```

Take a little time to look over this output and compare it with the code we wrote. There are a couple of things you can glean from the output. First of all, you can see that the **rewind()** method is the first thing called. That tells you that **foreach** will always try to iterate over all items in the object. However, the fact that you have control over the execution of that code means that you can decide whether you want to honor that behavior or not. In general you should, but if your object is a linked list that should not go back to the beginning, you can enforce that functionality in the object.

So far, we've looked only at echoing out the method names. Let's check out a simple implementation that uses the iterator functionality (Figure 5.4).

```
class User
{
    public $name;
}

class UserCollection implements Iterator
{
```

```php
    private $_users = array();
    private $_position = 0;

    public function __construct()
    {
        $names = array(
            'Bob',
            'David',
            'Steve',
            'Peter'
        );
        foreach ($names as $name) {
            $user = new User();
            $user->name = $name;
            $this->_users[] = $user;
        }
    }

    public function current()
    {
        return $this->_users[$this->_position];
    }

    public function key()
    {
        return $this->_position;
    }

    public function next()
    {
        $this->_position++;
    }

    public function rewind()
    {
        $this->_position = 0;
    }

    public function valid()
    {
        return isset(
            $this->_users[$this->_position]
        );
    }
}
```

```
$col = new UserCollection();
foreach ($col as $num => $user) {
        echo "Found {$num}: {$user->name}\n";
}
```

Figure 5.4: SPL iteration example

This code outputs:

```
Found 0: Bob
Found 1: David
Found 2: Steve
Found 3: Peter
```

No surprises. But there's a problem here. From a practical standpoint, this solution is not very beneficial because it really doesn't do anything different from a regular array. So why would you use it? One reason is that this type of functionality is quite useful when you want to load things on demand — a design known as lazy loading. Laziness is a programmer's virtue (except when it comes to leaving the coffee pot empty). So what could this look like from a practical standpoint?

Let's start with a database table (Figure 5.5).

```
CREATE TABLE 'users' (
  'user_key' INTEGER UNSIGNED NOT NULL AUTO_INCREMENT,
  'user_name' VARCHAR(64) NOT NULL,
  'user_email' VARCHAR(64) NOT NULL,
  'user_password' VARCHAR(64) NOT NULL,
  PRIMARY KEY ('user_key')
)
ENGINE = InnoDB;
```

Figure 5.5: CREATE statement for a sample user table

And some data (Figure 5.6).

```
INSERT INTO users (user_name, user_email, user_password)
  VALUES ('Steve', 'steve@localhost',
          '5baa61e4c9b93f3f0682250b6cf8331b7ee68fd8');
INSERT INTO users (user_name, user_email, user_password)
```

```
   VALUES ('Bob', 'bob@localhost',
          '5baa61e4c9b93f3f0682250b6cf8331b7ee68fd8');
INSERT INTO users (user_name, user_email, user_password)
   VALUES ('Peter', 'peter@localhost',
          '5baa61e4c9b93f3f0682250b6cf8331b7ee68fd8');
INSERT INTO users (user_name, user_email, user_password)
   VALUES ('David', 'david@localhost',
          '5baa61e4c9b93f3f0682250b6cf8331b7ee68fd8');
```

Figure 5.6: Four rows of data to insert

And now some code (Figure 5.7).

```
class User
{
    public $id;
    public $name;
    public $email;
    public $password;
}

class UserCollection implements Iterator
{
    private $_stmt;
    private $_user;

    public function current()
    {
        return $this->_user;
    }

    public function key()
    {
        return $this->_user->id;
    }

    public function next()
    {
        if (($row = $this->_stmt->fetch(
                     PDO::FETCH_ASSOC)) !== false) {
            $this->_user
                    = new User();
            $this->_user->id
                    = $row['user_key'];
```

```
                    $this->_user->name
                        = $row['user_name'];
                    $this->_user->email
                        = $row['user_email'];
                    $this->_user->password
                        = $row['user_password'];
            return;
            }
            $this->_user = null;
        }

        public function rewind()
        {
            $pdo = new PDO('mysql:dbname=book','root','');
            $this->_stmt = $pdo->prepare(
                            'SELECT * FROM users'
            );
            $this->_stmt->execute();
            $this->next();
        }

        public function valid()
        {
            return $this->_user instanceof User;
        }
    }
}

$col = new UserCollection();
foreach ($col as $id => $user) {
    echo "Found {$id}: {$user->name} {$user->email}\n";
}
```

Figure 5.7: Implementing a lazy loading collection using the Iterator interface

And finally some output:

```
Found 1: Steve steve@localhost
Found 2: Bob bob@localhost
Found 3: Peter peter@localhost
Found 4: David david@localhost
```

What does this code do? Any time the array is rewound, the database creates a prepared statement and attaches that statement to the class. Then, when asked to move to the next element, the object retrieves the next row from the database and populates the internal object of the type over which we are iterating. The benefit of this implementation is that you could technically iterate over a large number of records while maintaining a relatively small memory footprint.

The next problem is that this is a lot of code to write to do some basic things. Although it is nice to be able to load objects on demand as we have done here, from a practical standpoint we just don't need to do that all that often.

To resolve this issue, we're going to take a look at several helper classes. The first one, called **ArrayObject**, implements all the methods we've looked at already, plus some others we'll examine soon, plus several more that we'll just take a glance at. But first, the implementation of **ArrayObject** (Figure 5.8).

```
class UserCollection extends ArrayObject
{

    public function __construct()
    {
        $pdo = new PDO('mysql:dbname=book', 'root', '');
        $stmt = $pdo->prepare('SELECT * FROM users');
        if ($stmt->execute()) {
            $array = array();
            while (($row = $stmt->fetch(
                    PDO::FETCH_ASSOC)) !==false) {
                $user = new User();
                $user->id
                    = $row['user_key'];
                $user->name
                    = $row['user_name'];
                $user->email
                    = $row['user_email'];
                $user->password
                    = $row['user_password'];
                $array[] = $user;
            }
            parent::__construct($array);
        }
    }
}
```

Figure 5.8: Extending ArrayObject (no lazy loading)

And our output remains the same:

```
Found 1: Steve steve@localhost
Found 2: Bob bob@localhost
Found 3: Peter peter@localhost
Found 4: David david@localhost
```

With this example, we are loading everything up into memory, and so its purpose is different from the previous example. What if we wanted to add a user to this collection on the fly? Impossible, you say? Not at all. There are several methods that **ArrayObject** implements to enable you to do such things. Let's revisit our code that iterates over the list of users. This time, we'll add another user to the array (Figure 5.9).

```
$col = new UserCollection();

$me = new User();
$me->name = 'Kevin';
$me->email = 'kevin@localhost';
$col[] = $me;

foreach ($col as $id => $user) {
    echo "Found {$id}: {$user->name} {$user->email}\n";
}
```

Figure 5.9: Adding data to an ArrayObject instance

This code prints out:

```
Found 0: Steve steve@localhost
Found 1: Bob bob@localhost
Found 2: Peter peter@localhost
Found 3: David david@localhost
Found 4: Kevin kevin@localhost
```

The reason why this solution works is because of **ArrayObject**'s implementation of the **ArrayAccess** interface. **ArrayAccess** defines several additional methods:

- **offsetExists ($offset)**

- **offsetGet ($offset)**

- **offsetSet ($offset, $value)**

- **offsetUnset ($offset)**

When we execute the **$col[]** expression, the Zend Engine checks to see whether the array is an instance of **ArrayAccess**. If it is, it calls the **offsetSet()** method, which is implemented in **ArrayObject**, thereby setting the value in the object as if it were an array.

This brings up an interesting possibility. What if you wanted to build a collection object where you wanted to implement some kind of type-checking? Figure 5.10 shows one way you could do this.

```
class UserCollection extends ArrayObject
{

    public function addUser(User $user)
{

        $this[] = $user;
    }
}

class BadUser{}

$col = new UserCollection();

$me = new BadUser();
$col->addUser($me);
```

Figure 5.10: Adding some structure to ArrayObject

But a problem with this approach is that it throws a fatal error when you pass an incompatible object. The other problem is that we're trying to integrate this tightly into the PHP iterative implementation. There is nothing wrong with this method, and, in general, this is actually the way to go because it forces you to adhere to structure in your application. But sometimes you need things to be a little more loose, and rather than throwing a fatal error (catchable though it is, although not as an exception), you would rather capture an error in a **try/catch** block so you can more gracefully recover.

The solution is to override the **offsetSet()** method with your own (Figure 5.11).

```php
class UserCollection extends ArrayObject
{
      public function offsetSet($index, $newval)
      {
            if (!$newval instanceof User) {
                  throw new Exception(
                        'Only accepts User objects'
                  );
            }
            parent::offsetSet($index, $newval);
      }
}

class BadUser{}

$col = new UserCollection();

$me = new BadUser();
try {
    $col[] = $me;
} catch (Exception $e) {
    echo $e->getMessage() . "\n";
}
foreach ($col as $id => $user) {
    echo "Found {$id}: {$user->name} {$user->email}\n";
}
```

Figure 5.11: Overriding offsetSet() to provide type checking on array elements

When we run this code, we are able to nicely catch the error:

```
Only accepts User objects
Found 0: Steve steve@localhost
Found 1: Bob bob@localhost
Found 2: Peter peter@localhost
Found 3: David david@localhost
```

Using this method, we can realize both of our goals of type sensitivity and integration with PHP's iterative functionality.

Conclusion

This chapter is not intended to give a full treatment of SPL. SPL implementations are highly dependent on what your application needs, and for this reason it is difficult to provide useful or interesting examples. This chapter is here to inform you of the integration points that SPL, and the Zend Engine in general, have that you can exploit in your application.

6

Asynchronous Operations with Some Encryption Thrown In

One of the primary ways to increase the ability of your Web site to scale is to use asynchronous operations. Modern Web applications have a lot of logic to execute for each request, and the effect of this requirement is often slow requests. However, Web requests are intended to be snappy, partly because users demand it but also because Web sites need to be able to serve up content to large numbers of people on a moment's notice.

The problem of asynchronous operations will have a different solution depending on the type of application being written. What we're going to do here is look at an example of how you *could* implement this functionality in your application. I would not suggest that you take this code and throw it into a production environment, but, at the same time, the concepts demonstrated here are quite pertinent to what you *may* need in a production environment.

Application Overview

Our example will use a combination of different applications. The sample application we'll build is a simple credit card processor. This is probably the most common need I've seen for asynchronous operations. It may not be the most interesting example, but it probably is the most relevant. Also, because of the whole credit aspect, we need to throw in some encryption. When you first read this chapter's title, you may have thought, "How in the world are these two related?" Well, credit card processing is why. I could have chosen something like search to show an example, but some other company beat me to it.

Another question you may have is, "Why is this even a problem? Couldn't you just handle this in the Web server?" The answer is, "Yes, you could." But there is a caveat to that. The caveat is, "if you are not concerned with scalability or high load." For the most efficient use of a front-end Web server, you do not want to have it sitting idle waiting for PHP to handle the response to come back from the credit card processor. One reason for this is that if you have a high number of transactions, you can actually run out of spare processes to serve other requests. Without having some kind of asynchronous processing going on, your front-end Web servers could be overloaded while being completely idle if someone put in a Luhn-validated, but inactive, credit card number. This would be a very easy-to-implement denial-of-service attack. But by offloading any long-running functionality to a back-end queuing mechanism, the front end can remain snappy while any load is managed in the back end.

This brings us to what our architecture will look like. It will be relatively simple. The front end will be the Apache/PHP instance that you know and love. The back-end credit card handler will be running Zend Server's Job Queue. The Job Queue is a feature in Zend Server 5.0 and later that lets you run jobs asynchronously from the front end. We could write our daemon for this example, but daemons are the subject of another chapter. Here, we just need something that already works.

Figure 6.1 shows the basic flow of the queuing system.

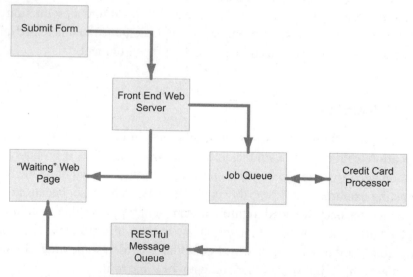

Figure 6.1: Basic flow chart of the queuing system

The way this works is that a form is submitted from the browser. This form should contain all the information needed to do a valid credit card transaction. To process the credit card transaction, we will use the Authorize.net payment gateway. Why? Because it came up first in a Google search and doesn't require you to have an actual merchant account to test its API.

Once the credit card form has been submitted, the Web server will do two things. First, it will call the Job Queue and pass the credit card information. Then, it will render a page that contains some JavaScript that connects to the message queue. This is the point where our logic separates.

The Web browser, once it has the HTML, will make an Ajax request, not to the Web server but to the message queue. Feel free to use any message queue you like; however, it should support some kind of HTTP request. However, what we're going to do is build a very small queue proxy whose only purpose will be to broker requests from the back-end job queue to the front-end listener. It will not have durability or any of the other features that a typical message queue would have. Other message queue software packages are available, but they tend to be a little difficult to set up for the simple demonstration we're going to have here. But if you end up using the methods described here, I recommend taking a look at some of the message queues that are already out there. Many of them already have HTTP-based messaging available.

Getting the Web page to properly display the data from the message queue is actually a bit of a pain due to the browser-domain, so-called security features. This is especially true if you just want a simple example that could possibly be reused. It's quite doable, as you can see, but because of the security restrictions in the browser, you may need some patience. The message queue's HTTP API is the reason for this, and it's not because of HTTP, but because of your browser. It doesn't matter whether you are on the same IP address with a different port or on a sub-domain; your browser will complain about cross-domain permissions issues.

In this example, we use JQuery 1.3.2 to handle processing the remote data. The way we do that is by taking the output of the job we run and wrapping it in a **mod_rewrite** call, which encapsulates the output in a JavaScript Object Notation (JSON) object, which is then attached to the window. What this basically means is that the output is attached to the browser by actually making it part of the

JavaScript code. It's not the most elegant solution, but it's simple, it works, and it doesn't have cross-domain issues.

Setting Up the Message Queue

First, we need to set up our message queue. To run this example, we will need two IP addresses: one for the Web server and one for the message queue. So, for our testing we will add the entries shown in Figure 6.2 to our hosts file.

```
127.0.0.1        localhost www.async.local jq.async.local
192.168.0.75     msg.async.local
```

Figure 6.2: Changes to our hosts file

You will note that the **www** and **jq** are on the same IP address. That is because the Zend Server Job Queue is actually run as an HTTP request. In this case, it will be on the same server, but in your own setup you should run it on a separate machine because the whole purpose of having a Job Queue is so your front end can scale more easily. Because I wanted an example that you should be able to replicate in a reasonable amount of time, I chose to do it on one local machine. If I were running an actual scalability test on it, with thousands of connections coming in, I would be more concerned with having many more servers, or virtual servers, to handle the different aspects of the queuing functionality.

The first thing we're going to do is build our message queuing application. Although technically we probably don't need to include this piece, I am a believer that code is a great teaching tool, and so we will include it. It will be very similar to the non-blocking I/O example in the networking chapter.

If I were to build this application as a production daemon, I would do it a little differently in that I would have more active connection management and would structure it a little better. I would also make it more conducive to unit testing. However, because it is just an example, we're going to keep it simple. For that reason, we will also not add a durability layer onto it. Durability simply means that your data would survive a crash. To provide durability, you would build a persistence layer — in other words, some kind of database. Because this is a simple key-value relationship, a solution such as the Berkeley DB library would be worth looking into.

The daemon works by supporting both **GET** and **POST** requests. A **GET** request is used to query a specific queue. A **POST** request is used to append data to a queue. The queue is specified by the Uniform Resource Identifier (URI) that is requested. So a **GET** request to the URL **http://msg.async.local/test** will create and query the queue **/test**, and a **POST** request to that same URL would create and submit data to that queue.

First, let's define the class that will be managing the queue connections with its data structures (Figure 6.3).

```
class Connection
{
        private static $_conns = array();
        private static $_qListen = array();
        private static $_qData = array();

        private $_sock;
        private $_readData = '';
        private $_writeData = '';
        private $_queue = '';
        private $_postSize = 0;
        private $_headers = array();
        private $_usableHeaders = array(
                'content-type'
        );

}
```

Figure 6.3: Property declaration for handling connections

The first three variables here are defined in the static context and are used for managing connections and data for the whole server.

The **$_conns** variable is used to manage all the connections for the daemon. The keys are a URI based on the host name and port, with the value being an instance of the **Connection** class.

The **$_qListen** variable is used to store all the active connections that are waiting for data to arrive on a queue. The keys will be the name of the queue and the value will be the **Connection** object. A connection object will be placed in this variable only if there is not data in the queue waiting for a listener. If data exists in the queue to which a new client connects, that data will be returned to the client instantly, and the client will disconnect. Only when a client connects to the queue and no data is available will the connection be placed into the $_qListen array. The connection is intended to be maintained until data is received for the queue or until the client disconnects.

The $_qData variable stores data for a queue that does not have a current listener defined. It is an associative multidimensional array, with the key being the name of the queue and the value being an array of data waiting to be received. So when the Job Queue does a **POST** to a queue for which no client is currently connected, that **POST** data will be placed here.

The final variables are defined in the object context and, as such, are intended to be unique on a per-object basis.

The $_sock variable is the socket resource that represents the connection. The $_readData variable stores data being read from a **POST** request. We have no guarantee that you can read all the data from such a request in a single read operation nor any assurance that the TCP buffer can hold all the data we need to store. Therefore, we need to be able to read in pieces. Any data that is read will be placed in this variable until we've read the full content from the stream and can process that data.

The $_writeData variable stores the data that needs to be sent to the client for its particular operation. For a **POST** request, this data would be a simple **200 OK** response. For a **GET** request, it would be a **200 OK** plus all the data that was appended to the queue by a previous **POST** request.

The $_queue variable stores the name of the queue as requested by the individual connection. $_postSize contains the size of the **POST** request. As you might assume, this value is used only for a **POST** request; it compares the length of the **POST** data read with the size of the data provided by the client.

The $_headers variable stores approved header fields from the request that need to be passed through to the front end. Those header values are taken from the $_usableHeaders variable.

Let's define some utility functions for the **Connection** class. The **getConnection** method (Figure 6.4) is used to retrieve a connection object for individual sockets.

```
public static function
  getConnection($sock, $sockId = null)
{
    if ($sockId === null) {
        $sockId = self::_getUri($sock);
    }
    if (!isset(self::$_conns[$sockId])) {
        socket_set_nonblock($sock);
        self::$_conns[$sockId] = new Connection($sock);
    }
    return self::$_conns[$sockId];
}
```

Figure 6.4: Code to retrieve Connection object for individual sockets

This method creates a new **Connection** object and registers it with the static **$_conns** variable, unless it's already been defined. This is the connection point between the selector and our connection management objects. To store the data from read and write operations between requests, we need to have something such as this because the selector returns only the socket variables and not the **Connection** object. The reason for the optional **$sockId** variable is because the server socket needs to be included for the selector's read operation. That way, we can specify the socket ID manually or use the TCP socket data to determine the ID, as we would for an incoming connection.

The **_getUri()** method (Figure 6.5) is used to provide a unique URI for each connection based on remote host and port. This should be sufficient to provide a predictable mechanism for determining the client while negating the possibility of a naming collision.

```
private static function _getUri($sock)
{
    $addr = $port = null;
    socket_getpeername($sock, $addr, $port);
    return "{$addr}:{$port}";
}
```

Figure 6.5: Code to determine a unique, repeatable connection handle

The **getReadConnections()** method is used to retrieve all the connections that are eligible for read operations. Because HTTP is a request/response protocol, we need to read only from connections that are "requesting." Once the request has been read, we just need to write to it (Figure 6.6).

```
public static function getReadConnections()
{
    $cons = array();
    foreach (self::$_conns as $con) {
        if (!$con->willWrite()) {
            $cons[] = $con->_sock;
        }
    }
    return $cons;
}
```

Figure 6.6: Retrieving connections that are ready to be read from

The **getWriteConnections()** method (Figure 6.7) does the exact opposite. It returns a list of all the connections that have data waiting to be written to.

```
public static function getWriteConnections()
{
    $cons = array();
    foreach (self::$_conns as $con) {
        if ($con->willWrite()) {
            $cons[] = $con->_sock;
        }
    }
    return $cons;
}
```

Figure 6.7: Retrieving connections that have writable data present

To see how these methods are used, let's look at our mainline code (Figure 6.8).

```
$sock = socket_create(AF_INET, SOCK_STREAM, SOL_TCP);
if (!$sock) die('Unable to create socket');
if (!socket_bind($sock, 'msg.async.local', 80))
    die('Unable to bind socket');
```

```
socket_listen($sock);
socket_set_nonblock($sock);
$counter = 0;
$time = time();
Connection::getConnection($sock, 'base');
$read = Connection::getReadConnections();
$write = $except = array();
while (socket_select($read, $write, $except, 1)
        !== false) {

    foreach ($read as $client) {
        if ($client === $sock) {
            $conn = Connection::getConnection(
                        socket_accept($sock)
            );
        } else {
            $conn = Connection::getConnection(
                        $client
                );
            $conn->read();
        }
    }
    foreach ($write as $client) {
        $conn = Connection::getConnection($client);
        $conn->write();
    }
    $read = Connection::getReadConnections();
    $write = Connection::getWriteConnections();
}
```

Figure 6.8: Mainline message server code

Most of this is quite similar to the non-blocking I/O example in the earlier chapter. So rather than spend time here explaining what is going on, I will leave it to you to review the explanation in that chapter if you need to.

In the **getConnection()** method, we create a new **Connection** object, but we haven't defined a constructor yet. The code in Figure 6.9 takes care of that.

```
private function __construct($sock)
{
    $this->_sock = $sock;
}
```

Figure 6.9: The constructor for the Connection class

Simple enough. We make the constructor private so that only the **getConnection()** method can create the object, but not any context outside the class. This ensures that the **Connection** class is the only place that is managing these types of connections.

Figure 6.10 shows the method that is used to determine whether the connection is in a condition for writing data. This can occur only after either **POST** content has been read or data has arrived in the queue for a **GET** request.

```php
public function willWrite()
{
        return strlen($this->_writeData) > 0;
}
```

Figure 6.10: Checking whether data is ready to be sent on the connection

Figure 6.11 shows the method that is used for reading when a socket has data waiting on it to be read.

```php
public function read()
{
  $data = socket_read($this->_sock, 1024);
  if ($data == '') {
        $this->_writeData = '';
        $this->close();
        return;
  }
  $this->_readData .= $data;

  if ($this->_postSize === 0
    && ($pos = strpos($this->_readData, "\r\n\r\n")) > 0
    || ($pos = strpos($this->_readData, "\n\n")) > 0) {

          $this->_handleHeadersReceived($pos);
  }

  if ($this->_postSize > 0
      && strlen($this->_readData) >= $this->_postSize) {

      $this->_handlePostReceived();
  }
}
```

Figure 6.11: Reading data from the socket

The first check we do is to read data in from the socket. If the socket is ready for a read, but has no data on it, that means that the connection has been closed. In that case, we remove any data that's going to be written and close the connection. We'll look at the method for that in a little bit.

Next, we check to see whether we have received a full HTTP header. If we have, we call the **_handleHeadersReceived()** method to set up the object according to the type of the request that is going to be read.

The next check determines whether the request is a **POST** request (**$_postSize > 0**) and whether the amount of received data matches what the **POST** claimed it was going to be sending.

At the end of each write operation, we call the **close()** method (Figure 6.12). It will close, however, only if there is no data.

```
public function close()
{
  if (!$this->_writeData) {
        unset(
                self::$_conns[self::_getUri($this->_sock)]
        );

        socket_close($this->_sock);
  }
}
```

Figure 6.12: Closing the socket if there is no data left to send

If there is data to write, we write to the socket (Figure 6.13). The **socket_write()** operation returns the number of bytes written to the buffer. We take this value and remove the bytes that have been sent.

```
public function write()
{
      if ($this->_writeData) {
            $writeLen = socket_write(
                                $this->_sock,
                                $this->_writeData
            );
```

```
                $this->_writeData = substr(
                                $this->_writeData,
                                $writeLen
                );
        }
        $this->close();
}
```

Figure 6.13: Code to write and remove written data from the internal buffer

The **_handleHeadersReceived()** method (Figure 6.14) is called after the headers
have been received from the client. The **$method** variable contains the first line
of the request, which should be something like **"GET /test HTTP/1.0"**. We get the
string in between the first and second space and store it as the queue name. After
that, we check to see whether the request is a **GET** or a **POST** request and handle it
accordingly.

```
private function _handleHeadersReceived($headerPos)
{
  $headers = trim(substr($this->_readData,
                    0, $headerPos));
  $method = trim(
        substr($this->_readData,
                0, strpos(
                        $this->_readData,
                        "\n"
                )
        )
  );

  $fs = strpos($method, ' ');
  $this->_queue = substr(
        $method,
        $fs + 1,
        strpos($method, ' ', $fs + 1) - $fs
  );

  if (stripos($method, 'GET') === 0) {
        $this->_setGet();
  } else if (stripos($method, 'POST') === 0) {
        $this->_setPost($headers);
  }
}
```

Figure 6.14: Code to execute once the HTTP headers have been received

The lovely piece of compact code shown in Figure 6.15 does a few things. First, it checks to see whether the static **$_qData** variable has any data in it. If it does, we call **setData()**, which creates the HTTP response header and places it in the class's write buffer. If there is no data in the queue, the connection is placed in the listen queue for the requested queue name.

```
private function _setGet()
{
    if (isset(self::$_qData[$this->_queue])
        && count(self::$_qData[$this->_queue]) > 0) {

        $this->setData(
                array_shift(self::$_qData[$this->_queue])
        );

        if (count(self::$_qData[$this->_queue]) === 0) {
                unset(self::$_qData[$this->_queue]);
        }
        $this->write();
        return;
    } else {
        if (!isset(self::$_qListen[$this->_queue])) {
                self::$_qListen[$this->_queue] = array();
        }
        self::$_qListen[$this->_queue][] = $this;
        return;
    }
}
```

Figure 6.15: Handling GET and POST requests

The **_setPost()** method (Figure 6.16) takes the headers that were passed in, looks for the **Content-Length** header, and sets it as the **$_postSize** for this connection. After it has that, it removes the headers by taking the end position of the headers and adds either 2 or 4 bytes, depending on whether it was a standards-based **"\r\n"** line terminator or a regular **"\n"** terminator.

```
private function _setPost($headers)
{
    $pos = strlen($headers);
    $headers = explode("\n", $headers);
    foreach ($headers as $header) {
```

```
            if (stripos($header, 'content-length') === 0) {
                $this->_postSize = (int)trim(
                    substr(
                        $header,
                        strpos($header, ':') + 1
                    )
                );
            }
        }
        $bodyPos = 4;
        if ($this->_readData[$pos] === "\n") {
            $bodyPos = 2;
        }
        $this->_readData =
            substr($this->_readData, $pos+$bodyPos);
    }
```

Figure 6.16: Handling POST requests

If the request is a **POST**, the **_handlePostReceived()** method (Figure 6.17) will be called once all the data has been received.

```
private function _handlePostReceived()
{
    if (isset(self::$_qListen[$this->_queue])
        && count(self::$_qListen[$this->_queue])) {

        $listener = array_shift(
            self::$_qListen[$this->_queue]
        );

        $listener->setData(
            $this->_readData,
            $this->_headers
        );
        $this->setData();

    } else {
        if (!isset(self::$_qData[$this->_queue])) {
            self::$_qData[$this->_queue] = array();
        }
        self::$_qData[$this->_queue][] =
        $this->_readData;
        $this->setData();
    }
}
```

Figure 6.17: Send POST data to a listener or store in a queue

This method first checks the listen queue for the specified queue. If a connection is waiting on that queue, it will remove it from the listen queue and set the waiting connection's data with the data it had received. It will then set its own data to empty, which creates an empty HTTP **200 OK** response and places it in the write buffer. If no existing connection is waiting on the queue, the data is placed in the **$_qData** variable for later retrieval by a **GET** request. **_handlePostReceived()** then sets its own data as empty and places an HTTP **200 OK** response in its buffer.

To set the return data, we use the **setData()** method (Figure 6.18). This method takes the raw data and generates the HTTP response for both the job queue and browser requests. The primary purpose is to get that **200 OK** on top.

```
public function setData($data = '', $headers = array())
{
      $strlen = strlen($data);
      $headersOut = '';
      foreach ($headers as $name => $value) {
            $headersOut .= "\n{$name}: {$value}";
      }
      $this->_writeData = <<<HTTP
HTTP/1.0 200 OK
Content-Length: {$strlen}
Connection: close{$headersOut}

{$data}
HTTP;

}
```

Figure 6.18: Creating an HTTP response

Now, what we need to do is test. To do that, we'll use the simple script shown in Figure 6.19.

```
$ctx = stream_context_create(
    array(
        'http'      => array(
            'content' => '<div>Hello World',
            'header'  => 'Content-Type: text/xml',
            'method'  => 'POST'
        )
    )
);

var_dump(file_get_contents(
    'http://msg.async.local/test', 0, $ctx));
```

Figure 6.19: Testing a POST to the queue

We request the URL **http://msg.async.local/test** with our browser, which sits there with its **Loading** icon spinning until we run our test script. Note that we are not using any JavaScript at this point. This is just a simple HTTP request for the browser. This script shown can be run from another browser window or from the command line. Its purpose is to populate the queue with the data our browser request is waiting for. Once we do that, our browser immediately returns the following:

```
<div>Hello World</div>
```

Seems like it worked. If it does not for you, I highly recommend running the daemon from within an integrated development environment (IDE), using a debugger to find out what the problem is.

Handling the Credit Card Processing

Now that we have our queue working, we're going to create a form to handle the credit card processing. To do that, we will use the **Zend_Form** component in Zend Framework. For information about that, you can go to *http://framework.zend.com* to start.

Figure 6.20 shows the code that creates the form to submit the credit card.

```
class Form_CreditCard extends Zend_Form
{
      public function init()
      {
            $this->setView(new Zend_View());
            $this->addElement(
                  'text',
                  'card_number',
                  array(
                        'label' => 'Card Number'
                  )
            );
            $this->addElement(
                  'text',
                  'exp_date',
                  array(
                        'label' => 'Expiration Date'
                  )
            );
            $this->addElement(
                  'text',
                  'amount',
                  array(
                        'label' => 'Amount'
                  )
            );
            $this->addElement(
                  'submit',
                  'Submit'
            );
      }
}
```

Figure 6.20: Creating a form to submit the credit card

The next thing to write is the script to handle our user interface (Figure 6.21). As with the daemon, if I were writing this for a production environment, I would structure things differently, but this example is for a book and as such is much simpler.

```php
$form = new Form_CreditCard();
$queue = false;
if ($_SERVER['REQUEST_METHOD'] == 'POST'
      && $form->isValid($_POST)) {

. . .We'll worry about this part later. . .

}
?>
<html>
<head>
<script type="text/javascript" src="jquery.js"></script>

<?php if ($queue): ?>

<script type="text/javascript">

function readMyQueue()
{
  $.getScript(
    "http://msg.async.local/<?php
      echo $queue
    ?>",
      function(){
        $("#message").html(content);
  });
}

$(document).ready(readMyQueue());

</script>
<?php endif; ?>

</head>
<body>
<div id="message">
<?php if ($queue): ?>
      Please wait while we process your request...
<?php else: ?>
      <?php echo $form ?>
<?php endif; ?>
</div>
</body>
</html>
```

Figure 6.21: Script to POST the credit card to the queue

This code basically acts as an interface between the main Web server and the message queue. The message queue, as you saw earlier, understands some very basic HTTP. The first request that the browser makes is simply to display the form. This is determined by whether the **$queue** variable is false or contains a queue name. The second request takes the form submission results, submits them to the job queue, and renders the results. As part of that functionality, we will set the **$queue** variable to a different value, which will keep the form from being rendered. However, there is an additional piece here because rendering the results, contrary to a typical Web page, actually is the start of the process, not the end. When the page is initially rendered, we do not print any of the JavaScript. But on the form submission, we print out some additional JavaScript that has the purpose of connecting to the message queue mini-HTTP server and printing the results.

Here, we use jQuery to handle the request. For Ajax calls, you generally would make a request to the same domain name and append the data using innerHTML or something like that. But one of the reasons I chose this example is because I want a solution that can scale much more than the typical Web server, not because of a lack of CPU but because we want to be able to stack a large number of concurrent, sleeping connections. However, because of that, we have that cross-domain problem that I described earlier in the chapter.

Encrypting the Data

Because we're going to be submitting credit card data for processing, we also need to be responsible and encrypt our data because it will not be stored encrypted in the queue while it's waiting for processing. In addition, because the front-end Web servers will be customer-facing, we don't want to use a synchronous encryption mechanism.

To achieve these things, we're going to use the OpenSSL extension with the **openssl_get_publickey()** and **openssl_public_encrypt()** methods on the front end and **openssl_get_privatekey()** and **openssl_private_decrypt()** on the Job Queue side. To start, we'll need to create a private key, with a passphrase and a public key based on that private key. There are plenty of descriptions about how to do this on that thing called the Internet, so I'll just show the basics of getting it done.

We use the **openssl** command with the **genrsa** option to create our private key (Figure 6.22). This is the key that would be distributed along with our job queue. We'll take the key and put it into a file named **private.key**.

```
$ openssl genrsa
Generating RSA private key, 512 bit long modulus
...........++++++++++++
......++++++++++++
e is 65537 (0x10001)
-----BEGIN RSA PRIVATE KEY-----
MIIBOwIBAAJBAMM+M2jnpiowNxc6qmeCgNOHiasLcB76OsP+gDzmL8nB
+qTOBaURGYNywR6i41RY9Z39KmfQMEL8Ip5vOlpnMLkCAwEAAQJBAJNB
VZr4pE3LgbGGcMGTHOgViFK2VME4b5wlVmkYH9DlqLxNRw+a+rO3Fk1X
BBnlouaGQ6bpRpuppdfxvWOJWbUCIQDgRAN5EAEx+NOOmxEgrte/5H6I
fvXmk2gxD7nNy5kiiwIhAN7e2DiHOEwudq8FN6AYzI6fsPkMPKsPLa3B
Ez7lmnZLAiA4ThspG/GQ4FB5Uq1cLUmRrgZusqF+QGgaWT5nAsTxvQIg
V9tLKOXGxDFQOf/hhLgh81taXWMIi3ppTGSfXJOQfe8CIQCxI63HrlE9
Hvrmz2T QB4U2gos6yVmSNJIoNOK1+kTMfA==
-----END RSA PRIVATE KEY-----
```

Figure 6.22: Creating a private key

We then take that private key and create the public key so that we can encrypt any data we want to send to the job queue (Figure 6.23).

```
$ openssl rsa -in private.key -out public.key -pubout
writing RSA key
```

Figure 6.23: Creating the public key from the private key

Figure 6.24 shows what we see when we look at the output of the **public.key** file.

```
-----BEGIN PUBLIC KEY-----
MFwwDQYJKoZIhvcNAQEBBQADSwAwSAJBAMM+M2jnpiowNxc6qmeCgNOH
iasLcB76OsP+gDzmL8nB+qTOBaURGYNywR6i41RY9Z39KmfQMEL8Ip5v
Ol pnMLkCAwEAAQ==
-----END PUBLIC KEY-----
```

Figure 6.24: Output of the public key

We can now use public/private key encryption.

The next thing we're going to look at is the actual code on the front-end machine that connects with the Job Queue. This is the code that we omitted from the previous HTML/PHP code. If I were truly doing this for a production environment, I would be building out a whole abstraction layer. What am I saying? While there is nothing wrong with this code, it should be written in a manner that is more "library-oriented" than script-oriented. That would make it more manageable and more reusable.

Figure 6.25 presents the code to encrypt the request and send it to the queue.

```php
if ($_SERVER['REQUEST_METHOD'] == 'POST'
    && $form->isValid($_POST)) {
    $queue = uniqid(php_uname('n') . '-');

    $publicKeyTxt = file_get_contents('public.key');
    $publicKey = openssl_get_publickey($publicKeyTxt);

    $encryptedParams = array('card_number',
                             'exp_date');

    $params = array(
      'card_number' => $form->getValue('card_number'),
      'exp_date'    => $form->getValue('exp_date'),
      'amount'      => $form->getValue('amount'),
      'encryptedParams' => $encryptedParams,
      'queue'       => $queue
    );
    foreach ($encryptedParams as $enc) {
        openssl_public_encrypt(
            $params[$enc],
            $params[$enc],
            $publicKey
        );
        $params[$enc] = base64_encode($params[$enc]);
    }

    $jq = new ZendJobQueue();
    $e = $jq->createHttpJob(

        'http://jq.async.local/Test'
        . '/Async/jobs/run_credit_card',
        $params

    );
}
```

Figure 6.25: Code to encrypt the request and send it to the queue

This code first checks to see whether the request is a **POST** and, if so, whether the form is valid. If the request is a **POST** and the form is valid, the next thing it does is generate a new queue on which it will listen. The queue name is based on the host name for the location machine plus some randomness.

The next thing we need to do is connect to the Job Queue and run the job, but the problem is that in order for us to be somewhat secure about the whole thing, we need to encrypt some of the data. If I were building a more full processing system, what I most likely would do is serialize a payment object and encrypt the whole thing. But, again, to keep things simple we're going to just encrypt a bit of the data. We state which parameters we want to encrypt, and after creating a resource that points to our public key, we encrypt each of those and encode them as base64. (The reason for that is simply because the Job Queue didn't like having 8-bit data passed as a parameter, most likely because a URL needs to be ASCII-encoded.)

Once we've done that, we create a new Job Queue object. If you are not using the Zend Server Job Queue, this portion of code will be different for you. The Zend Server Job Queue works by calling the URL of a back-end machine that will run the request for you. So, we call **createHttpJob()** with the URL and pass in the parameters. That's all we need to do with the front-end portion. Once this code is executed, it will continue on, rendering the JavaScript that will make the connection back to the message queue.

Constructing the Back End

We've got our front-end piece written. Now we need to write the code to make the back-end piece work.

Figure 6.26 shows the script to send the request to the credit card processor.

```php
if (isset($params['encryptedParams'])
 && is_array($params['encryptedParams'])) {

    $privateKey = file_get_contents('../private.key');
    $privateKey = openssl_get_privatekey($privateKey,'');
    foreach ($params['encryptedParams'] as $enc) {
        $params[$enc] = base64_decode($params[$enc]);
        $dec = '';
        openssl_private_decrypt($params[$enc],
                                $dec,$privateKey);
```

```
              $params[$enc] = $dec;
      }

}

$submittedParams = array(
      'x_version'    => '3.1',
      'x_login'      => 'xxxxxxxxx',
      'x_tran_key'   => 'xxxxxxxxxxxxxxxx',
      'x_amount'     => $params['amount'],
      'x_card_num'   => $params['card_number'],
      'x_exp_date'   => $params['exp_date'],
      'x_delim_data' => 'TRUE'
);

$query = http_build_query($submittedParams);

$ctx = stream_context_create(
      array(
            'http'        => array(
                  'content' => $query,
                  'header'  => 'Content-Type: application'
                              . '/x-www-form-urlencoded',
                  'method'  => 'POST'
            )
      )
);

$response = file_get_contents(
      'https://test.authorize.net/gateway/transact.dll',
      0, $ctx
);

$response = explode(',', $response);
echo "{$response[3]}<br />\n";

if ($response[6]) {
      echo "Transaction ID: {$response[6]}<br />";
}
```

Figure 6.26: Script to send the request to the credit card processor

This code first decrypts any pertinent data and places it back in the parameter variable; then we build our **POST** data. Because we're not using this example to demonstrate Authorize.net and this code is not particularly complicated, I will only say that when it works it prints out something like this:

```
This transaction has been approved.
Transaction ID: 2151615800
```

However, we're not just printing it out. We are sending it through a message queue which, by the browser definition, is on a different domain. Because we're connecting to a different domain, we have browser considerations to take into account. We can't simply connect to the message queue, receive some HTML, and embed it in our browser. But although you are not able to load static HTML from a third-party domain, you can execute JavaScript from a third-party domain. To get around this limitation, we need to have an additional small layer in between the job that's going to handle the integration.

Basically, what we're going to implement is a sort of Model-View-Controller (MVC) layer that will take the output of a given job and wrap it in a JavaScript variable so we can access it from our parent page. It's an ugly, but simple, way to handle it. And it is really the only way of doing it across domains.

Figure 6.27 shows the script to **POST** job output to the queue from the job queue.

```php
$params = ZendJobQueue::getCurrentJobParams();
if (!isset($params['queue'])) {
    die('Missing queue name');
}

$queue = $params['queue'];

$dirName = dirname(__FILE__);
$scriptDir = dirname($_SERVER['SCRIPT_NAME']);
$requestedURI = $_SERVER['REQUEST_URI'];

if ($requestedURI === $_SERVER['SCRIPT_NAME']) {
    header('Not Found', true, 404);
    exit;
}
```

```
$jobName = substr(
                $requestedURI,
                strlen($scriptDir))
                . '.php';

$jobFile = realpath(
        $dirName . DIRECTORY_SEPARATOR . $jobName
);
if (strpos($jobFile, $dirName) !== 0) {
        die('Security Violation');
}

ob_start();
require $jobFile;
$content = ob_get_flush();
$content = 'window.content
        = '.json_encode($content).';';

$header  = 'Content-Type: application/javascript';

$ctx = stream_context_create(
        array(
                'http'      => array(
                        'content' => $content,
                        'header'  => $header,
                        'method'  => 'POST'
                )
        )
);

echo file_get_contents(
        'http://msg.async.local/'.$queue, 0, $ctx);

ZendJobQueue::setCurrentJobStatus(ZendJobQueue::OK);
```

Figure 6.27: Script to POST job output to the queue from the job queue

This script first of all gets all the parameters that were provided by the front-end request. If the variable for holding the queue name is not set, it just dies because it doesn't know which queue to send the data to. Next, it tries to figure out the name of the script based on the requested URL. If the name of the URL is the same as the broker file name, the script dies with a 404. This behavior protects against recursive inclusion in case someone requests a job by using the same script name as the job script bootstrap file. The 404 is there simply to hide the fact that the job script bootstrap file exists. I kind of like doing that in case someone tries to access something that he or she should not know about that is not an entry point for a script. If it is an entry point but the person lacks access, a 403 is more pertinent. However, if nobody will ever know about it and no one should be directly accessing it, a 404 helps to protect against spiders and such. Not a great deal of protection, but some.

Once we've determined what the requested path name is, we check to make sure that the path to the requested job and the actual job path match exactly. Otherwise, someone might be trying to include a script that is local on the computer, but not one of the approved jobs. So this is a security check.

Once we've verified that the file is okay to run, we include it after starting the output buffer. The reason for doing this is so that we can capture all the output and place it into the JavaScript variable. We take the content, after the file has been included, and put it into a window variable called **content** as JSON. Why not as a simple text string? Because then we would have to worry about properly escaping it and such. We don't want to fuss with that, so we encode the content as JSON and let PHP and JavaScript create and interpret it properly.

Next, we create a **POST** context for our upcoming HTTP request that has the content stored in there along with the appropriate headers. As I said earlier, if I were building a production system, this would be a little more complicated, with better error handling and more structure. Once we have everything set, we call **file_get_contents()**, with the **POST** context, which then **POST**s the request to the message queue. Because the URL has the queue name appended to it, the message queue will take that queue name and check to see whether there is currently a waiting connection on the queue that can take the data and send it to that listener. Otherwise, it will just store it in its data queue until a valid listener comes in.

Testing It Out

That covers the functional aspects of our example, so all that's left now is to test it. When we fill in a credit card number, expiration date, and an amount and hit submit, our front-end code returns the HTML code shown in Figure 6.28.

```
<html>
<head>
<script type="text/javascript" src="jquery.js "></script>
<script type="text/javascript">

function readMyQueue()
{
  $.getScript(
    "http://msg.async.local/LAP-KEVIN-4b6d89ad5ea02",
      function(data, textStatus){

        $("#message").html(content);
  });
}

$(document).ready(readMyQueue());

</script>

</head>
<body>
<div id="message">
      Please wait while we process your request...
</div>
</body>
</html>
```

Figure 6.28: Generated browser script to read from the queue

As you can see, the queue name was created and appended to the URL. You can also follow the request chain in the browser by using Firebug (Figure 6.29).

⊞ **POST process.ph**	200 OK	localhost	451 B (?)	25ms
⊞ **GET jquery.js**	304 Not Modified	localhost	117.9 KB	18ms
⊞ http://msg.async.local/LAP-KEVIN-4b6d89ad5ea02? =1265469869476				518ms

Figure 6.29: Firebug output showing the JavaScript queue request

First, the post is made to the **process.php** file, which is our front-end code. Then, the browser does a **GET** request to the **msg.async.local** URL, which is where our queuing daemon is listening. The request comes back relatively fast at 518 ms. However, compared to the 25 ms that the previous request took, it is clear that more was going on behind the scenes. That "more" was the request back to

Authorize.net. If we look at the response to the **GET** request (Figure 6.30), we can see our output from the job.

```
window.content = "This transaction has been
approved.<br \/>\nTransaction ID: 2152144198<br \/>";
```

Figure 6.30: Script output sent to the queue

And then when we look at the output on the browser side, we see:

```
This transaction has been approved.
Transaction ID: 2152144198
```

Conclusion

When all of this is put together, you can see that we submitted a form, the data was then sent to a Job Queue script, the message queue was connected to by the browser, the job connecting to Authorize.net was run, and that job retrieved transaction data from the credit card processor, which was then submitted to the message queue, which found the connection to that individual queue, which returned the results to the browser. And we did it all without polling the Web server.

Structured File Access

In the desktop world, structured files are relatively commonplace. But in the Web world, we tend not to deal with them much. When we work with structured data, we usually do so via a database. Often, it doesn't make much sense for a Web developer to store data that is structured according to a proprietary format. A database does for us what we generally need to do. In addition, we typically work with string data as opposed to binary data, which is something that structured data files tend to use more.

But there are times when knowing how to figure out the internal format of a file can be useful. Other times, being able to write to those files, or even being able to write your own format, could have benefit. And, as with networking, it is just good to have an understanding of how to do things that aren't in your regular tool belt.

If you are not familiar with structured files, I caution you to read this chapter slowly. There is a lot of detail, and it is very easy to get lost. So read slowly, take breaks, and try writing out some of the code yourself. And don't expect to get it all in one shot. This chapter actually took me a very long time to write. You shouldn't expect to understand it all at once. In fact, it would probably be a good idea to read each individual section separately, interspersing other chapters in between as you move forward through this one. This chapter will probably be the most difficult one to get through, so take your time.

We'll begin by looking at some file formats that follow open standards.

Tar Files

The tar format — "tar" is short for "tape archive" — initially was used for the purpose of storing backup data on tape drives, but, as any developer who touches a Linux system knows, it has expanded well beyond that use. Tar is a relatively simple format that lets us store individual files in one file for easy transport. The use of the gzip application has become virtually synonymous with tar, although we won't look at that topic in great depth simply because gzipping a tar file is just the simple act of taking the raw tar file and compressing it.

We'll be examining an existing tar file that contains the source code for PHP 5.2.11. Before going into the actual file itself, let's check out the structure of a file header record. Files often include a file header containing metadata about the file. Depending on the file, this metadata could include the file version number, author, bit rate, or any number of other parameters. The tar file headers are actually just simple text strings, but they are stored in a structured format. In other words, they are text strings, but they are fixed-length text strings, similar to a **char** text field in SQL.

Table 7.1 shows the header record format for a tar file.

Table 7.1: Tar header record format		
Offset	Size	Description
0	100	File name
100	8	File mode (permissions)
108	8	Numeric user ID
116	8	Numeric group ID
124	12	File size in bytes
136	12	Last modified Unix timestamp
148	8	Header checksum
156	1	Record type
157	100	Linked file name

Table 7.2 lists the seven possible values for the record type.

Table 7.2: Tar record types	
Value	**Type**
0	Regular file
1	Unix link
2	Unix symbolic link
3	Character device (virtual terminal, modem, COM1)
4	Block device (disk partition, CD-ROM drive)
5	Directory
6	First-in-first-out (FIFO) or named pipe

Reading a single header record is quite easy, as you can see from the code shown in Figure 7.1.

```php
$fh = fopen('php-5.2.11.tar', 'r');

$fields = readHeader($fh);

foreach ($fields as $name => $value) {
    $value = trim($value);
    echo "{$name}: {$value}\n";
}

function readHeader($resource)
{
    $data = fread($resource, 512);
    return strunpack(
            '100name/8mode/8owner/8group/'
            . '12size/12ts/8cs/1type/100link', $data);
}

function strunpack($format, $data)
{
    $return = array();
    $fieldLengths = explode('/', $format);
    foreach ($fieldLengths as $lens) {
        $name = preg_replace('/^\d+/', '', $lens);
        $lens = (int)$lens;
        if (ctype_alpha($name)) {
            $return[$name] = substr($data, 0, $lens);
```

```
        } else {
                $return[] = substr($data, 0, $lens);
        }
        $data = substr($data, $lens);
        if (strlen($data) === 0) {
                break;
        }
    }

    return $return;
}
```

Figure 7.1: Reading the tar header

The tar block size is 512 bytes, and so even though we use only about 250 bytes, we read the entire 512-byte block. As you look at more structured files, you'll find this block-based approach a very common occurrence.

Most of this code is there simply to make reading string-based data easier. Because the **unpack()** method returns an array of individual characters rather than full strings, this method gets a little cumbersome when you're dealing with anything beyond simple string operations. That is the purpose of the **strunpack()** function. **strunpack()** takes characters that are returned individually and groups them in a single record. You might think you could use a function such as **fscanf()**, but **%s** does not like **NULL** characters. Because a tar file contains many **NULL** characters, this approach will not work well for us. So, most of this code is here to handle reading the file information, but we will use it a fair amount later on.

Figure 7.2 shows the code's output.

```
name: php-5.2.11/
mode: 0000755
owner: 0026631
group: 0024461
size: 00000000000
ts: 11261402465
cs: 012435
type: 5
link:
```

Figure 7.2: Output of reading a single header

Okay, so we have read the first record, but that doesn't help if we have more than one file in the tar file. How do we read to the next record, and the next record, and so on? Very simply. We take the size and advance the file pointer that points to the entry size to the start of the 512-byte block that follows the end of the 512-byte block at the end of the file. Make sense? No? Let's look at some code (Figure 7.3).

```php
$fh = fopen('php-5.2.11.tar', 'r');
$fileCount = 10;


for ($c = 0; $c < $fileCount; $c++) {

    $fields = readHeader($fh);
    $newPosition = ftell($fh);

    $name = trim($fields['name']);
    echo "Name: {$name}\n";

    $size = octdec($fields['size']);
    if ($size === 0) {
        continue;
    }
    $remainder = $size % 512;
    $totalSize = $size + (512 - $remainder);

    fseek($fh, $totalSize, SEEK_CUR);
}
```

Figure 7.3: Reading the next record

Because there are several thousand files in this tar file, we are going to limit ourselves to only 10 for now. The first thing we do is read the 512-byte header. This is the same as what we did earlier. The first time the **$newPosition** constant is assigned a value, it will be the number **512** because that is exactly how many bytes we read. Because **$fields['name']** is 100 characters, null-padded, we trim it to get the correct value and then echo it. After that, we take the size field. However, the sizes are specified not in bytes, but in octal. So we call the **octdec()** function to convert the number from octal to decimal. If the size of the file is zero bytes, we have no data to read. Usually, a file of zero bytes will actually be a directory.

After we have gathered our data, because we are not reading the file content itself, we need to manually advance the file pointer to the start of the next header record.

We do that by getting the modulus of the size against the size of the standard tar block, 512 bytes. The result of this calculation should exactly match the number of null bytes padded at the end of the file data. We do that by taking our found size and adding 512 minus the padded data. After that, the file pointer should be at the start byte of the next file header.

When we run this code, we get the output shown in Figure 7.4.

```
Name: php-5.2.11/
Name: php-5.2.11/.gdbinit
Name: php-5.2.11/acconfig.h
Name: php-5.2.11/acconfig.h.in
Name: php-5.2.11/acinclude.m4
Name: php-5.2.11/aclocal.m4
Name: php-5.2.11/build/
Name: php-5.2.11/build/build.mk
Name: php-5.2.11/build/build2.mk
Name: php-5.2.11/build/buildcheck.sh
```

Figure 7.4: Output for reading the individual records

Clearly, the code works.

There's more information we can glean from there. Earlier, we saw that additional information was contained in the header record. However, because we have already parsed that information out and made it available in the return value from **readHeader()**, there is no need to show how to do that. Just take the desired value, such as the size or the owner's name, from the **readHeader()** return value if you need it.

The additional information is from a tar format extension called Uniform Standard Tape Archive (UStar). Perhaps you noticed a bit of an incongruity earlier on. The header record is 512 bytes long, but we parsed only 257 bytes. At byte 257, you can test for the UStar indicator, which is just a string that says "ustar". If it is present, there are some additional pieces of information you can glean. Table 7.3 lists the format of these additional details.

Table 7.3: Format of additional information in the tar header		
Offset	Size	Description
257	6	UStar indicator
263	2	UStar version
265	32	Owner name
297	32	Group name
329	8	Device major number
337	8	Device minor number
345	155	File name prefix

To obtain this information, the first thing we need to do is modify how we read the header to test whether it is a UStar-formatted header. Figure 7.5 shows the code to read UStar-formatted data.

```php
function readHeader($resource)
{
    $data = fread($resource, 512);
    if (strlen($data) !== 512) {
        trigger_error('Invalid tar file header');
        return array();
    }
    if (ord($data[257]) !== 0x00
        && substr($data, 257, 6) === 'ustar ') {

        return strunpack(
                '100name/8mode/8owner/8group/'
                . '12size/12ts/8cs/1type/100link/'
                . '6isustar/2usver/32user/32group/'
                . '8devmaj/8devmin/155prefix', $data);

    } else {

        return strunpack(
            '100name/8mode/8owner/8group/'
            . '12size/12ts/8cs/1type/100link', $data);

    }
}
```

Figure 7.5: Reading UStar-formatted data

Then, in our loop, we simply test for UStar data (Figure 7.6).

```php
$name = trim($fields['name']);
echo "Name: {$name}\n";
if (isset($fields['isustar'])) {
    $user = trim($fields['user']);
    $group = trim($fields['group']);
    echo "\tUser: {$user}\n";
    echo "\tGroup: {$group}\n";
}
```

Figure 7.6: Testing for UStar data

Figure 7.7 shows the output of this code.

```
Name: php-5.2.11/
    User: kevin
    Group: mkgroup-l-d
Name: php-5.2.11/.gdbinit
    User: kevin
    Group: mkgroup-l-d
Name: php-5.2.11/acconfig.h
    User: kevin
    Group: mkgroup-l-d
Name: php-5.2.11/acconfig.h.in
    User: kevin
    Group: mkgroup-l-d
Name: php-5.2.11/acinclude.m4
    User: kevin
    Group: mkgroup-l-d
Name: php-5.2.11/aclocal.m4
    User: kevin
    Group: mkgroup-l-d
Name: php-5.2.11/build/
    User: kevin
    Group: mkgroup-l-d
Name: php-5.2.11/build/build.mk
    User: kevin
    Group: mkgroup-l-d
Name: php-5.2.11/build/build2.mk
    User: kevin
    Group: mkgroup-l-d
Name: php-5.2.11/build/buildcheck.sh
    User: kevin
    Group: mkgroup-l-d
```

Figure 7.7: Outputting file header with UStar data

As you can see, the tar file is a relatively simple format. For that reason, it is a good place to start. Now, though, it's time to make things a little more complicated.

WAV Files

The second file format we'll look at is WAV, the Waveform Audio File Format. WAV is a relatively simple format for storing uncompressed audio data. It is easy to interpret, and I happen to have a WAV file on my desktop, so it makes good sense for me to use it as an example.

The key to working with almost any binary file structure is interpreting that structure. That is what we will do with our **unpack()** function call. Looking at the WAV file specifications, we are told the sizes of the fields and the fact that the WAV file format uses little-endian byte ordering. From there, we can figure out which format characters we need to use. Table 7.4 lists the **pack()/unpack()** format characters.

Table 7.4: Format constants for the pack() and unpack() functions	
Code	**Description**
a	NUL-padded string
A	SPACE-padded string
h	Hex string, low nibble first
H	Hex string, high nibble first
c	Signed char
C	Unsigned char
s	Signed short (always 16-bit, machine byte order)
S	Unsigned short (always 16-bit, machine byte order)
n	Unsigned short (always 16-bit, big-endian byte order)
v	Unsigned short (always 16-bit, little-endian byte order)
i	Signed integer (machine-dependent size and byte order)
I	Unsigned integer (machine-dependent size and byte order)
l	Signed long (always 32-bit, machine byte order)
L	Unsigned long (always 32-bit, machine byte order)
N	Unsigned long (always 32-bit, big endian byte order)
V	Unsigned long (always 32-bit, little endian byte order)
f	Float (machine-dependent size and representation)

Table 7.4: Format constants for the pack() and unpack() functions, continued	
Code	**Description**
d	Double (machine-dependent size and representation)
x	NUL byte
X	Back up one byte
@	NUL-fill to absolute position

For a quick illustration of how endianness works, consider the code in Figure 7.8.

```
$int = 256;
$str = pack('n', $int);
echo "Big Endian: ";
printBytes($str);

$str = pack('v', $int);
echo "Little Endian: ";
printBytes($str);

$data = unpack('vdata', $str);
echo "\n";
var_dump($data['data']);

function printBytes($data)
{
        $len = strlen($data);
        for ($c = 0; $c < $len; $c++) {
                if ($c % 8 === 0) echo "\n";
                $hex = str_pad(dechex(
                        ord($data[$c])), 2  , 0, STR_PAD_LEFT);

                echo "0x{$hex} ";
        }
        echo "\n";
}
```

Figure 7.8: A test demonstrating endianness

We use the number **256** because it cannot be represented in a single byte. What this code does is take the **256** value and split it into both a 16-bit (short) little-endian and big-endian formatted value and convert it back. Figure 7.9 shows the output.

```
Big Endian:
0x01 0x00
Little Endian:
0x00 0x01

int(256)
```

Figure 7.9: Output of endian test

If the concept of packing and unpacking bytes was a little foggy before, I hope this helps to explain it.

One of the nice things about binary files is that they tend to be relatively rigid in their structure. Table 7.5 shows the header for the WAV format.

Table 7.5: WAV file header			
Field	Length	Type	Contents
File type ID	4	String	**"RIFF"**
Size	4	Unsigned long	Length + 4
Wave ID	4	String	**"WAVE"**
Data	n		Rest of the file

So let's look at the hex data and compare it with what we've seen so far. Figure 7.10 shows the WAV file raw data.

```
52 49 46 46   78 cd 27 04   57 41 56 45   66 6d 74 20    RIFFxÍ'.WAVEfmt
12 00 00 00   01 00 02 00   44 ac 00 00   10 b1 02 00    ........D¬...±..
04 00 10 00   00 00 4a 55   4e 4b ca 0f   00 00 00 00    ......JUNKÊ.....
```
Figure 7.10: WAV file raw data

As expected, the first four bytes contain the string **"RIFF"**, which stands for Resource Interchange File Format. The next four bytes are the length of the file in little-endian format. The four after that are the string **"WAVE"**.

You might be looking at the file size of **0x78CD2704** (positions 4–8) and thinking that this is a huge file because that evaluates to 2,026,710,788 bytes. This is where the concept of endianness is important. We did some basic examination of endianness when we discussed network protocols. But because most IP-implemented protocols use the same endianness as IP, which is big-endian, it hasn't been much of an issue.

With WAV files, however, all the integers are in little-endian format, which means that the least significant byte comes first. With big-endian, the *most* significant byte is first. So, if we were to take the file size stated in the second field and flip it to big-endian, it would look like **0x0427CD78**. This size evaluates to 69,717,368 bytes, or about 66.5 MB.

To read the bytes from the file and get the proper interpretation of the structure, we will use **unpack()** and specify the **'V'** format. **'V'** tells **unpack()** to read four bytes and return the long value from a little-endian formatted byte array, which we read as a string. Figure 7.11 shows the code to read the WAV header file.

```
$filename = 'test.wav';
$fh = fopen($filename, 'r');

$typeId = fread($fh, 4);
$lenP = unpack('V', fread($fh, 4));
$len = $lenP[1];
$waveId = fread($fh, 4);

if ($typeId === 'RIFF' && $waveId === 'WAVE') {
        echo "We have a WAV file\n";
        echo "Chunk length: {$len}\n";
} else {
        die("Invalid wave file\n");
}
```

Figure 7.11: Reading the WAV header file

Running this code produces the output shown in Figure 7.12.

```
We have a WAV file
Chunk length: 69717368
```

Figure 7.12: Output of reading the WAV header file

When we compare the actual length of the file with the chunk length, we get the chunk plus eight. What this means is that the chunk length will be the file length minus the eight bytes that were needed to determine the chunk length. A chunk, in case you are not familiar with the term, is just a block of data of a defined length. HTTP can use chunks to start downloading a file of indeterminate length. In HTTP, the length of the next chunk is appended after the end of the last chunk. Chunk, block, they all kind of mean the same thing except chunks tend to be a little more variable in length, although that is by no means a rule.

After we have read the header, the next step is to read chunk data. There are three types of chunks in a WAV file: the format chunk, the fact chunk (used for compression), and the data chunk. Right now, we're just interested in the format chunk because it gives us our metadata about the nature of the data in the file.

Table 7.6 shows the format of the format chunk.

Table 7.6: WAV file metadata format			
Field	**Length**	**Type (pack)**	**Contents**
Chunk ID	4	String	**"fmt "**
Size	4	Unsigned long (V)	**0x16, 0x18**, or **0x40**
Format	2	Unsigned int (v)	
Channels	2	Unsigned int (v)	
Sample rate	4	Unsigned long (V)	
Data rate	4	Unsigned long (V)	
Block size	2	Unsigned int (v)	
Bits/sample	2	Unsigned int (v)	
Extension size	2	Unsigned int (v)	**0 or 22**
Valid bits/sample	2	Unsigned int (v)	
Channel mask	4	Unsigned long (V)	
Subformat	16	Unsigned char (c16)	

To read the data in that format, we need to **unpack()** it. To do so, we append the code shown in Figure 7.13 to the code we had before.

```
$chunkId = fread($fh, 4);
if ($chunkId === 'fmt ') {

    $size = unpack('V', fread($fh, 4));
    if ($size[1] == 18) {
        $d = fread($fh, 18);
        $data =
            unpack('vfmt/vch/Vsr/Vdr/vbs/vbis/vext', $d);
        $format = array(
                0x0001 => 'PCM',
                0x0003 => 'IEEE Float',
                0x0006 => 'ALAW',
                0x0007 => 'MuLAW',
                0xFFFE => 'Extensible',
        );
        echo "Format: {$format[$data['fmt']]}\n";
        echo "Channels: {$data['ch']}\n";
        echo "Sample Rate: {$data['sr']}\n";
        echo "Data Rate: {$data['dr']}\n";
        echo "Block Size: {$data['bs']}\n";
        echo "Bits/Sample: {$data['bs']}\n";
        echo "Extension Size: {$data['ext']}\n";
    }
}
```

Figure 7.13: Code to read the metadata

First, we read the four bytes to identify the chunk. Then, we read the size. In this case, the size returned is 18 bytes. As we saw in the preceding table, the size can be 16, 18, or 40 bytes long. That table is the 40-byte version of the header. Because my sample file uses only the 18-byte header, we will parse only that one out. That means reading up to and including the extension size field.

When we run the code, we get the output shown in Figure 7.14.

```
We have a WAV file
Chunk length: 69717368
Format: PCM
Channels: 2
```

```
Sample Rate: 44100
Data Rate: 176400
Block Size: 4
Bits/Sample: 4
Extension Size: 0
```

Figure 7.14: Output of reading the metadata

So we have a PCM (pulse-code modulation) WAV file with two channels, a sample rate of 44.1 KHz, and a bit rate of 176.4 kbit/second.

So far, so good. But that was with a relatively simple file format. What we have done here is read the basics of a format that was "more binary" than the tar format. Tar has a structured format, but it is based on structured text fields. The WAV format is structured but has more binary data in it. We could continue on with the WAV file, but because we generally do more Web-based work and the rest of the file is simply chunked data that would be output to an audio interface, the usefulness of the WAV file as an example is a little limited. With that in mind, let's move on to a format that is not so simple.

Ext2

Next, we're going to take a look down a path you will probably never go in PHP, but one that is interesting nonetheless. That path is directly reading a disk partition. To perform this task, we're going to create a simple ext2 partition of about 100 MB in size and then copy the raw data to our workspace. The ext2, or second extended file system, is a file system for the Linux kernel.

Why not ext3? Because I didn't want to work with the additional features of ext3. The purpose of this section is not actually to tell you how to read an ext2 file system, but rather to stimulate your imagination as to what you might do. This point is important to understand because I don't want to get letters from people complaining that this example wasn't practical. It's not meant to be. As I've noted elsewhere, many PHP developers are used to working directly with text-based protocols — HTTP, XML, and such. A fair chunk of this book is written to give you insight into the lower-level programming that is possible so you can apply that understanding in more day-to-day contexts, and that is why this topic is here. However, if you want to build a fully functional file system in PHP, have at it.

Experimentation is always fun. I also highly recommend that you use a debugger in this section. There is a lot of jumping around between blocks on the disk, and a debugger will make it much easier to understand. In addition, I recommend reading through the whole section first before coding anything.

I also should not have to remind you (but I will anyway) not to do anything you see here on a production system. This caution is especially important if the file system on which you are working is mounted. It is a bad idea. Fun? Yes. But a bad idea nonetheless.

We'll start with the **mkfs.ext2** program, the program responsible for setting up the basic format of the partition. Figure 7.15 shows this program's output.

```
[root@localhost ~]# mkfs.ext2 /dev/sdb1
mke2fs 1.39 (29-May-2006)
Filesystem label=
OS type: Linux
Block size=1024 (log=0)
Fragment size=1024 (log=0)
26208 inodes, 104432 blocks
5221 blocks (5.00%) reserved for the super user
First data block=1
Maximum filesystem blocks=67371008
13 block groups
8192 blocks per group, 8192 fragments per group
2016 inodes per group
Superblock backups stored on blocks:
        8193, 24577, 40961, 57345, 73729

Writing inode tables: done
Writing superblocks and filesystem accounting
 information: done

This filesystem will be automatically checked every
 34 mounts or 180 days, whichever comes first.
 Use tune2fs -c or -i to override.
```

Figure 7.15: Output of mkfs.ext2

For an ext2 file system, the primary superblock is always going to be at position 1024. Bytes 0–511 are the boot record, if one is required. Bytes 512–1023 are additional, optional, boot record data. Because the disk we are creating does not have a boot record, we will simply jump to position 1024 and read the superblock.

Table 7.7 shows part of the format of the superblock. The format is partial because we are going to concern ourselves only with the basic functionality. We can glean that information from the first 80 bytes.

Table 7.7: Format of the superblock			
Offset	**Size**	**Type***	**Description**
0	4	**ULONG**	Inode count
4	4	**ULONG**	Block count
8	4	**ULONG**	Reserved block count
12	4	**ULONG**	Free blocks count
16	4	**ULONG**	Free inode count
20	4	**ULONG**	First data block
24	4	**ULONG**	Block size
28	4	**LONG**	Fragment size
32	4	**ULONG**	Blocks in each block group
36	4	**ULONG**	Fragments in each block group
40	4	**ULONG**	Inodes in each block group
44	4	**ULONG**	Last mount time
48	4	**ULONG**	Last write time
52	2	**USHORT**	Mount count
54	2	**USHORT**	Maximum mount count
56	2	**USHORT**	Declare ext2
58	2	**USHORT**	Current state
60	2	**USHORT**	How to report errors
62	2	**USHORT**	Minor revision
64	4	**ULONG**	Last checked
68	4	**ULONG**	Maximum check interval
72	4	**ULONG**	Which OS?
76	4	**ULONG**	File system revision
***ULONG** = Unsigned long (32-bit); **LONG** = Signed long (32-bit); **USHORT** = Unsigned short (16-bit)			

The code to read and report that header information is relatively simple, although a bit verbose (Figure 7.16).

```
$device = 'sdb1';

$fh = fopen($device, 'r');
fseek($fh, 1024);
$superblock = fread($fh, 1024);

$format = 'Lic/Lbc/Lrbc/Lfbc/Lfic/Lfdb/Llbs/'
        . 'Ilfs/Lbpg/Lfpg/Lipg/Lmtime/Lwtime/'
        . 'Smntcnt/smaxmntcnt/Smagic/Sstate/'
        . 'Serrors/Sminrev/Llastcheck/Lcheckint/'
        . 'Sos/Srev';
$sb = unpack($format, $superblock);

$sb['lbs'] = 1024 << $sb['lbs'];
$sb['lfs'] = 1024 << $sb['lfs'];
$sb['mtime'] = date('r', $sb['mtime']);
$sb['wtime'] = date('r', $sb['wtime']);
$sb['lastcheck'] = date('r', $sb['lastcheck']);
$sb['magic'] = '0x'.strtoupper(dechex($sb['magic']));

echo "Inode Count: {$sb['ic']}\n";
echo "Block Count: {$sb['bc']}\n";
echo "Reserved block count: {$sb['rbc']}\n";
echo "Free blocks count: {$sb['fbc']}\n";
echo "Free inode count: {$sb['fic']}\n";
echo "First data block: {$sb['fdb']}\n";
echo "Block size: {$sb['lbs']}\n";
echo "Fragment size: {$sb['lfs']}\n";
echo "Blocks in each block group: {$sb['bpg']}\n";
echo "Fragments in each block group: {$sb['fpg']}\n";
echo "Inodes in each block group: {$sb['ipg']}\n";
echo "Last mount time: {$sb['mtime']}\n";
echo "Last write time: {$sb['wtime']}\n";
echo "Mount count: {$sb['mntcnt']}\n";
echo "Maximum mount count: {$sb['maxmntcnt']}\n";
echo "Declare ext2: {$sb['magic']}\n";
echo "Current State: {$sb['state']}\n";
echo "How to report errors: {$sb['errors']}\n";
echo "Minor Revision: {$sb['minrev']}\n";
echo "Last checked: {$sb['lastcheck']}\n";
echo "Maximum check interval: {$sb['checkint']}\n";
echo "Which OS?: {$sb['os']}\n";
echo "Filesystem revision: {$sb['rev']}\n";
```

Figure 7.16: Code for reading the superblock

Most of the numbers we see here are pretty self-explanatory, such as block size and inode count. I believe that when you look at the different formats and compare them with what the **pack()** documentation states, you should be able to see the correlation between the number of bytes and the data type. There are, however, a few items to note.

First, block size and fragment size. The way to calculate the block size is to take the number 1024 and shift it *X* bits to the left. The fragment size is calculated the same way.

Next, the modification, write, and last checked timestamps. These are Unix timestamps, and because it is not easy for a human to read a Unix timestamp, these values are converted to the RFC 2822 format in the **date()** function.

Last, the "magic" value. This is the value that states what the file system type is and is usually rendered in a hexadecimal format. To make it easier for a human to read, we convert it to that. The ext2/ext3 value should be **0xEF53**. Why? Because the format document says that an ext2/ext3 file system will have this value at that position.

When we run the code on the new partition, we get the output shown in Figure 7.17.

```
Inode Count: 26208
Block Count: 104432
Reserved block count: 5221
Free blocks count: 99565
Free inode count: 26196
First data block: 1
Block size: 1024
Fragment size: 1024
Blocks in each block group: 8192
Fragments in each block group: 8192
Inodes in each block group: 2016
Last mount time: Mon, 23 Nov 2009 08:03:54 -0500
Last write time: Mon, 23 Nov 2009 08:03:59 -0500
Mount count: 1
Maximum mount count: 34
Declare ext2: 0xEF53
Current State: 1
How to report errors: 1
Minor Revision: 0
```

```
Last checked: Mon, 23 Nov 2009 08:03:42 -0500
Maximum check interval: 15552000
Which OS?: 0
Filesystem revision: 0
```

Figure 7.17: Output of reading the superblock

Table 7.8 compares this output with that of **mkfs.ext2** from earlier on.

Table 7.8: Comparing our data with mkfs.ext2	
mkfs.ext2	**PHP**
Block size=1024 (log=0)	Block size: 1024
Fragment size=1024 (log=0)	Fragment size: 1024
26208 inodes	Inode count: 26208
104432 blocks	Block count: 104432
5221 blocks (5.00%) reserved for the super user	Reserved block count: 5221
8192 blocks per group	Blocks in each block group: 8192
8192 fragments per group	Fragments in each block group: 8192
2016 inodes per group	Inodes in each block group: 2016

It looks like we have an exact match. That's a good place to be.

The next thing to look at is how the individual blocks are mapped. Mapping blocks and inodes is done by mapping individual bits in the block bitmap or the inode bitmap to a specific block on the drive. A bitmap is just that: a series of bits that map to some other structure. In this case, those bits map to individual blocks on the drive. Figure 7.18 illustrates this concept.

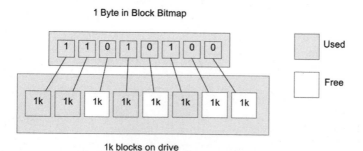

Figure 7.18: What is a bitmap?

The purpose of having the bitmap is for easy access to information on free or used disk blocks. So, our first exercise is going to be to read those bits and report on how many free blocks there are. The code to achieve this, shown in Figure 7.19, would replace everything after the initial **unpack()** string.

```
echo "Blocks Per Group: {$sb['bpg']}\n\n";

$blockSize = 1024 << $sb['lbs'];

$bgDesc = fread($fh, $blockSize);
$descTableRecordFormat
    = 'Lbid/Linodebid/Linotblbid/Sfreeblks/'
    . 'Sfreeino/Suseddirs/';

for ($c = 0; $c < $blockSize; $c += 32) {
    $data = unpack(
        $descTableRecordFormat,
        substr($bgDesc, $c, 32)
    );
    if ($data['bid'] === 0) {
        break;
    }
    $loc = $data['bid'] * $blockSize;
    fseek($fh, $loc);
    $bBm = fread($fh, $blockSize);
    $bBm = unpack('C*', $bBm);

    $usedBlockCount = 0;

    for ($bc = 0; $bc < $blockSize; $bc++) {
        $usedBlockCount += countBits($bBm[$bc]);
    }

    echo "Block ID: {$data['bid']}\n";
    echo "Used Blocks: {$usedBlockCount}\n";
    echo "Free Blocks: {$data['freeblks']}\n";
    echo "Total: " . ($usedBlockCount +
                    $data['freeblks']) . "\n\n";
}

function countBits($byte)
{
    $count = 0;
    if ($byte & 0x01) {
        $count++;
    }
```

```
    if ($byte & 0x02) {
        $count++;
    }
    if ($byte & 0x04) {
        $count++;
    }
    if ($byte & 0x08) {
        $count++;
    }
    if ($byte & 0x10) {
        $count++;
    }
    if ($byte & 0x20) {
        $count++;
    }
    if ($byte & 0x40) {
        $count++;
    }
    if ($byte & 0x80) {
        $count++;
    }
    return $count;
}
```

Figure 7.19: Reading the bitmap

The first thing we read is **$bgDesc = fread($fh, $blockSize)**. This is an array of each and every block group on the disk. Because each and every block group is found in the block group descriptor table and the table size is limited by the block size, you can actually determine the maximum size of the partition you are working on.

To read this array, we iterate over each block group descriptor. A block group descriptor is a series of 32 bytes that provides information about the location that the block group is in. Table 7.9 shows the format.

Table 7.9: Block group descriptor format		
Offset	Length	Description
0	4	Location of block group bitmap
4	4	Location of inode bitmap
8	4	Location of inode table
12	2	Free blocks in the block group
14	2	Free inodes in the block group
16	2	Count of inodes allocated to directories
18	2	Padding
20	12	Reserved

This information is represented by the format of **Lbid/Linodebid/Linotblbid/ Sfreeblks/Sfreeino/Suseddirs**. Because the padding and reserved fields don't have any specific use, we are going to ignore them. Using this format, we iterate over each 32-byte record in the block group descriptor table. If we find a block group with a block ID of zero, we have reached the end of the block group records.

The next thing to do is jump to the individual block group and retrieve all the bits that represent the blocks in the block group. Each block group can address **$blockSize * 8** blocks. This formula is simply a function of each byte in the block size being eight bits long. The way to retrieve this bitmap block is to **fseek()** to the block ID multiplied by the block size. So, if the block ID is 259 and the block size is 1024, the actual position to seek to is 265,216. That will bring us to the precise point in the file system that contains information about that block group.

To read the information about the individual block group, we then **fread()** **$blockSize** bytes from the file system. Each bit in that data set represents one block in the block group. To test which blocks are used and which ones are free, we **unpack()** each byte and pass it to the **countBits()** function. For each bit that is turned on, we increase the counter by one.

After we have iterated over all the bytes we've read in, we simply print out the results (Figure 7.20), and we can see how many blocks are being used on the system for each block group.

```
Block Per Group: 8192

Block ID: 259
Used Blocks: 528
Free Blocks: 7664
Total: 8192

Block ID: 8451
Used Blocks: 4600
Free Blocks: 3584
Total: 8184

Block ID: 16385
Used Blocks: 8184
Free Blocks: 0
Total: 8184

Block ID: 24835
Used Blocks: 8184
Free Blocks: 0
Total: 8184

Block ID: 32769
Used Blocks: 8184
Free Blocks: 0
Total: 8184

Block ID: 41219
Used Blocks: 8184
Free Blocks: 0
Total: 8184

Block ID: 49153
Used Blocks: 8184
Free Blocks: 0
Total: 8184

Block ID: 57603
Used Blocks: 7272
Free Blocks: 912
Total: 8184
```

```
Block ID: 65537
Used Blocks: 6489
Free Blocks: 1695
Total: 8184

Block ID: 73987
Used Blocks: 8095
Free Blocks: 97
Total: 8192

Block ID: 81921
Used Blocks: 3108
Free Blocks: 5084
Total: 8192

Block ID: 90113
Used Blocks: 254
Free Blocks: 7938
Total: 8192

Block ID: 98305
Used Blocks: 2311
Free Blocks: 5873
Total: 8184
```

Figure 7.20: Reading the block groups

The first piece of information displayed is the block group size at 8192. However, we see that while the size of the block group is 8192, several block groups have 8 KB less than the maximum. This is likely due to the fact that there is a fair amount of additional information that needs to be stored, such as superblock backups, inodes, directory structures, and such. So, let's take a look at some of those.

To obtain directory information, we need to know something about where the start of the directory structure is. The root directory inode is located in the second inode table entry. Why? Because the format document says so. The inode table resides at the location of the third field in the block descriptor table. We'll see how that looks in the code in a bit.

Inodes themselves do not contain any file name information, only meta information, but we need to find the root inode so that we can find the block that contains the directory structure records for each file in the root node. Each individual inode contains the structure shown in Table 7.10.

Offset	Size	Description
Table 7.10: Inode structure		
Offset	Size	Description
0	2	Mode
2	2	Owner
4	4	Size
8	4	Access time
12	4	Create time
16	4	Modification time
20	4	Delete time
24	2	Group
26	2	Link count (symbolic links N/A)
28	4	Reserved block count
32	4	Flagged behavior
36	4	Reserved
40	15 x 4	Blocks used
100	4	Used for Network File System (NFS)
104	4	File access control list (ACL)
108	4	Dir ACL
112	4	File fragment
116	12	Reserved (kind of)

Table 7.11 highlights a few of these fields. Only the "blocks used" field is really important to what we are doing.

Table 7.11: Description on inode fields	
Field	**Description**
Mode	The **chmod** value of the file. Most of the values correspond to the regular **chmod** settings with which you're familiar (e.g., 644, 755), with the exception of the file format values that are stored in the most significant byte position:

Value	Description
0xC000	Socket
0xA000	Symbolic link
0x8000	Regular file
0x6000	Block device
0x4000	Directory
0x2000	Character device
0x1000	FIFO

Link count	The number of links back to this inode. This value counts only hard links; symbolic links are not counted.
Blocks used	Fifteen long values that indicate which blocks are used to house the raw data of this individual inode. The first 12 blocks are direct references to **$blockSize** blocks that contain the data. On our 1 KB block sized partition, that means that we can directly reference 12 KB worth of data. The 13th block is a reference to another block that contains an indirect array of blocks. The 14th contains an array of double-indirect blocks (an array of arrays of blocks). The 15th is a triple-indirect array of blocks. If this sounds complicated, don't worry about it. We are not going to go into that level of depth. Once you understand the direct blocks, figuring out the indirect blocks is not difficult.

Whew! Seems like a bit to know, but it's not all that difficult. Let's look at our code and explain what we're doing, starting at the superblock (Figure 7.21).

```
$sb = unpack($format, $superblock);
$blockSize = 1024 << $sb['lbs'];

$bgDesc = fread($fh, $blockSize);
```

```
$descTableRecordFormat
    = 'Lbid/Linodebid/Linotblbid/Sfreeblks/'
    . 'Sfreeino/Suseddirs/';

$inodeFmt = 'Smode/Suid/Lsize/Latime/Lmtime/Ldtime/'
          . 'Sgid/Slnkcnt/Lblknum/Lflg/Losdl/L15blks/'
          . 'Lversion/Lfacl/Ldacl/C12osd2';

$dirFmt   = 'Linode/Sreclen/Cnamelen/Ctype';
$c = 0;

$data = unpack(
    $descTableRecordFormat,
    substr($bgDesc, $c, 32)
);
fseek($fh, $data['inotblbid'] * $blockSize);
$inodeData = fread($fh, $blockSize);

$rootInode = unpack($inodeFmt,
                substr($inodeData, 128, 128));

foreach ($rootInode as $key => $value) {
    if (strpos($key, 'blks') === 0 && $value > 0) {
        $startPos = $value * $blockSize;
        fseek($fh, $startPos);
        while (ftell($fh)
                < $startPos + $rootInode['size']) {

            $dirEntry = fread($fh, 8);
            $dirFields = unpack($dirFmt, $dirEntry);
            $entry = fread(
                        $fh,
                        $dirFields['reclen'] - 8
            );

            var_dump(
                substr(
                    $entry,
                    0,
                    $dirFields['namelen']
                )
            );
        }
    }
}
```

Figure 7.21: Code to read an inode

We've already seen everything up to **$c = 0**, so let's start after that. The data for the root inode will be found in the first inode table record in the first block table. That is why we start at zero. We **unpack()** the data and retrieve the block ID of the inode table, which we named **inotblbid**. Then, we move the file pointer to the value of **inotblbid * $blockSize** to get the exact byte position where the inode table starts.

The first inode table has several reserved inodes, one of which is important to us. Table 7.12 lists the reserved inodes.

Table 7.12: Reserved inodes and their corresponding inode number	
Inode	**Description**
1	Inode containing bad blocks
2	Inode containing the root directory
3	ACL index
4	ACL data
5	Boot loader
6	Undelete directory

For what we're doing here, we are interested only in the second inode. You might be thinking that there is some kind of fancy way to find the actual location of that information, but, nope, the inode number is simply a reserved sequential inode in the inode table.

For this reason, when we want to find the root directory node, we do the **substr(128, 128)**. Inodes are 128 bytes long, and we want the second one, so we get only the one that starts at the 128th position.

After we have our properly sized inode data, we **unpack()** it using the format we defined earlier in **$inodeFmt**. Our purpose in reading the inode is to find the blocks that contain the directory structure information. We specified the format of the inode data in our format variable as **L15blks** — in other words, 15 unsigned long integers. Each result of that will be prefixed with the word **'blks'**. That is why we iterate over the array. We don't necessarily *know* what the block names will be. So we do a **foreach** over the inode values, and if the name starts with **'blks'**, we know that we are working with one of the byte's references to either a direct or an indirect block.

If we were to look at what **$rootInode** contained, it would be similar to the contents of Figure 7.22.

```
array(41) {
  ["mode"]=>
  int(16877)
  ["uid"]=>
  int(0)
  ["size"]=>
  int(1024)
  ["atime"]=>
  int(1259000738)
  ["mtime"]=>
  int(1258998194)
  ["dtime"]=>
  int(1258998194)
  ["gid"]=>     int(0)
  ["lnkcnt"]=>
  int(0)
  ["blknum"]=>
  int(262144)
  ["flg"]=>
  int(2)
  ["osd1"]=>
  int(0)
  ["blks1"]=>
  int(0)
  ["blks2"]=>
  int(513)
  ["blks3"]=>
  int(0)
  ["blks4"]=>
  int(0)

. . .continued
```

Figure 7.22: Output of the root inode

The "size" value is important because it tells us how large the record is. This value will likely match the block size. The "blks2" value is also important. That is the block ID that contains the directory table. Because our directory listing is small enough to fit in one block, only one block ID has any value in it.

To read that block, we seek to the block ID multiplied by **$blockSize** and loop until we reach the end of the record, which is indicated by the start position plus the size, as noted by the root inode (again, likely the block size of the file system).

We then read eight bytes. Why eight bytes? Because the directory structure record has eight fixed bytes. The file name is a variable-length field. Table 7.13 shows the structure of the directory record.

Table 7.13: Directory structure format		
Offset	**Size**	**Description**
0	4	Inode location for file
4	2	The total length of the record
6	1	The actual length of the name
7	1	The type of file system entity
8	0-255	File name

The entity type can be one of the values listed in Table 7.14.

Table 7.14: Type values for the individual directory structure entry	
Value	**Description**
0	Unknown file type
1	Regular file
2	Directory file
3	Character device
4	Block device
5	Buffer file
6	Socket file
7	Symbolic link

Next, we read to the end of the record minus eight, to account for the eight bytes that we have already read and then retrieve the substring of the result starting at zero and going until **'namelen'**. Why not just read until **'namelen'**? Because we want the file pointer to be at the right position to read the next record without an additional seek. Usually **'reclen'** and **'namelen'** do not match up because the file name is padded. That is the reason why we read to the end of the record and then do a **substr()** on the result.

Figure 7.23 shows the result of this code.

```
string(1) "."
string(2) ".."
string(10) "lost+found"
string(8) "testdata"
string(10) "php-5.2.11"
```

Figure 7.23: Result of reading the root inode and immediate children

Excellent! But we're not quite there. We found the root directory node, but this is not a single-level file system. In other words, there are directories. There are also files in those directories. So why don't we finish up the code by reading the file system to locate the file **php-5.2.11/ext/com_dotnet/com_dotnet.c** (I have to do *something* for the Windows folk).

To do this, we are going to move our code into a class to encapsulate the functionality. The reason for this step is that it just makes things easier to manage. Because we use a fair amount of recursion, having everything within a defined container rather than having some things as parameters, some as globals, and some as local variables makes for a more complicated example, and this is complicated enough as it is.

Our class (Figure 7.24) first reads the superblock and the data from all the blocks.

```
class Filesystem
{
  private $_sb = array();
  private $_blockGroups = array();
  private $_fh;

  public function __construct($device)
  {
  $this->_fh = fopen($device, 'r');
  fseek($this->_fh, 1024);
  $superblock = fread($this->_fh, 1024);
```

```
    $this->_sb = unpack(
        'Lic/Lbc/Lrbc/Lfbc/Lfic/Lfdb/Llbs/'
        . 'Ilfs/Lbpg/Lfpg/Lipg/Lmtime/Lwtime/'
        . 'Smntcnt/smaxmntcnt/Smagic/Sstate/'
        . 'Serrors/Sminrev/Llastcheck/Lcheckint/'
        . 'Sos/Srev',
        $superblock
    );

    $this->_sb['lbs'] = 1024 << $this->_sb['lbs'];
    $this->_sb['lfs'] = 1024 << $this->_sb['lfs'];
    $this->_sb['mtime'] = date('r', $this->_sb['mtime']);
    $this->_sb['wtime'] = date('r', $this->_sb['wtime']);
    $this->_sb['lastcheck']
                = date('r', $this->_sb['lastcheck']);

    $bgDescTable = fread($this->_fh, $this->_sb['lbs']);
    $pos = 0;

    while ($pos < $this->_sb['lbs']) {
        $blockGroupDesc = unpack(
            'Lbid/Linodebid/Linotblbid/Sfreeblks/'
            . 'Sfreeino/Suseddirs/',
            substr($bgDescTable, $pos, $pos + 32)
        );
        if ($blockGroupDesc['bid'] > 0) {
            $this->_blockGroups[]
                        = $blockGroupDesc;
        }
        $pos += 32;
    }
  }
}
```

Figure 7.24: Base of class for reading the file system

If we do a **var_dump()** on an instance of this class, we get the results shown in Figure 7.25.

```
object(Filesystem)#1 (3) {
  ["_sb:private"]=>
  array(23) {
    ["ic"]=>
    int(26208)
```

```
  . . .snip

  ["rev"]=>
  int(0)
}
["_blockGroups:private"]=>
array(13) {
  [0]=>
  array(6) {
    ["bid"]=>
    int(259)
    ["inodebid"]=>
    int(260)
    ["inotblbid"]=>
    int(261)
    ["freeblks"]=>
    int(7664)
    ["freeino"]=>
    int(2004)
    ["useddirs"]=>
    int(2)
  }
  [1]=>
  array(6) {
    ["bid"]=>
    int(8451)
    ["inodebid"]=>
    int(8452)
    ["inotblbid"]=>
    int(8453)
    ["freeblks"]=>
    int(3584)
    ["freeino"]=>
    int(82)
    ["useddirs"]=>
    int(52)
  }

  . . .snip

}
["_fh:private"]=>
resource(3) of type (stream)
}
```

Figure 7.25: var_dump() of an instance of a Filesystem object

Having the blocks stored in a numerical array in this manner is actually about what we need. This is because when we start looking for file name, we need to start traversing inodes. Inodes are sequential in number. Unlike with blocks, you cannot skip directly to them by taking the number and multiplying them by the block size. You need to calculate the inode number and then do some simple math to figure out which block group the inode is in. It is that information that you can use to find the block that has the directory information records stored in it.

We are going to take the next few method definitions one at a time because there is a fair amount of jumping around. Our first method is called **getFile()**. It is the entry point for trying to find the file contents (Figure 7.26).

```php
public function getFile($filename)
{
    // Reset to the root inode
    $inode = $this->readInode(
        $this->_sb['lbs']
            * $this->_blockGroups[0]['inotblbid']
        + 128
    );

    foreach ($inode as $key => $value) {

        if (strpos($key, 'blks') === 0 && $value > 0) {
            $blocks = $this->readFileInode(
                $value * $this->_sb['lbs'],
                '/',
                $filename
            );
            if (is_array($blocks)) {
                break;
            }
        }
    }

    if ($blocks) {
        return $this->readBlocks(
                $blocks['size'],
                $blocks['blocks']
        );
    }

    return null;
}
```

Figure 7.26: Entry point for reading an individual file name

What this code does is read in the root inode, which is found in the inode table of block 0 at inode position 2. Inode entries, remember, are 128 bytes long. Thus, the **inotblbid + 128.**

Once we have the root inode, which will be the root directory, we iterate over all the directory structures stored in the block. For a typical root directory, this should be a small number of blocks to search through. That is why we check to see whether the key over which we are iterating is a key that starts with **'blks'** and we verify that the value of that item is larger than zero. Once we find one, we take its value, which is a block ID, not a file position, and multiply it by the block size, which is a file position, and pass it to the **readFileInode()** method along with the current node we are on and the file name we're looking for. The return value of that method will be an array containing the size of the file and a list of all the blocks on which the file contents reside. If no blocks are returned, the file has not been found.

But to parse the information to search the root directory, we need to read the root inode. We do that in the **readInode()** method. This is virtually the same code we used earlier, just put into a more reusable container (Figure 7.27).

```php
public function readInode($pos = null)
{
    if ($pos !== null) {
        fseek($this->_fh, $pos);
    }
    $fmt = 'Smode/Suid/Lsize/Latime/Lmtime/Ldtime/'
        . 'Sgid/Slnkcnt/Lblknum/Lflg/Losdl/L15blks/'
        . 'Lversion/Lfacl/Ldacl/C12osd2';
    $data = fread($this->_fh, $this->_sb['lbs']);
    return unpack($fmt, $data);
}
```

Figure 7.27: Code to read the inode, now in the class definition

We use the **readFileInode()** method (Figure 7.28) to take the current block and find the inode that is specified in that block.

```php
public function readFileInode($startPos, $cwd, $dest)
{
  $blocks = array();
  $cwdLen = strlen($cwd);
  $destLen = strlen($dest);
  $currentNode = substr($dest, $cwdLen,
                        $destLen - $cwdLen);
  $ds = strpos( $currentNode, '/');
  if ($ds) {
        $currentNode = substr($currentNode, 0, $ds);
  }
  fseek($this->_fh, $startPos);
  while (ftell($this->_fh) <
          $startPos + $this->_sb['lbs']) {
    $dirEntry = fread($this->_fh, 8);
    $dirFields = unpack(
                    'Linode/Sreclen/Cnamelen/Ctype',
                    $dirEntry
    );
    $entry = fread($this->_fh,
                  $dirFields['reclen'] - 8);
    $node = substr($entry, 0,
                  $dirFields['namelen']);
    if ($node === $currentNode) {
      $blockGroup = (int)
              (($dirFields['inode'] - 1)
              / $this->_sb['ipg']);

      $groupInode = ($dirFields['inode'] - 1)
                            % $this->_sb['ipg'];
      $thisNode = $cwd . $node;

      $pos =
          $this->_blockGroups[$blockGroup]['inotblbid']
            * $this->_sb['lbs'];
      $pos += $groupInode * 128;
      $inode = $this->readInode(
            $pos
      );
```

```
foreach ($inode as $key => $value) {
    if (strpos($key, 'blks') === 0
        && $value > 0) {
        if ($dest === $thisNode) {
            if (!$blocks) {
                $blocks = array(
                    'size' =>
                        $inode['size'],
                    'blocks' =>
                        array()
                );
            }
            $blocks['blocks'][]
                = $value;
        } else {
            return $this->readFileInode(
                $value
                    * $this->_sb['lbs'],
                $thisNode . '/',
                $dest
            );
        }
    }
}
if ($blocks) return $blocks;
}
}
}
```

Figure 7.28: Finding the inode for a given file

The first thing this block of code does is find out what the current node is that it is looking for. We do that simply so that we know what to match later on when we read the directory structure from the block. Then, we start to iterate over all the directory entries in the block that the previous inode had described.

It is important to note that this code does not handle indirect blocks. As such, there are limits on the number of directory entries and blocks it can read. However, the purpose of the exercise is *not* to build an ext2 file system reader, but rather to look at the ext2 file system as an example of what a structured file would look like. You can take this code and extend it to read indirect blocks and so be able to fully read the file system. But we will not be doing that here simply because I do not believe it would add much. It is for this same reason that we will not be writing to the file system.

The directory structures, as we saw earlier, start with an 8-byte header that states the inode, record length, name length, and type. The file name after that is a variable-length field. So we read the first eight bytes, parse, and then read the remaining bytes from the record. If that value matches the value of the current node, then we need to find the inode of that directory, which contains the blocks of the next directory structure that we need to search.

To get the inode for the next directory structure, we must first figure out which block group that next inode is in. If you remember, in our constructor we have already parsed out all the block groups after reading the superblock. We can find out which block group our inode is in by taking the quotient of the inode in the directory record divided by the number of inodes in each block group. Then, we can also calculate the exact inode within the block group that we are going to use. To do that, we calculate the modulus of the previous operation.

To calculate the final file position, we take the location of the inode table and multiply it by the block size to get our base file position. That is the position at the start of the inode table. However, because we can also calculate the exact inode, we then increase the pointer by the inode number in the block group multiplied by 128, the size of an inode record. Once we have that calculated, we read the inode and start iterating over the results.

As we iterate over the results of the inode, we check to find the individual blocks for that inode. If the inode contains the file we were looking for, the blocks will be data blocks that contain the file contents. If it is just another directory, those blocks will contain the directory structures through which we need to search. If they are the directory structures, we will recursively call **readFileInode()** either until there is no match any more, indicating that the file could not be found, or until we find a match, at which point we can read the data blocks. Once we have found the node we're looking for, we aggregate all the blocks and return them. That aggregation is the actual reading of the file. As I noted before, this code does not handle indirect blocks and so can only deal with a limited size of file.

Once we have a list of all the direct blocks, we then need to read them into a variable so we can return them. To do that, the return value of the **readFileInode()** method will be a multidimensional array noting the final size of the file and an array of the blocks that contain the file. The **readBlocks()** method (Figure 7.29) accomplishes the reading of the blocks.

```
public function readBlocks($size, array $blockList)
{
    $data = '';
    foreach ($blockList as $block) {
        fseek($this->_fh, $block * $this->_sb['lbs']);
        $data .= fread($this->_fh, $this->_sb['lbs']);
    }

    return substr($data, 0, $size);
}
```

Figure 7.29: Reading the blocks for a given file

Simple enough. Take all the blocks, read them, and then return the substring of the final size. The reason for this is because file length may not match the allocated space because the space is allocated in blocks, in this case blocks of 1 KB. So there will likely be padding at the end. The call to **substr()** removes that padding.

The last thing we need to do, then, is test the code. To do that, we'll use the small test script shown in Figure 7.30.

```
$fs = new Filesystem('sdb1');

$file = $fs->getFile('/php-5.2.11/ext/com_dotnet/
                      com_dotnet.c');

$lines = explode("\n", $file);

echo count($lines) . " lines\n";
echo "First 10 lines: "
    . implode("\n", array_slice($lines, 0, 10))
    . "\n";
```

Figure 7.30: Reading the first 10 lines from the specified file

When we run this code, we get the output shown in Figure 7.31.

```
320 lines
First 10 lines: /*
   +-----------------------------------------------------+
   | PHP Version 5                                       |
   +-----------------------------------------------------+
   | Copyright (c) 1997-2009 The PHP Group               |
   +-----------------------------------------------------+
   | This source file is subject to version 3.01 of the |
   | PHP license, that is bundled with this package in   |
   | file LICENSE, and is available through the          |
   | world-wide-web at the following url:                |
   | http://www.php.net/license/3_01.txt                 |
```

Figure 7.31: Output of reading the first 10 lines

We see that it works, which is good, but I think there is a benefit to seeing a timeline of *how* this works. If paper could have video on it, this would probably be a little easier, but you can use your imagination for a bit. Or, if you are using a debugger (which you should be), you can follow along that way.

Table 7.15 shows the execution flow for reading the file.

Table 7.15: Execution flow for reading the file		
Step	**Function**	**Reading ext2; sequence of events**
1	**main()**	Create new **FileSystem** object, reading the superblock and the block group description table.
2	**main()**	Call **getFile('/php-5.2.11/ext/com_dotnet/com_dotnet.c')**.
3	**getFile()**	Read the root inode. This is the second inode in block group 0.
4	**getFile()**	Iterate over the blocks in the root inode. In this case, it is block number 513.
5	**getFile()**	Translate the block number to the file position by multiplying the block number by the block size. This evaluates to 525,312. Call **readFileInode()** with that position specified.
6	**readFileInode()**	Calculate the current node value, which is **php-5.2.11**.
7	**readFileInode()**	Iterate over the directory structures until the directory node matches the current node value.
8	**readFileInode()**	If the current node is found, calculate the block group (1) and the group inode (0).

Step	Function	Reading ext2; sequence of events
		Table 7.15: Execution flow for reading the file, continued
9	**readFileInode()**	Take the table block ID for the calculated group and multiply it by the block size. This value is calculated to position 8,655,872 in the file. Add the value of the group inode multiplied by 128. In this case it is zero, so the position stays the same.
10	**readInode()**	Seek to the inode position in the file, read only that inode, and return the structure.
11	**readFileInode()**	Iterate over the inode data, and find the keys that manage the blocks and have a value greater than zero.
12	**readFileInode()**	If the current path does not match the final path, calculate the file position based on the block ID provided by the inode and re-call **readFileInode()** with the new values, which will send you to step 6 for this new block.
13	**readFileInode()**	If the current path does match the final path, the blocks in this inode will contain the raw data. Put each block in the return array, and, once all the inode blocks have been iterated over, return the value. Because of **if ($blocks) return $blocks;**, this operation will cascade down to the root node.
14	**getFile()**	If **readFileInode()** returns an array, call **readBlocks()**.
15	**readBlocks()**	For each block ID, **fseek()** to the block ID multiplied by the block size and read block size data. Trim the concatenated blocks to the inode-specified file size, and return the string.
16	**getFile()**	Return the string provided by **readBlocks()**.

As I noted earlier, writing to ext2 takes a little more effort, and the purpose of this chapter is not how to work with ext2 but to give you some basic insight into reading from a complex file. In this case, a very complex file. By working through this exercise, I hope you can start to see how binary structured data files are actually quite understandable from within a PHP-based context.

Writing Your Own

Chances are, you will not need to write your own structured file format. There are so many other ways to store your data that you probably won't need to. Nevertheless, you might have to do it someday — plus, it's kind of fun. And, as with ext2, it is probably a good idea to go over the section a few times before you start coding yourself.

So, what are some of the things you need to consider when designing a format? Here is a quick, although incomplete, list:

- What is the usage profile? Will it be primarily read operations, or will it need to handle high write concurrency?

- How much data will you be storing in it? In other words, will you need to allocate space and development time for an index? An additional consideration is whether or not operating system file size limitations will come into play.

- What type of data will you be storing? Storing text as opposed to images may have some different implications.

- What are the potential value ranges going to be for record fields? For example, it would be pointless to create a 255-byte field if the field is going to be storing a value between 1 and 8.

- Are you going to allow deletion or updating of data, or will the file be rewritten when changes are made?

In general, structured file formats have some kind of header record; in other words, they don't just dive into the data. The header might hold format version numbers, encoding, authoring information, or any number of other pieces of information. Even if you don't currently have any header information that you want to store, it is a good idea to reserve a block of space so that you can add header information later if needed.

As an example of doing this, we're going to write a data file to store simple binary data. It will be similar to a simple key/value storage engine, except that the values will be growable, while the keys will be relatively static. As an additional point of fun, when an individual growable record is read, it will be deleted automatically, like a first-in-first-out (FIFO) file. This will also not be the perfect example of building a scalable, fast file structure. Its purpose is to illustrate the basics, as well as some of the problems you might encounter.

Figure 7.32 shows the execution flow for our custom structured file.

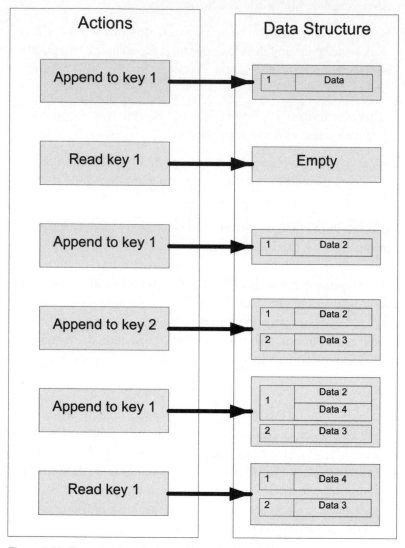

Figure 7.32: Execution flow for our custom structured file

This is actually an extremely easy problem to solve, until you get past the last block on the diagram. That is because up until that point you will simply be able to reuse disk space. After that, you'll have to manage deleted space in the file. This is why defragmentation programs are available for various operating systems.

The actual structure of the file is going to be quite simple. It will have three record types: key, value, and unused. The "unused" type will denote space on the drive that previously had *X* bytes of data stored but is now unused. For the purpose of predictability, we are going to divide up the file into 32-byte blocks, very similar to our example with the ext2 file system but with a much smaller block size because we are not going to need to store large pieces of data and we likely will not have the ability to use a full disk. Our storage mechanism needs to use disk space more efficiently.

The storage mechanism will also be implemented like a linked list. A linked list is a concept in which you can iterate over a list in one direction without having to scan the disk, or memory. However, you cannot randomly seek to a point on a linked list. That's because each item on the list knows only about the next item on the list. If you wanted to be able to go backward, you would need a doubly linked list, which means that an item in the list would need to know something about the next item as well as its predecessor. Because we are building a FIFO, all we really need is a singly linked list.

Each record in the list will be at least 32 bytes long, null-padded, and each will start with the same 9-byte header. Table 7.16 shows the record header format.

Table 7.16: Record header format		
Byte	**Length**	**Description**
0	1 byte	Type: key (**0x01**), value (**0x02**), or unused (**0x03**). Retrieved using **pack()**'s **C** format character.
1	4 bytes	Position in file of the next record. Retrieved using **pack()**'s **N** format character.
5	4 bytes	For a key record, this field will be the location of the first value record. For the value record and the unused record, the field will denote the raw length of the data that is, or was, stored. Retrieved using **pack()**'s **N** format character.

The first thing to do is to put some of this data into a class. We're going to be super-creative and call that class **File** (Figure 7.33).

```
class File
{
 const TYPE_KEY    = 0x01;
 const TYPE_DATA   = 0x02;
 const TYPE_UNUSED = 0x03;

 const FORMAT_READ_KEY    = 'Ctype/Nnextrecord/Nloc';
 const FORMAT_READ_NONKEY = 'Ctype/Nnextrecord/Nlength';

 const FORMAT_WRITE_KEY   = 'CNNxxxa20';
 const FORMAT_WRITE_DATA  = 'CNN';

 private $_fd;
 private $_fileName;
}
```

Figure 7.33: Base class for handling records

Here, we see the values for each individual type, the format for reading the header for each record, the format for writing the data to the file, and then a private variable that is used to store the file descriptor, or the variable containing the reference to the actual stream.

When we create an instance of the **File** class, we will provide the name of the file to the constructor. It can be a relative or an absolute file name. We just need a file name:

```
$file = new File('storage');
```

To make this do anything, we next need to create our constructor (Figure 7.34).

```
class File
{

    public function __construct( $fileName )
    {
        $this->_fileName = realpath($fileName);
        touch($this->_fileName);
```

```
            $this->_fd = fopen($this->_fileName, 'r+');
            if (filesize($fileName) < 1024) {
                  fseek($this->_fd, 0);
                  // Leave 1 KB reserved for future use
                  fwrite($this->_fd, pack('a1024', ''));
            }
      }
}
```

Figure 7.34: Constructor for our File class

We **touch()** the file first, which will modify the timestamp and create the file if it does not exist. After that, we **fopen()** it with the mode **'r+'** so that we can read and write; any writes that occur will be wherever we **fseek()** to. If the file size is less than 1 KB, we will overwrite any file contents and write 1 KB worth of null bytes to the disk. This is just in case we need some space at a later time for some meta information. Predictability is good in a binary file.

The first thing we want to do is to be able to write data to the file system. If we can't write data, we can't read data, so it makes sense to start there.

We know that we have two different types of data. We have the key, and we have the value. But we have a bit of a problem. The key is not predictable. Why not? Because it comes from outside the class. Therefore, it would be a good idea to homogenize it. To do that, we are going to create a **sha1()** hash of the key value. The reason for this is that **sha1()** always returns either a 40-byte ASCII value or a 20-byte binary value. Always. Ironically, we are using a mechanism designed to be unpredictable (without knowing the original value) to gain predictability for our data format. We will simply put this functionality in a helper function so that we can override it in the future relatively easily (Figure 7.35).

```
class File
{
      private function _hashKey($key)
      {
            return sha1($key, true);
      }
}
```

Figure 7.35: Hashing function

Now, we start getting into some of the more difficult things. For that reason, we will go deeper into the class and work our way toward the front. The deeper things are simpler and will be built upon by the more complicated things.

One of the important things we need to do is find out where a key is located. We need to do this so that we know where the starting point is for each FIFO we have. Each individual key will have its own FIFO. But even before we determine that, we need a mechanism we can use to find space in the file that is not currently occupied. That functionality will reside in a method called **_getFirstFreeSpace()**, which will take the needed size as an argument. We need to provide the size because although we can predict the size of the key, we cannot do so with the value.

Figure 7.36 shows the code to find the first free block of space in the file.

```php
private function _getFirstFreeSpace($size)
{
    $seek = 1024;
    fseek($this->_fd, 1024);

    clearstatcache();
    $lastRecordPos = ceil(
        filesize($this->_fileName)/32) * 32;

    while ($seek < $lastRecordPos - 32) {

        $currentRecordPos = ftell($this->_fd);
        $record = fread($this->_fd, 9);

        if (!$record) return $currentRecordPos;

        $type = ord($record[0]);
        if ($type !== self::TYPE_KEY) {

            $data = unpack(
                self::FORMAT_READ_NONKEY,
                $record
            );
            $maxRecordLength
                = (ceil($data['length']/32)*32) - 9;
```

```
                    if ($type === self::TYPE_UNUSED
                        && ($size <= 23
                                || $maxRecordLength >= $size
                        )) {

                        return $currentRecordPos;

                    } else if ($type === self::TYPE_DATA) {
                        if ($data['length'] > 23) {
                                $seek += $maxRecordLength+9;
                        } else {
                                $seek += 32;
                        }
                    }

            } else {
                    $seek += 32;
            }
            fseek($this->_fd, $seek);
        }
        return $lastRecordPos;
}
```

Figure 7.36: Finding the first free block in the file

The first thing we need to do when finding free space is to start at the beginning. If we simply append to the end of the file, we could run out of space very quickly because we would not be reclaiming unused space upon deletion of data. Of course, what we could do as well is use some kind of algorithmic magic to figure out where to put data, but I think that would miss what we're trying to accomplish here.

Because we are starting at the beginning, the first thing we do is **fseek()** to position 1024 (remember the reserved space?). What we are going to do is keep iterating over records until we either find some space or reach the end of the file. For this reason, most of our code is in a loop.

The first thing we do in the loop is get the current position. This is important because if the data in the current position is available, all we need to do is return the value in **$currentRecordPos**. If we can't find any free space, we return the next record position past the end of the file. Once we have that data, the first thing we do is read the first nine bytes from that position onward. Remember that our header is nine bytes long. The **fread()** function returns an empty string if it reaches the end of the file, so if the results evaluate to false, we simply return the record position at which we started.

If we have data, the next thing we do is check the value of that data. We could use **unpack()** to do this, but **ord()** on the first character is just as good. And just because we have one byte does not mean that we will have all nine.

Next, we check what type of record this is. If it is a key record, we simply advance the pointer 32 bytes and go through the next loop because the record has not been marked as unused. If it is not a key, we need to determine whether it is a value record or a record marked as unused. If it is a value record, we need to find where the end of that record is. To do that, we divide the length of the data plus nine bytes (to account for the header, which is not included in the length) by 32 and take the next highest integer value from that calculation. The result will tell us how many 32-byte blocks the data occupies. To get to the end, we do an **fseek()** on the result multiplied by 32, the size of our block.

If the record type is unused, we need to check to make sure that either the size of the data is less than 23 (32-byte length minus nine bytes for the header) or the length of the unused block will be able to store the requested amount of data. If it will, we return the current record position.

When we add our content, if a base location for the specified key is not found, we will need to create a new one. We do so by calling the **_createNewKeyLocation()** method (Figure 7.37) with the hash of the requested key provided as an argument.

```
private function _createNewKeyLocation($hashKey)
{
    $position = $this->_getFirstFreeSpace(32);
    fseek($this->_fd, $position);
    $data = pack(
        self::FORMAT_WRITE_KEY,
        self::TYPE_KEY,
        0,
        0,
        $hashKey
    );
    fwrite($this->_fd, $data);
    return $position;
}
```

Figure 7.37: Finding a new position for a key

In this method, we get the first available block in the file and seek to that position. Then we write, using the format we defined earlier, the type, the next record (which doesn't exist), and the location of the first data element (which also doesn't exist yet), followed by our 20-byte key.

We've got our functionality to write a new key, but what about a new value? Because we have a similar structure for key and value records, the base functionality to write a value is quite similar to writing a new key (Figure 7.38).

```
private function _writeValue($value)
{
    $size = strlen($value);
    $valueLocation = $this->_getFirstFreeSpace($size+9);
    fseek($this->_fd, $valueLocation);
    $data = pack(
            self::FORMAT_WRITE_DATA,
            self::TYPE_DATA,
            0,
            $size
    )
    . $value;
    fwrite($this->_fd, $data);
    return $valueLocation;
}
```

Figure 7.38: Writing a new value to the file

There are a few differences, though. Rather than requesting exactly 32 bytes, we request the size of the value we want to store plus nine bytes for the header. We take that location and **fseek()** to it. Once there, we write the value header, stating that it is a value type, and set the next record to zero because new values do not know anything about the next record until it is added. Then we specify the size, which would not include the header size. To that data we then append the actual data and write it to the file system, returning the location to which that value was written.

Why do we need to return where the data was written? Because we have only the code that actually writes the values to the disk. We have not implemented the code that ties the key and the value together. To do that, we need another method, called **_getKeyValueLocation()** (Figure 7.39). When the next value for a key is requested or a new value is added to a key, this is the method we'll use to find and, if necessary, create, the location of that individual key.

```
private function _getKeyValueLocation($key)
{
$key = $this->_hashKey($key);
    fseek($this->_fd, 1024);

    do {
        $recordPos = ftell($this->_fd);
        $recordMin = fread($this->_fd, 32);
        if (!$recordMin) {
            return array(
                $this->_createNewKeyLocation($key),
                0
            );
        }
        $data = unpack(self::FORMAT_READ_KEY,
                    $recordMin);
        if ($data['type'] === self::TYPE_KEY
            && $key == substr($recordMin, -20)) {

            return array($recordPos, $data['loc']);
        }
        if ($data['nextrecord'] > 0) {
            fseek($this->_fd, $data['nextrecord']);
        } else {
            $position = $this->_createNewKeyLocation(
                            $key
             );
            fseek($this->_fd, $recordPos + 1);
            fwrite($this->_fd, pack('N', $position));
            return array($position, 0);
        }
    } while (true);
}
```

Figure 7.39: Getting the first key value location

This method goes back to the start of the file, position 1024, and starts looking for an existing key location that matches. This activity occurs in a loop, starting at the beginning and iterating over each record until we find a match. If we do not find a match, we create a new key location. But the first thing we do is read in a full 32-byte record. Why the whole 32 bytes and not just nine as we did before? It's because the key is the first thing to be written to the file, and therefore we can assume that the record will be a key record and not a value. Because of that, we need to compare the key found with the key that was requested. There is no point in doing two file operations for that, so we read the full 32 bytes so that the pointer is automatically positioned at the next record.

When doing the read, we check to see whether it evaluates to a Boolean false. If so, that means we have reached the end of the file and no record has been found. In that case, we create a new key location and return the result. The return value is a two-value array. The first value is the file location of the record for the key, and the second value is the location for the first value record. Because we created a new key location here, we return a location of **0** (zero) for the first value location.

The first check we do after **unpack()**ing the data is to make sure we have the right type of record (we should) and check to see whether the key matches the one in the record. If it does, we return the current record position and then the **'loc'** item in the data array, which corresponds to the file location of the first value record.

If we don't have a match, we check to see whether **'nextrecord'** is greater than zero. If it is, we seek to the next record and start the loop over again. If the value is **0**, we know that we have reached the end of the key linked list, although not the end of the file. So we create a new key location and take the result of that operation and seek to the previous key record's position plus one. Position 1 is the type; position 2 is where the next record is stored. We take that result and overwrite the last key record's **'nextrecord'** value, which should be **0**.

To append a new value to the linked list, we need to find another location: the last item in the linked list. For this purpose, we have another method, called **_findLastValueLocation()**, that takes a start position as an argument. The start position should be the first value record in the linked list. The method, shown in

Figure 7.40, iterates over all the values for a given key and returns once it reaches the end of the linked list.

```php
private function _findLastValueLocation($position)
{

    while (true) {
        fseek($this->_fd, $position);
        $data = unpack(
            self::FORMAT_READ_NONKEY,
            fread(
                $this->_fd,
                9
            )
        );
        if ($data['nextrecord'] > 0) {
            $position = $data['nextrecord'];
        } else {
            break;
        }
    }
    return $position;
}
```

Figure 7.40: Finding the last value position for a hash key

The final stage in hitching them together is to take the return value of the **_getKey ValueLocation()** call and merge it with the **_writeValue()** call. We do this work in our public method, **addValue()** (Figure 7.41).

```php
public function addValue($key, $value)
{
    list ($keyLocation, $firstValueLocation)
        = $this->_getKeyValueLocation($key);
    $writePosition = $this->_writeValue($value);

    if ($firstValueLocation) {

        $position = $this->_findLastValueLocation(
                        $firstValueLocation
                    );
        fseek($this->_fd, $position + 1);
        fwrite($this->_fd, pack('N', $writePosition));
```

```
    } else {

        fseek($this->_fd, $keyLocation + 5);
        fwrite($this->_fd, pack('N', $writePosition));

    }
}
```

Figure 7.41: Adding a value for a key

The reason for the conditional statement in there is because there may or may not be a previous value record to attach to. If there is not, we need to write the location of the value record to the key record. If a previous value for the key exists, we need to link the new value record to the previous value record instead of the key record.

This is all well and good, but does it work? Let's start with a simple test (Figure 7.42).

```
$file = new File('storage');
$file->addValue('book', 'You want to do WHAT with PHP?');
```

Figure 7.42: Adding a value to the file

Running this code produces no errors, so that's good, but it also produces no output. To really test it, we need to open up a hex editor, load the file **storage**, seek to position 1024, and see what it says. Figure 7.43 shows the results.

```
0x0400 - 01 00 00 00 00 00 00 04 20 00 00 00 e7 e6 94 c5
0x0410 - 8c d5 0e 03 24 ec 96 91 88 00 bc 35 cd 17 62 9b
0x0420 - 02 00 00 00 00 00 00 00 26 59 6f 75 20 77 61 6e
0x0430 - 74 20 74 6f 20 64 6f 20 57 48 41 54 20 77 69 74
0x0440 - 68 20 50 48 50 3f
```

Figure 7.43: Bytes on disk for the new record

Let's take this output apart piece by piece. Remember that the first nine bytes are used for header information; they are followed by three null bytes (the **'xxx'** in our **pack()** format) and then the hashed key value.

Figure 7.44 depicts the bytes for the new key record header.

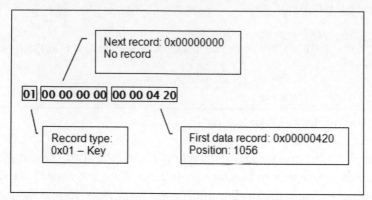

Figure 7.44: Examining the bytes for the new key record header

The hashed value for the key is stored following three null bytes, which serve simply as padding (Figure 7.45).

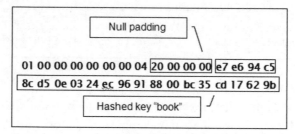

Figure 7.45: Hash value after the header bytes

The next data in our hex editor is that of the individual field value. This data starts at hex position **0x0420**, just as we saw in the "first data record" field (Figure 7.46).

```
0x0420 - 02 00 00 00 00 00 00 00 26 59 6f 75 20 77 61 6e
0x0440 - 74 20 74 6f 20 64 6f 20 57 48 41 54 20 77 69 74
0x0460 - 68 20 50 48 50 3f
```

Figure 7.46: Bytes for the first data record

"But wait a sec," you say. "I thought that the fields were 32 bytes in length." No, the fields are allocated in blocks of 32 bytes. And because this is at the end of the file, we did not pad with nulls because doing so is not necessary. It would happen automatically if we were to write another record. Let's look at this individual record's header (Figure 7.47).

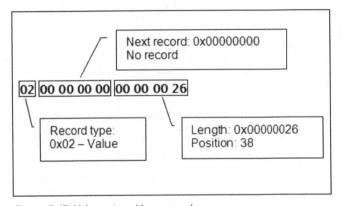

Figure 7.47: Values stored in a record

The rest of the record — **59 6f 75 20 77 61 6e 74 20 74 6f 20 64 6f 20 57 48 41 54 20 77 69 74 68 20 50 48 50 3f** — is simply the ASCII code for "You want to do WHAT with PHP?"

So what happens to these two records if we add another record? Figure 7.48 shows the addition we'll make.

```
$file = new File('storage');
$file->addValue('book', 'You want to do WHAT with PHP?');
$file->addValue('book', "IBM i Programmer's Guide to PHP");
```

Figure 7.48: Code to add another record

This test results in the values shown in Figure 7.49.

```
0x0400 - 01 00 00 00 00 00 00 04 20 00 00 00 e7 e6 94 c5
0x0410 - 8c d5 0e 03 24 ec 96 91 88 00 bc 35 cd 17 62 9b
0x0420 - 02 00 00 04 60 00 00 00 26 59 6f 75 20 77 61 6e
0x0430 - 74 20 74 6f 20 64 6f 20 57 48 41 54 20 77 69 74
0x0440 - 68 20 50 48 50 3f 00 00 00 00 00 00 00 00 00 00
0x0450 - 00 00 00 00 00 00 00 00 00 00 00 00 00 00 00 00
0x0460 - 02 00 00 00 00 00 00 00 28 49 42 4d 20 49 20 50
0x0470 - 72 6f 67 72 61 6d 6d 65 72 27 73 20 47 75 69 64
0x0480 - 65 20 74 6f 20 50 48 50
```

Figure 7.49: Data of added record

Note that the key record stays the same. That is because there is no additional key. We added only one item, and it was for the same key. Look at the header for the value record starting at position **0x0420** at the position for the next record field (Figure 7.50).

```
02 00 00 04 60 00 00 00 26
```

Figure 7.50: Updated primary header field

It states that the next record is going to be at position **0x0460**, or 1120. In Figure 7.51, what do we see at position **0x0460**? Another value record (**0x02**) with a length of 40 characters with no "next record."

```
02 00 00 00 00 00 00 00 28
```

Figure 7.51: Header value of new record

It seems as though our disk-based linked list mechanism is working. It also looks like nulls are being filled in properly. But we need one last test to make sure that key records are being properly linked. That means that when we create items with different keys, those records are properly being linked together. For that, we'll do one last test that is slightly different from the last one (Figure 7.52).

```
$file = new File('storage');
$file->addValue('b1', 'You want to do WHAT with PHP?');
$file->addValue('b2', "IBM i Programmer's Guide to PHP");
```

Figure 7.52: Adding a new value with a different key

As you can see, all we're doing is giving each item its own key that it will be attached to. Figure 7.53 shows what our file looks like after we run this test.

```
0x0400 - 01 00 00 04 60 00 00 04 20 00 00 00 7e 83 ca 2a
0x0410 - 65 d6 f9 0a 80 9c 85 70 c6 c9 05 a9 41 b8 77 32
0x0420 - 02 00 00 00 00 00 00 00 26 59 6f 75 20 77 61 6e
0x0430 - 74 20 74 6f 20 64 6f 20 57 48 41 54 20 77 69 74
0x0440 - 68 20 50 48 50 3f 00 00 00 00 00 00 00 00 00 00
0x0450 - 00 00 00 00 00 00 00 00 00 00 00 00 00 00 00 00
0x0460 - 01 00 00 00 00 00 00 04 80 00 00 00 32 f2 8e a0
0x0470 - 3b 1b 20 12 66 29 d2 ca 63 fc 66 65 b0 bb b6 04
0x0480 - 02 00 00 00 00 00 00 00 28 49 42 4d 20 49 20 50
0x0490 - 72 6f 67 72 61 6d 6d 65 72 27 73 20 47 75 69 64
0x04A0 - 65 20 74 6f 20 50 48 50
```

Figure 7.53: Data for multiple key values

Rather than having three records as before, we now have four records, starting at positions **0x0400** (type **0x01** – key), **0x0420** (type **0x02** – value), **0x0460** (type **0x01** – key), and **0x480** (type **0x02** – value). Also, if we look at the record starting at **0x0400**, we can see that it has a "next record" entry pointing to **0x00000460**. It looks like our linked list mechanism is working for both keys and values.

That brings us to our next feature: the ability to read and subsequently delete any read item automatically. This is actually a much easier thing to do, and because we can build on our earlier code, the amount of code we need to write is much smaller. Figure 7.54 shows the code to read and delete records.

```
public function getValue($key)
{
    list ($keyLocation, $firstValueLocation)
        = $this->_getKeyValueLocation($key);

    if (!$firstValueLocation) {
        return null;
    }
    fseek($this->_fd, $firstValueLocation);
    $recData = unpack(
        self::FORMAT_READ_NONKEY,
        fread($this->_fd, 9)
    );
```

```
    $value = fread($this->_fd, $recData['length']);
    fseek($this->_fd, $keyLocation + 5);
    fwrite(
        $this->_fd,
        pack(
            'N',
            $recData['nextrecord']
        )
    );
    fseek($this->_fd, $firstValueLocation);
    fwrite($this->_fd, pack('C', self::TYPE_UNUSED));
    return $value;
}
```

Figure 7.54: Code to read and delete records

The first thing we do here is get the key and first value location for that key. The reason we need both is so that we can easily update the value location in the key record and also seek to the next value record if one exists. If a value record does not exist for the key, we simply return null.

However, if there is a value, we seek to that location and read the nine bytes for the header from the file system. Here, we should be doing some more error checking, such as making sure that **fread()** is returning data and not empty strings. But what we are working with here is an example, and it is going to assume that the file has not been corrupted. If we were to use this solution in a production environment, we would have a lot more checking going on to ensure that data being returned has not been corrupted.

Once we have the header for the value record, we can read the entire length of the record. This step will not read to the end of the 32-byte block but only to the end of the valid data. This is important to note, as you'll see in a bit.

After we have read the data, we take the "next record" value for the value record we just read. We then seek to the value record's key record plus five bytes, because the "location" field is five bytes into the key record, and overwrite the current location with the new one. After that, we seek back to the current location and change its record type from **0x02** (value) to **0x03** (unused). The length will be left unmodified.

There is one structural weakness in this method. It is that it is possible for a data record that is longer than the 32-byte block length to be deleted and reused, but not fully reused, so there could be some orphaned data that might be mistaken for valid data when looking for free space on another subsequent write. However, this situation would be problematic only in cases where the data that was at the start of the next 32-byte block was **0x01**, **0x02**, or **0x03**. What that would mean is that you would be storing binary data as a value, if the value at position 24 of the value (32 bytes of record length minus nine bytes for header data plus one byte to move to the next record) was a **0x01**, **0x02**, or **0x03** and that value had been previously deleted. It's a pretty big long shot, but it is possible, so bear the possibility in mind.

So, now that we have our code set to read, and delete, items in a linked list, let's try a little test (Figure 7.55).

```
$file = new File('storage');
$file->addValue('book', 'You want to do WHAT with PHP?');
echo $file->getValue('book') ."\n";
```

Figure 7.55: Reading the value

Figure 7.56 shows the output produced when we run this code.

```
You want to do WHAT with PHP?
```

Figure 7.56: Outputting the value

Just as expected, but the interesting part is in our data file (Figure 7.57).

```
0x0400 - 01 00 00 00 00 00 00 00 00 00 00 00 e7 e6 94 c5
0x0410 - 8c d5 0e 03 24 ec 96 91 88 00 bc 35 cd 17 62 9b
0x0420 - 03 00 00 00 00 00 00 00 1d 59 6f 75 20 77 61 6e
0x0430 - 74 20 74 6f 20 64 6f 20 57 48 41 54 20 77 69 74
0x0440 - 68 20 50 48 50 3f
```

Figure 7.57: Data after a value has been outputted

We see that our data is still there, but our type is now "unused" (**0x03**), with our data length of **0x0000001D** being preserved (Figure 7.58).

```
0x0420 - 03 00 00 00 00 00 00 00 1d 59 6f 75 20 77 61 6e
0x0430 - 74 20 74 6f 20 64 6f 20 57 48 41 54 20 77 69 74
0x0440 - 68 20 50 48 50 3f
```

Figure 7.58: Changed data

The block is now available for reuse. What would that look like? Figure 7.59 shows the test code.

```
$file = new File('storage');
$file->addValue('book', 'You want to do WHAT with PHP?');
echo $file->getValue('book') ."\n";
$file->addValue('book', 'Test');
```

Figure 7.59: Code to test adding data after data has been deleted

Figure 7.60 shows our newly modified data file, with record type **0x02** (value), a new length of **0x00000004**, and the ASCII code for the word "Test": **0x54 0x65 0x73 0x74**. The rest is basically junk.

```
0x0400 - 01 00 00 00 00 00 00 04 20 00 00 00 e7 e6 94 c5
0x0410 - 8c d5 0e 03 24 ec 96 91 88 00 bc 35 cd 17 62 9b
0x0420 - 02 00 00 00 00 00 00 00 04 54 65 73 74 77 61 6e
0x0430 - 74 20 74 6f 20 64 6f 20 57 48 41 54 20 77 69 74
0x0440 - 68 20 50 48 50 3f
```

Figure 7.60: Modified data overwriting an unused block

At this point, one thing you might be wondering about is performance. There seems to be a lot of "starting over" that happens, which could cause some I/O contention in a heavy write scenario. Well, let's conduct another test. Writing new values to an existing key is relatively fast and is unlikely to cause a massive pileup of data. Creating new keys, however, could be much different. Figure 7.61 shows our test.

```
$file = new File('storage');
$times = array();

for ($c = 0; $c < 1000; $c++) {
    $start = microtime(true);
    $file->addValue($c, $c);
    $times[((int)($c/100))] += (microtime(true)-$start);
}

foreach ($times as $time) {
    $time /= 100;
    echo "{$time}\n";
}

$start = microtime(true);
$file->addValue('book', 'You want to do WHAT with PHP?');
echo (microtime(true) - $start);
```

Figure 7.61: Adding a bunch of data and timing it

This is just some simple code that writes out the average insertion time for blocks of 100 inserts and then does a single final timing to see what the worst insert time is. Figure 7.62 shows the output.

```
0.013955991268158
0.040138781070709
0.066643755435944
0.09318589925766
0.11952744960785
0.14659163236618
0.17252885818481
0.19908903121948
0.22374948978424
0.25011153459549
0.26544117927551
```

Figure 7.62: Timing of adding a bunch of data

The increase is almost exactly linear to the number of keys that are in the file. And we're lucky. This file is small enough that it can easily fit into the operating system's disk page cache. So even though we're doing a lot of reads, most of them aren't actually touching the disk. If this were a much larger file — one that was too large to be cached — we would have a significant performance problem.

So, what to do? The clear solution would be to build an index. But where? For that answer, we're going to go to a neat little feature in Zend Server 5 called Code Tracing. (We'll look at this feature in some more depth in a later chapter.) Code tracing lets you obtain runtime instrumentation on a function-by-function basis, including parameters and return values. Figure 7.63 shows some summary information.

Function Name	# of Calls	Total Running Time	
		Incl. Children	**Just Own**
fopen()	1	0.24 ms	0.24 ms
File::addValue()	1	20.06 ms	0.02 ms
File::_getKeyValueLocation()	1	12.39 ms	4.73 ms
File::_hashKey()	1	0.01 ms	0.01 ms
fread()	5003	0.21 ms	0.21 ms
File::_createNewKeyLocation()	1	7.59 ms	0.05 ms
File::_getFirstFreeSpace()	2	15.18 ms	15.03 ms
File::_writeValue()	1	7.65 ms	0.02 ms

Figure 7.63: Code tracing output

This trace was run on the following code:

```
$file = new File('storage');
$file->addValue('book', 'You want to do WHAT with PHP?');
```

There is some interesting information in here. First of all, note that the elapsed time on the actual read operations on the file system amounts to squat. Even though **fread()** is called 5,003 times, it is not the source of our problem because its total elapsed time is one-fifth of a millisecond. The vast majority of the time is spent in **_getFirstFreeSpace()**. Even though **_getKeyValueLocation()** is on par with **_getFirstFreeSpace()** in terms of elapsed time, the "own time," or time spent in its own code apart from other function calls, is just under 5ms compared with 15ms in the free space function. So it would seem as though we need to be able to index freed space. And even though our **fread()** calls are not the specific cause of our performance problem, because of the high call count they are a strong indicator of the cause. So, our goal is going to be to lower the number of read operations, not because they are slow but because they are a result of inefficient functionality. Even if we delete an item and add a new item to the end of the list, we still have 4,002 calls to **fread()**.

But aren't indexes supposed to point you to data? I suppose. But here we're not interested in data; we're interested in non-data. My definition of an index is "something that shows you where to get what you want, faster (or more efficiently)." I am sure the computer science majors are groaning right now, but from a functional perspective that is *all* that an index is. All you want to know is where the data is or, in this case, where the data is not.

So the first index we're going to write will be for shortcuts to finding unused space. I will say up front that this indexing mechanism will have several limitations in it. Making a very efficient index is not an easy job and really does not belong in a book like this. One of the problems I run into constantly is PHP developers doing iterative functionality. Often, that iterative functionality is looping over an array and looking for a specific value, which is often recursive. Therefore, the purpose of this exercise is not to teach you how to write a good index. The purpose is for you to think of ways in which you can more efficiently access your data. In this case, an index is probably the best way to go. So we are going after two birds here: 1) the basics of quickly accessing data in a structured file and 2) giving you food for thought about how to more efficiently find data.

The most basic principle of indexing is not segment size, RAM caching, or any other things you might be thinking. This is the type of exposure you may have had due to work you've done with database systems. No, the most basic principle of an index is to get to where you want in the fewest number of steps possible. The best way to implement that goal is through predictability.

To make our index predictable, we are going to have our index segments split up into 512-byte blocks. To make it work within our existing file format, it will contain a header as well, but the header will be only five bytes. One byte will denote the type of record, and an additional four bytes will contain the position of the next index segment.

In each 512-byte block, there will be 32-byte records that will contain a list of empty file positions for each individual size block that can be allocated. Reclaimed space that is 15 bytes and reclaimed space that is 20 bytes would end up being in the same record list. There is a limitation here that you need to be aware of. Because there are only 32 bytes and each location will require four bytes, there is a limitation of eight blocks that can be stored in the index for a specific block length. Although we are not going to do it, one way around this limitation would be to have the final record contain the position to another 32-byte record that could be appended to. However, that approach adds complexity without buying much in terms of education.

Figure 7.64 shows what the index structure will look like.

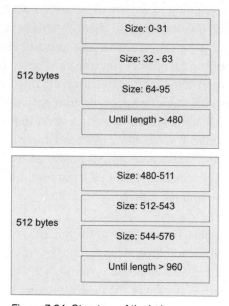

Figure 7.64: Structure of the index

We have several modifications to make to our code. First are some additions to the private member variables of our **File** class (Figure 7.65).

```
class File {
    private $_indexSegmentLength  = 512;
    private $_blockLength         = 32;
}
```

Figure 7.65: Adding class members for the index

The second is a change to the constructor (Figure 7.66).

```
public function __construct( $fileName )
{
      touch($fileName);
      $this->_fileName = realpath($fileName);



      $this->_fd = fopen($this->_fileName, 'r+');

      if (filesize($fileName) < 1024) {
            ftruncate($this->_fd, 0);
            $this->_appendIndexSegment(1);
            fseek($this->_fd, 512);
            fwrite(
                  $this->_fd,
                  pack('a512', '')
            );
      }
}
```

Figure 7.66: Code adding a starting index segment

We are going to use that first 1,024 bytes that we reserved earlier as the starting point for our index. For that reason, if the file size is smaller than 1,024 bytes, we truncate the file and call a previously undefined method called **_appendIndexSegment()**. The argument for this method is the length of data for which we need to have an index segment. Because we only want to initialize the index, we enter the number 1. After we have created that index, we append 512 bytes instead of the previous 1,024 because with the creation of the primary index record, we already have 512 bytes of data written to the file system.

The next thing to look at is the mechanism for appending an index segment (Figure 7.67).

```
private function _appendIndexSegment($size)
{
      $capacity = floor(($this->_indexSegmentLength - 5)
                              / $this->_blockLength)
                        * $this->_blockLength;
      clearstatcache();
```

```
    if (filesize($this->_fileName) === 0) {
        // Special case for a new file
        fseek($this->_fd, 0);
        fwrite(
            $this->_fd,
            pack(
                self::FORMAT_WRITE_INDEX,
                self::TYPE_INDEX,
                0,
                ''
            )
        );
        if ($capacity >= $size) {
            return 0;
        }
    }

$offset = 0;
$maxSize = 0;
while ($maxSize < $size) {
    fseek($this->_fd, $offset);

    $data = fread($this->_fd, 5);
    $data = unpack(
        self::FORMAT_READ_INDEX,
        $data
    );
    if ($data['nextrecord']) {
        $offset = $data['nextrecord'];
    } else {
        fseek($this->_fd, $offset + 1);
        clearstatcache();
        $fileSize = filesize($this->_fileName);
        if ($fileSize < 2048) {
            $fileSize = 2048;
        }
        $offset = ceil(
                $fileSize / $this->_blockLength
                )
                * $this->_blockLength;
        fwrite(
            $this->_fd,
            pack('N', $offset)
        );
```

```
                    fseek($this->_fd, $offset);
                    fwrite(
                        $this->_fd,
                        pack(
                            self::FORMAT_WRITE_INDEX,
                            self::TYPE_INDEX,
                            0,
                            ''
                        )
                    );
                }

                $maxSize += $capacity;
            }
            return $offset;
        }
```

Figure 7.67: Code to append to an index segment

Lots of code, huh? Actually, it's not that much in terms of logic. The first thing we do is calculate the overall capacity of the individual index segments. The capacity is the value of the maximum size that can be stored in the last record without overflowing the 512-byte boundary. To calculate that, we take the segment size and subtract five from it, which is the size of the index record header (one byte for type and four bytes for the next record). We divide that number by the length of the block, round it down, and multiply it by the length of the block.

After that, we check to see whether the file size is zero, which would mean that we're starting from scratch. If we are, then we write the basic index header to the file system and return zero. We have no "next record," and so we enter that as zero as well.

That's fine for when we create the new index, but what if we want to store a 65 KB document? That's where the loop comes in. We reset everything back to zero and start reading our first index segment. We read our first index segment and see whether we have the next index segment written to the record. If we do, we seek to it, incrementing the **$maxSize** variable by the capacity of the index segment, which will always be the same. If the maximum size in the current index segment is greater than the requested size, then we have determined what the position is for that segment and so we return it.

If we have not defined an index segment for that size, we have a little bit of work to do. The first thing we do is seek to the current offset plus one. The reason for this is that if an index segment has not been found, the easiest place to put it is at the end of the file. Technically, we could use the index to look for a free 512-byte segment, but that would add enough complexity to this example to make it more difficult to understand.

The next thing we do is test the size of the file. If it is a new file, it is going to want to write to position 1024. However, that is where our root key is supposed to be, so we can't write it there. We could write it at the next 32-byte block at position 1056, but for symmetry's sake we will just move it to position 2048 if the file size is smaller than 2048.

Once we have our next position, what we want to do is make sure that it is at the precise block point, and so we calculate the next position at the start of the next 32-byte block at the end of the file. We do this because we do not guarantee that a value write operation will write an exact 32-byte amount. We guarantee only that it will be within the constraints of a 32-byte field. We then take that calculated position and write it to the current position of the file descriptor, which should be at the previous index segment position plus one: the "next record" position. After we have written that, we write our empty index segment to the offset that we calculated.

That is all that needs to be done to allocate the space. But you might be thinking that we have a problem. That problem would be that our **_getFirstFreeSpace()** method will have trouble with that 512-byte size because we don't have a "length" field in there. Actually, we're going to completely rewrite that method. It is used both when we create a new key and when we add a new value, so its impact should be immediate. But to find free space, we need to first know where to look. That is handled by the **_getIndexLocationForSize()** method (Figure 7.68).

```
private function _getIndexLocationForSize($size)
{
    $offset = $this->_findIndexOffset($size);

    $capacity = floor(
        ($this->_indexSegmentLength - 5)
        / $this->_blockLength
```

```
        ) * $this->_blockLength;

        $startSize = floor(
                        $size / $capacity
                    )
                    * $capacity;

        $sizeRecord = $offset + (
            ceil(
                ($size - $startSize)/$this->_blockLength
                ) * $this->_blockLength
        ) + 5;

        return $sizeRecord;
}
```

Figure 7.68: *Finding the location of an index segment for a given size*

We use **_findIndexOffset()** to get the starting position of the proper index segment. Then, using the same formula we used before, we determine the capacity of each index segment. Then, we get to the interesting stuff. We get the start position by normalizing the size according to the capacity to its lower 32-byte position. After that, we find the location by taking the difference between the requested size and the beginning of the 32-byte size that would hold it, normalizing it against the block size, adding it to the offset, and adding five bytes to handle the header offset.

Now, we can look at our new **_getFirstFreeSpace()** method (Figure 7.69).

```
private function _getFirstFreeSpace($size)
{
    $sizeRecord = $this->_getIndexLocationForSize($size);
    fseek($this->_fd, $sizeRecord);
    $data = fread($this->_fd, $this->_blockLength);
    $data = unpack(
        'Na/Nb/Nc/Nd/Ne/Nf/Ng/Nh',
        $data
    );
    $key = 0;
    foreach ($data as $datum) {
        if ($datum > 0) {
            fseek($this->_fd,
```

```
                    $sizeRecord + ($key * 4));
            fwrite($this->_fd, pack('N', 0));
            return $datum;
        }
        $key++;
    }
    clearstatcache();
    $fileSize = filesize($this->_fileName);
    $offset = ceil($fileSize / $this->_blockLength)
            * $this->_blockLength;
    return $offset;
}
```

Figure 7.69: A rewritten method to find the first free disk space

What we do here is retrieve the exact location in the file for the index record
and read all 32 bytes from it. We iterate over the result, and if we find one that is
greater than zero, we seek to its position, overwrite its value with zeros, and return
the value. If we can't find any free positions, we return the next 32-byte offset of
the end of the file. That's it.

How does this compare with our previous version? Figure 7.70 shows the average
elapsed time over 100 add operations.

Without index	With index
0.013955991268158	0.0034213018417358
0.040138781070709	0.0078161549568176
0.066643755435944	0.012926840782166
0.09318589925766	0.017557938098907
0.11952744960785	0.022148966789246
0.14659163236618	0.027034678459167
0.17252885818481	0.03189195394516
0.19908903121948	0.036531779766083
0.22374948978424	0.041740772724152
0.25011153459549	0.046525557041168

Figure 7.70: Performance difference between indexed and non-indexed data

Performance is 4.5 times faster with a relatively empty file and 5.3 times faster for a file with 1,000 keys in it. Not bad. And if we do our previous test using Code Tracing, we have 1,002 **fread()** operations, virtually all which are used to find the key, not empty space. If we do a write operation on an existing key, we have only 200 or so **fread()** operations, down from more than 4,000.

But we have one last thing to do in our free space calculations. We need to have our class actually write to the index when a block is freed up. To do that, we will add one line to the end of our previously defined **getValue()** method (Figure 7.71).

```
public function getValue($key)
{

      list ($keyLocation, $firstValueLocation)
            = $this->_getKeyValueLocation($key);
. . .snip

      $this->_freeBlock(
            $firstValueLocation,
            $recData['length']+ 9
      );
      return $value;
}
```

Figure 7.71: Call to method that frees a block of data

The free block method is actually quite similar to our method to get the free space from the index, except that it is exactly opposite (Figure 7.72).

```
private function _freeBlock($position, $size)
{
   $sizeRecord = $this->_getIndexLocationForSize($size);
   fseek($this->_fd, $sizeRecord);
   $data = fread($this->_fd, $this->_blockLength);
   $data = unpack(
         'Na/Nb/Nc/Nd/Ne/Nf/Ng/Nh',
         $data
   );
   $key = 0;
   foreach ($data as $datum) {
```

```
        if ($datum == 0) {
                fseek($this->_fd, $sizeRecord+($key*4));
                fwrite($this->_fd, pack('N', $position));
                return;
        }
        $key++;
    }
}
```

Figure 7.72: Actually freeing the block in the index

We do the same thing we did before by getting the exact position for the size of block and iterating over all the data stored there. If we find a field that equals zero (in that it has no block data in it), we write the freed block number to that record.

When we look at the Code Tracing output, it is clear that read operations still have a fair number of reads when the key is way down on the list. But I will let you look into how to index that. Using the **sha1()** hash means that your keys will likely be more dispersed than if you were to simply take the raw data. Use this fact to your advantage. You have 20 bytes of data that you can work with. Even the worst key index should be able to find any key of the 1.35146128375 55926871896863388277e+48 possible hashed key values from the result of a **sha1()** call within 20 or so disk seeks. But with a good index, you could do it much quicker.

Another thing you can do is allocate larger blocks for key and index data. Rather than have hundreds of read operations, state that keys will be in the same format but will be contained in 512-byte blocks like the indexes. Then, you could read the block once and simply jump from key to key.

Conclusion

As you can see, building an index does not necessarily need to be a massive undertaking for basic operations, especially if the data format is predictable. Writing to your own structured file is not overly difficult either. But both are things that PHP developers don't often do. Now, having read this chapter, don't immediately think that you need to be building out your own indexes or files for your applications. In fact, much of what we've covered can be better handled by other applications, such as a database. However, by starting to think more along these types of lines, you will put yourself in a much better position to optimize your application.

8

Daemons

In reading this chapter, you might get the idea that I'm telling you to use PHP to build large-scale, daemon-based applications. While I definitely am of the opinion that PHP can be used for this purpose, the language was not designed for it. For me, the question of whether PHP can be used as a daemon comes out of the "use the best tool for the job" discussion that often happens online. Usually, this topic comes up as an argument after one person bested another in some kind of language shootout. The looser of the argument (regardless of the actual merits of his or her chosen language) half-concedes by saying, "Well, you just use the best tool for the job." Meaning, "You got me, but I won't be made to look the fool." Or, "It's not worth arguing with this idiot." Chances are it's the latter.

The problem is that there are lots of jobs that need to be done that are outside the specialty of a given language. Following the "best tool for the job" mentality, you might have part of your infrastructure running PHP, part of it running Ruby on Rails, part of it running .NET, and part of it running Java. I've got nothing against any of those languages, but absolutely *none* of them do *everything* well.

Java is a good example. I personally like programming in Java. However, to have a Web site running in Java, you need to have layer upon layer upon layer of application server upon application server upon application server to make it run. Will it run? Yes. Will it run fast? Yes. Are Web pages what Java was designed to do? With due respect to JavaServer Pages (JSP) developers, no.

Same thing with Ruby. Ruby is really good if you can afford to have very little flexibility. The benefit of Ruby on Rails comes at the price of inflexibility. If you need specific control over aspects of your application, Ruby is probably not the best choice for you.

Where am I going with this discussion? The question of using "the best tool for the job." A heterogeneous environment is not a good one to build for or to manage. Getting one of those to work should be the goal of academics. Real life, with all its warts, does much better with a fuller understanding of a smaller subset of features. This is because as soon as you have more than one type of architecture in your organization, you need to have more than one skill set. Having more skill sets means it's hard to find experts. And fewer experts means more time spent on support calls with other people whose knowledge base is also too wide.

What's the solution? I would contend that there is not one. Just as there is no vehicle that serves all needs, there is no programming language that serves all needs. In addition, the people you have around are important factors. If you have developers who are good, but not great, at PHP, Ruby, Python, Java, and .NET (who also need to know Flash), where will you have the skill set internally to handle a problem for which you can't find an answer on Google? It's like buying a Peugeot in Wyoming. I believe that if you have several languages and infrastructures that you support, your developers are going to have more problems and be less creative.

Creativity for the sake of creativity is not good. However, creativity enables innovative solutions to difficult problems. Far too many people pick up a language and work with it, thinking that they are experts, because someone else said the language was cool. However, the more languages you know, the less of an expert you will be in each.

This takes us back to the earlier statement about using "the best tool for the job." I would contend that this philosophy is wrong, or at least, problematic. I'd go the route of saying "use the best tool for the organization" instead. That organization might be your place of business, a nonprofit you work for, the Web site of a friend who's starting a new business, your church, anything. How do you decide which tool you are going to use for a specific problem?

What you base the decision on is not set in stone. In fact, it's unlikely that your organization made an intentional decision beyond, "Hey, we're building a Web site;

we should use PHP, right?" If your organization has a significant Web presence, then that is probably the right call. PHP does Web good. But what if you need something else? Say, for example, you need a simple message queue. You have several options. One is to obtain some kind of third-party messaging software. There are plenty of options available for you, and they probably are going to be better than what you would build.

But there is often a problem with using off-the-shelf software, both proprietary and open source. Half the time, it's complicated enough that once you install it, you need even more experts to manage it. So, say you have simple needs. You need a message queue, but your organization does not have the skill to support another language.

That is where building a PHP daemon comes in.

Starting Out

If we're going to be building a daemon, one of the primary goals is to build something that can handle multiple tasks at one time. To do that, we need to be able to handle multiple connections at once. Building an application that can handle multiple connections at once is actually very simple. So simple, in fact, that we've already done it, back in the chapter on networking and sockets. However, we have two problems, one old and one new. Both deal with how to use the resources on the system in the best way possible.

The old problem is the question of how to efficiently use CPU time when we may have significant parts of our work that require other services and, thus, have wait times. These can be tasks such as database calls, network calls, or even file system access. Even though disks are relatively fast these days, I/O contention does occur. This isn't just a problem that happens for larger organizations with high performance environments; smaller shops that have inefficient data structures on disk or just high-performance data requirements also face this issue. So, how do we do other things while waiting for slower things to do their thing?

The newer problem is probably one with which you're already familiar. With processors opting now for multi-core, multi-CPU, hyper-threaded architectures, a big issue to solve is that of using all of those CPUs and cores. PHP has a simple architecture that is great for HTTP. But it doesn't work so well once you start building a daemon-ized architecture. PHP has no internal mechanism for doing things asynchronously. Why should it? In PHP's native arena, Apache handles that work. And even the default **prefork** Multi-Processing Module (MPM) in Apache doesn't really do a lot of asynchronous processing because each process is separate from the others and handles only one request at a time.

So the first problem we need to solve is how to handle doing more than one thing at a time. There are two ways to do this, and the method you choose will depend on what type of system you're working on. If you are building a daemon, handling many incoming connections, then using a forking, or rather, a pre-forking, method is likely the best option.

In our prior examples using non-blocking I/O, we had to have a relatively complex piece of logic to handle data coming in from multiple sources. When you use pre-forking, this is not required, depending on how you do it. That's because forking actually lets the operating system manage the connections instead of you doing it yourself.

When a process is forked, the system copies the allocated resources into a new segment of memory, and both processes are resumed after the **fork()** call. The only difference between the two is the return value of the call. The parent process receives the process ID of the child, and the child receives a process ID of **0** (zero). If an error occurs, **-1** is returned.

Because the process being copied is mostly identical, some shared resources remain somewhat shared. An example of this is a socket that was opened prior to the forking. If a socket was created before the forking, you likely do not need to worry about non-blocking I/O. That is because existing connections are duplicated during the forking operation. When a new socket is accepted, the socket is unique to the individual forked process, even though the server socket is shared. Each forked process represents a resource that is available to do a specific unit of work. Because blocking operations on one work unit will not affect the operations on another work unit we can build our functionality without having to come up with an architecture that is tolerant of wait times on disk and network I/O.

To handle multiple work units, any solution we implement will likely need to work similarly to the pre-forking method. But there is, of course, the problem of how to do that on Windows. Windows does not support forking. To get around this limitation, we would need to create a daemon to act as a broker between the incoming requests and the worker processes that will ultimately handle the work. That type of broker would require very few CPU resources and would need to run as a single process/thread. Clearly, PHP doesn't do this, but the broker functionality is relatively simple, and as such it wouldn't matter that it uses only a single core. The operating system would take care of allocating the other cores automatically because they would be distinct processes from each other.

The second problem is going to be how to share data. But before examining that challenge, let me state something that you should keep in the back of your mind. Try to *not* share data, especially writeable data. That is a tall order, indeed. However, sharing data, particularly sharing data that needs to be written to, is one of the Achilles' heels of modern programming. It is far too easy to read data that is in the process of being overwritten. That is not to say that you shouldn't share data, but only that you should proactively minimize the use of shared resources. Consider defining as many resources as you can as read-only.

Also, try to write your data historically rather than overwriting values. When you overwrite data, you generally need to lock the resource. Fine-grained locks are not desirable. Locks are often necessary, but try to minimize them.

Another thing to consider is loading as many of your resources up front as possible. Consistency can be a problem in a shared environment. By front-loading as much data as you can, you reduce the likelihood of a collision between current and out-of-date data in the same data set. Inconsistency is probably a bigger threat than wasting some compute time processing old data.

As a language, PHP is very good at serialization, while other languages tend to restrict you more. The purpose of this restriction in other languages is mostly for security. Serializing data exposes that data to the outside world. It is quite possible that the data in question may be available in a context in which there are no security considerations to be had. Myself, I am somewhat unconvinced that this restriction truly buys a solid layer of security — the reason being that if your system is compromised to the point where an attacker can read serialized data, your problems are probably bigger than an attacker being able to read serialized data.

Using data serialization, you can easily pass virtually any data between PHP processes. One exception to this rule would be anything that has a resource variable in it. So things such as file handles or database connections cannot be passed. But passing regular serialized data is relatively easy and can be done by using a very simple protocol. Basically, you send four bytes (or eight bytes) that state the length of the serialized object and then send the raw object. Sometimes, the binary data in a serialized object can be problematic for some mechanisms, but as long as you use **fread()**, **fwrite()**, and so on in combination with sending the serialized data length, you should be fine. This point is important because some functions may not like reading the binary content because serialization operations can generate null characters which could be interpreted as the end of the string.

One of the benefits of serialization is that it lets you pass data within the context of your entire application. Say you need to pass information about a user. Yes, you could use Soap and have all the mappings done between the Soap call and native code, but passing serialized data is just nice, efficient, and native. Modern applications seem to be sold on how many layers are required to make it run. There's something about "here's your frigging data" that's kind of refreshing as many of the problems I've seen are due to overly complex application layers.

These are all points that you will have to take into consideration if you are to build your own PHP daemon. With PHP 5.3's new garbage collection mechanism, the walls preventing long-running PHP daemons are slowly being torn down. The last major wall is that of architecting your application to make full use of your CPU resources — in other words, how to do more than one thing at a time.

Our Example

For simplicity's sake, I am going to focus on building a pre-forking daemon, similar in approach to the Apache **prefork** MPM. It is rather unlikely that PHP developers deploying to Windows are going to run PHP as a daemon any time soon. Linux developers are more likely to do that, even though they are only slightly less unlikely to do it. So, with apologies to all the PHP developers on Windows (and there are a bunch), this example will focus on Linux. The same thing can be achieved on Windows using a proxy architecture similar to FastCGI.

Our example will be a simple spider. It will run in the background while PHP runs on the Web server. When someone makes a request stating the desire to spider a Web site, the PHP on the Web server will create an object representing that request and pass it off to the daemon, which will then handle the spidering of the Web site.

The first class definition is for the **Url** class, which will be used by both the front end and the back end to initiate the spider request. The front end uses it to pass the basic information about the URL to the back end and then disconnect. The back end uses it to spawn the request for each individual URL it finds on the site.

Figure 8.1 shows the code to define the **Url** class.

```
class Url
{
        private $_url;
        private $_recursive;
        private $_disconnect;

        public function __construct(
                $url,
                $recursive        = false,
                $disconnect       = true
        )
        {
                $this->_url               = $url;
                $this->_recursive         = $recursive;
                $this->_disconnect        = $disconnect;
        }

        public function getUrl()
        {
                return $this->_url;
        }
```

```
    public function isRecursive()
    {
        return $this->_recursive;
    }

    public function willDisconnect()
    {
        return $this->_disconnect;
    }
}
```

Figure 8.1: URL container class

For handling the responses, we have a simple class, **UrlResponse** (Figure 8.2), that will be used to pass data from a worker back to the dispatcher process.

```
class UrlResponse
{

    private $_body;
    private $_links = array();

    public function __construct($body,
                                array $links = array())
    {
        $this->_body = $body;
        $this->_links = $links;
    }

    public function getBody()
    {
        return $this->_body;
    }

    public function getLinks()
    {
        return $this->_links;
    }
}
```

Figure 8.2: Data class for holding the response from a URL

Our front end will consists of a single form (Figure 8.3). I use **Zend_Form** because the actual form HTML is kind of irrelevant, and the code used here should be easy to conceptualize even if you are not familiar with Zend Framework.

```php
class UrlForm extends Zend_Form
{

    public function init()
    {
        $this->setMethod('POST');
        $this->addElement(
            'text',
            'url',
            array('label' => 'URL')
        );
        $this->addElement(
            'checkbox',
            'recursive',
            array(
                'label'=> 'Do recursive spider'
            )
        );
        $this->addElement(
            'submit'
        );
    }
}
```

Figure 8.3: A Zend_Form based class for submitting the URL

When it is submitted, the PHP script on the server side will serialize the URL object and submit it to the back-end daemon for processing (Figure 8.4).

```php
$form = new UrlForm();
$form->setView(new Zend_View());

if ($_SERVER['REQUEST_METHOD'] === 'POST'
        && $form->isValid($_POST)) {
    $url = new Url(
        $form->getValue('url'),
        $form->getValue('recursive'),
        true
    );
```

```
        $serverSock = fsockopen('tcp://dev', 10000);
        $data = serialize($url);
        $data = pack('N', strlen($data)) . $data;
        fwrite($serverSock, $data);
        fflush($serverSock);
        echo "URL submitted";
} else {
        echo $form;
}
```

Figure 8.4: Code to submit the URL to the daemon socket

We take the data from the form submission and create a new **Url** object. From there, we serialize it and then build the data stream by prepending the size as a 32-bit unsigned long. You will notice that we build the entire string instead of sending it in pieces. That is because we don't want to give the network the opportunity to flush bits of data. The purpose of this example is to write a decently scalable networking application without the connection management of non-blocking I/O. For this goal, we need to be able to read the full string from the stream. Making two write calls can cause separate packets to be sent. In the Web–PHP portion of the script, this didn't seem to be much of an issue, but on the command-line interface (CLI) it is.

Now for the fun stuff. The daemon will be a class called **Daemon** (no points for creativity). It will contain an interface to the **Zend_Search_Lucene** search engine in Zend Framework. I used this solution for the simple reason that it was already written. Figure 8.5 shows the starting definition for the **Daemon** class.

```
class Daemon {

    private $_sSock;
    private $_workerCount = 0;

    /**
     *
     * @var Zend_Search_Lucene_Interface
     */

    private $_index;

}
```

Figure 8.5: Base Daemon class

In here, we have a property that holds the server socket resource, a property that holds the count for the number of forked processes we'll start up, and then the object for the index. When a connection is made to the daemon from the Web server, the pre-forked process that answers the request manages the spidering of the Web site, farming out the individual HTTP requests to other pre-forked processes while taking the results and storing them in the Lucene index. The "answering" process loads the first page, retrieving all the URLs on the page that match the current docroot and passing them off to individual workers. That is defined in a function called **execute()** (Figure 8.6).

```php
public function execute($host, $port, $workerCount)
{
    $this->_index = Zend_Search_Lucene::create(
        '/tmp/index'
    );
    $this->_workerCount = $workerCount;
    $this->_sSock = socket_create(
        AF_INET,
        SOCK_STREAM,
        SOL_TCP
    );
    socket_set_option(
        $this->_sSock,
        SOL_SOCKET,
        SO_REUSEADDR,
        1
    );

    if (!socket_bind($this->_sSock, $host, $port)) {
        throw new Exception("Unable to bind socket");
    }

    if (!socket_listen($this->_sSock)) {
        throw new Exception("Unable to listen on socket");
    }

    for ($c = 0; $c < $workerCount; $c++) {
        if (($pid = pcntl_fork()) === 0) {
            $this->_execute();
        } else {
            echo "Child {$pid} started...\n";
        }
    }

    socket_close($this->_sSock);
    pcntl_wait($status);
}
```

Figure 8.6: Code to execute the daemon

This method primarily does two things: it creates the server socket, and it pre-forks the correct number of processes.

Creating the socket is similar to what we saw in the networking and sockets chapter, but we have an additional function call here to **socket_set_option()**, setting the socket option **SO_REUSEADDR** to 1. The purpose of this step is so that if the daemon goes down without properly closing the server socket, we can immediately bring it back up. When a daemon goes down and the socket is still open, the socket will be in a **TIME_WAIT** state if there are clients attached to it. What this means is that the socket has closed, and the client side connection has closed, but the socket is waiting for a timeout to occur. This is normal TCP behavior. However, by default, Linux will not let you bind to a socket that's listening on the same port as a socket in the **TIME_WAIT** state until the socket times out and is removed. By setting **SO_REUSEADDR**, we can re-bind to that socket while it is still in a **TIME_WAIT** state. If it is in the **LISTEN** or **ESTABLISH** state, it will not bind. Only if it is in **TIME_WAIT** or if the socket has timed out can we re-bind.

The second thing the **execute()** method does is perhaps the most important part of our discussion. It occurs in the **for()** loop. Here, we will create all the individual pre-forked processes. When we call the **pcntl_fork()** process, Linux takes the memory allocated to the application and copies it to a new memory space. This includes objects, classes, sockets, and so on. The return value of **pcntl_fork()** will differ depending on whether you are the child process or the parent process. If you are the child, it will return zero. If you are the parent, it will return the parent of the child.

After that, we close the socket for the parent process and sit on **pcntl_wait()**. The reason we close the socket is because we don't want this process to answer any connections, and we want to keep it in the foreground so we can easily kill the process for testing reasons. The **pcntl_wait()** function call will wait until one of the children receives some kind of signal, such as an interrupt or a kill. We could actually use this mechanism to manage the children, however in this example we're just using it to keep the parent process from dying. With this code, killing just one child process will cause the parent process to exit because **pcntl_wait()** is called only once. One of the things we could do is have it sit on **pcntl_wait()** and if a child goes down have it spawn another one. But I didn't want to do a whole bunch of process management stuff because that can get to be a little confusing, particularly in print. Calling **pcntl_wait()** just once lets the parent process hang around so we can simply hit **Ctrl-C** and have the parent, plus all the children, terminate in one action.

Once a process has been forked, and it is a child, we need to be able to manage the incoming connections. The **_execute()** method call handles that work (Figure 8.7).

```php
private function _execute()
{
    while (true) {
        $sock = socket_accept($this->_sSock);

        $obj = $this->_readData($sock);
        if (!$obj instanceof Url) {
            socket_close($sock);
            continue;
        }
        echo 'PID '
            . posix_getpid()
            . ' received URL '
            . $obj->getUrl()
            . "\n";

        try {
            $url = Zend_Uri_Http::fromString(
                $obj->getUrl()
            );
            if ($obj->willDisconnect()) {
                socket_close($sock);
            }
            $reqData = @file_get_contents($url);
            $this->_processPage(
                $obj,
                $url,
                $reqData,
                $sock
            );

        } catch (Exception $e) {
            echo $e->getMessage() . "\n";
        }
        if ($sock && is_resource($sock)) {
            socket_close($sock);
        }
    }

}
```

Figure 8.7: Code to handle child process requests

As you can see, we put ourselves into an infinite loop. We then sit on a **socket_accept()** call on the socket that we created earlier. This is the primary method of handling multiple connections. Because we copied the memory from the parent process after creating the socket, the kernel will handle dispatching the request to each individual child process as a new connection on the server socket comes in. From there, we call the **_readData()** method, which reads the initial data from the socket. We'll see that step in a bit.

Because the request must be made with a serialized version of **Url**, if the data is not an instance of **Url** then we simply close the connection. After printing some informational data (which technically should go to a log file), we parse the URL to make sure it is valid. Then, we check to see whether the client cares about the response, by calling **willDisconnect()**. An example of this would be the front-end Web server. The Web server does not want to hang around while a site is spidered. And so, the daemon immediately disconnects once it has read and parsed the request. On the other hand, the dispatch process that manages the spider operation will want to stay around so it can retrieve the body and the list of links from the worker process.

Having done all that, we then call **file_get_contents()** on the URL and pass all that data on to the **_processPage()** method. However, before we look at the **_processPage()** method, let's take a quick look at **_readData()** (Figure 8.8).

```php
private function _readData($sock)
{
    $data = socket_read($sock, 4);
    if (!$data) {
        return false;
    }

    $data = unpack('N', $data);
    $len = array_shift($data);
    $data = socket_read($sock, $len);
    $obj = @unserialize($data);

    return $obj;
}
```

Figure 8.8: Reading data from the server socket

This is really a very simple method. We know that the first four bytes are a 32-bit long unsigned integer. So we read four bytes and unpack that data. We then know exactly how much data we need to read from the socket when we call **socket_read()**. Because we're using blocking I/O and letting the kernel handle the asynchronous operations, the code is much simpler than it would be had we used non-blocking I/O. After we read the data, we unserialize it. If the data we read is malformed, **unserialize()** will throw an error and return **false**. Good or bad, we return the value.

Pretty easy. Now that we have that operation out of the way, let's look at the **_processPage()** call (Figure 8.9).

```php
private function _processPage(
    Url $obj,
    Zend_Uri_Http $url,
    $reqData,
    $sock
)
{
    $links = $this->_getLinks(
            $reqData,
            $url->getHost(),
            $url->getPath()
    );
    $farmedLinks = array();
    foreach ($links as $link) {
            $farmedLinks[$link] = false;
    }
    // Don't re-spider the original URL
    $farmedLinks[$obj->getUrl()] = true;
    if (!$obj->willDisconnect()) {
            $response = new UrlResponse(
                    $reqData,
                    $links
            );
            $data = serialize($response);
            $data = pack('N', strlen($data)).$data;
            socket_write($sock, $data);
            socket_close($sock);
    }
    if ($obj->isRecursive()) {
            $this->_farmLinks($farmedLinks);
            $this->_index->commit();
```

```
                    echo "Data received.  Optimizing index...\n";
                    $this->_index->optimize();

                    echo "Optimizing Complete.\n";
            }
    }
```

Figure 8.9: Indexing a page and gathering links

The first thing **_processPage()** does is call the **_getLinks()** method, which uses XML Path Language (XPath) to query the HTML page. We'll look at that step shortly. From there, **_processPage()** captures all the links and places them in an associative array so that they can be returned as part of the **UrlResponse** object. This is only done if the client intends to disconnect. The front-end request will disconnect. But if for some reason it doesn't want to, this mechanism could be used to report back the links that were found on the page. However, it is most likely to be used by the dispatch process so it can process the links and hand them off to other worker processes.

If the request is a recursive request, meaning a full spider of the URL, the method passes off the links to a method called **_farmLinks()**, which is where the actual dispatching occurs.

The **_getLinks()** method (Figure 8.10) is a relatively long method, but it's primary purpose is to get all the **href** attributes and return fully formatted URLs. That's where most of the length comes in.

```
private function _getLinks($data, $host, $path)
{
    $currentDir = dirname($path);

    $doc = new DOMDocument();
    @$doc->loadHTML($data);
    $links = array();
    $xPath = new DOMXPath($doc);
    $nodeList = $xPath->query('//a[@href]');
    foreach ($nodeList as $node) {
      $link = $node->getAttribute('href');
```

```
        if (!$link) $link = $path;
        if (stripos($link, 'http://') === 0) {
            if (stripos($link,'http://'.$host.'/')!== 0) {
                continue;
            }
        } else if (stripos($link, 'https://') === 0) {
            if (stripos($link,'https://'.$host.'/')!== 0){
                continue;
            }
        }
        if (($ancPos = strpos($link, '#')) !== false) {
            $link = substr($link, 0, $ancPos);
        }

        if (strlen($link) >= 2
            && $link[0] == '.'
            && $link[1] == '/') {

            $link = substr($link, 2);
        }
        if (!$link) {
            continue;
        } else if ($link[0] === '/') {
            $link = 'http://'
                        . $host
                        . $link;
        } else if (stripos($link, 'http://') !== 0
                    && stripos($link, 'https://') !== 0) {
            $link = 'http://'
                        . $host
                        . $currentDir
                        . '/'
                        . $link;
        }

        if (array_search($link, $links) === false) {
            try {
                $l = Zend_Uri_Http::fromString($link);
                $links[] = $link;
            } catch (Exception $e) {}
        }
    }

    return $links;
}
```

Figure 8.10: Retrieving all the links from a page

We make a good effort to format the data as best we can. Next, we check to see whether we already have that link found. Then, we do a final check using **Zend_ Uri_Http** to make sure that the format is correct. If we were not able to generate a properly formatted URL, we simply ignore it via the empty **catch** statement.

The **_farmLinks()** method (Figure 8.11) takes the links that were supplied and sends them to the worker connections to do the actual downloading and parsing of content for the remote page.

```php
private function _farmLinks($farmedLinks)
{

    $connCount = (int)($this->_workerCount / 3);

    $addr = $port = null;
    socket_getsockname($this->_sSock, $addr, $port);

    $req = array();
    $write = $except = array();
    while (($link = array_search(false, $farmedLinks))
                !== false
                || count($req) > 0) {

        if ($link !== false) {
            $farmedLinks[$link] = true;
            $sock = $this->_sendPacket(
                'localhost',
                $port,
                $link
            );
            $req[$link] = $sock;
        }
        $timeout = 0;
        if (count($req) >= $connCount
            || array_search(false, $farmedLinks)
                === false) {
            $timeout = null;
        }
        $conn = $req;
        socket_select($conn, $write, $except, $timeout);
        foreach ($conn as $c) {

            $obj = $this->_readData($c);
```

```
        $connKey = array_search($c, $req);
         socket_close($c);
         unset($req[$connKey]);
         $farmedLinks[$connKey] = true;
         if ($obj instanceof UrlResponse) {

           $doc =
            Zend_Search_Lucene_Document_Html::loadHTML(
                $obj->getBody()
                );
                $doc->addField(
        Zend_Search_Lucene_Field::keyword(
                'url',
                $connKey
             )
                );
                $this->_index->addDocument($doc);

                foreach ($obj->getLinks() as $link) {
                        if (!isset($farmedLinks[$link])){
                                $farmedLinks[$link]=false;
                                unset($req[$link]);
                        }
                }
             }
          }
       }
}
```

Figure 8.11: Sending the requests to parse the links to child workers

The first thing the **_farmLinks()** method does is determine how many workers it is going to use. In this case, we choose a third of them, although as long as you choose a fraction that is at least a few less than the number of connections you should be fine. The call to **socket_getsockname()** is there only so we can get the actual port on which the server is listening.

After that, it's time to start iterating over the results. We do this by trying to find the first instance in **$farmedLinks** whose value is false. Earlier, we iterated over all the links, changing the values (which were the URLs) to be the keys and setting the **$link** value to false for each one. False values would mean that the URL had not been spidered yet, whereas true values would mean that it had. So we retrieve the next URL or, if there are no more links to be found, check to see whether we have some connections open. If either of these conditions is true, we iterate over the array, sending data to the workers.

If **$link** is not false, it means that we found a link that has not been spidered yet. In that case, we initiate a connection by calling **_sendPacket()**. This quick and easy helper function is shown in Figure 8.12.

```
private function _sendPacket($host, $port, $link)
{
    $sock = socket_create(AF_INET, SOCK_STREAM, SOL_TCP);
    socket_connect($sock, $host, $port);
    $url = new Url($link, false, false);
    $data = serialize($url);
    $data = pack('N', strlen($data)) . $data;
    socket_write($sock, $data);
    return $sock;
}
```

Figure 8.12: Code to send the response back

The function's sole purpose is to take the URL and place it into a **Url** object, connecting to a worker process and sending the serialized **Url** object. After sending the object, **_sendPacket()** takes the socket that was created and returns it so that the **_farmLinks()** method can manage it.

Once we have that socket back, we place it into the **$rec** array so we can manage it later on. The next thing we need to do is determine what our read timeout is. One thing we do not want to do is poll TCP connections. That would mean we would have to do a read on each socket, let it time out, and go on to the next one — a very inefficient process. Instead, we use the **socket_select()** function, just as we did with non-blocking I/O, and have it select on the sockets that are in the **$rec** array.

If data has been received on any of the sockets, we can call the **_readData()** method on the socket that was returned as part of **$conn**. This is a blocking call, but because the socket was returned from the select operation, we know that there will be data on it, so no read timeout is needed. If a data stream were longer than the TCP packet size, a delay could occur. On a remote machine on an Ethernet network, that size, called the Maximum Transmission Unit (MTU), is 1,500 bytes. However, we are connecting over the local interface, so in our case any lag would be negligible. In addition, the MTU for the local interface is usually larger than an Ethernet one. Mine is 16,436 bytes. If we were doing this over a larger network, non-blocking I/O might be more pertinent, but here it is not. Another reason for opting to connect over the local interface is because I wanted a simpler example than what we would have had to do with non-blocking I/O over multiple connections on a pre-forked server. It's moderately easy to do, but also very easy to get lost if it is a new concept. So I sacrificed a small increase in efficiency for clarity of code.

Once we receive and process the data, we close the socket, unset the variable in **$req**, and set the value to true in **$farmedLinks** so we don't download the data again. If we get a response back of **UrlResponse**, that means that the request was successful and we can now place the URL into our Lucene index. We do that by creating a document object of a type that was specifically created for HTML and adding an additional field so we can get the URL for search results.

That encompasses most of our functionality. The last thing we need to do is create the **Daemon** object and execute it. Figure 8.13 shows how simple this is to do.

```
require_once 'Zend/Loader/Autoloader.php';
Zend_Loader_Autoloader::getInstance()
                    ->setFallbackAutoloader(true);

$d = new Daemon();
$d->execute('0.0.0.0', 10000, 10);
```

Figure 8.13: Kicking off the daemon

Because we are using several Zend Framework components, we make sure to load the autoloader and then execute the **Daemon** object, telling it to listen on all interfaces, on port 10000, with 10 workers.

Does it work? Figure 8.14 shows the output generated when we start the daemon.

```
[apache@localhost Daemon]#
  /usr/local/zend/bin/php daemon.php
Child 3000 started...
Child 3001 started...
Child 3002 started...
Child 3003 started...
Child 3004 started...
Child 3005 started...
Child 3006 started...
Child 3007 started...
Child 3008 started...
Child 3009 started...
```

Figure 8.14: Output after starting the daemon

And if we do an **lsof -i -P** to list the Internet sockets and port numbers (not port names), we see all of them listening on the correct socket (Figure 8.15).

```
[root@localhost conf.d]# lsof -i -P | grep 10000
php  3000  apache  16u  IPv4 9591   TCP *:10000 (LISTEN)
php  3001  apache  16u  IPv4 9591   TCP *:10000 (LISTEN)
php  3002  apache  16u  IPv4 9591   TCP *:10000 (LISTEN)
php  3003  apache  16u  IPv4 9591   TCP *:10000 (LISTEN)
php  3004  apache  16u  IPv4 9591   TCP *:10000 (LISTEN)
php  3005  apache  16u  IPv4 9591   TCP *:10000 (LISTEN)
php  3006  apache  16u  IPv4 9591   TCP *:10000 (LISTEN)
php  3007  apache  16u  IPv4 9591   TCP *:10000 (LISTEN)
php  3008  apache  16u  IPv4 9591   TCP *:10000 (LISTEN)
php  3009  apache  16u  IPv4 9591   TCP *:10000 (LISTEN)
```

Figure 8.15: All the forked processes listening on the same socket

Does it run? I placed the PHP manual on my server so that I could test indexing a decent-sized volume of information. If I go to the form I created earlier, type the URL where the documentation is available, set the "recursive" checkbox to true, and submit the page, the Web page immediately returns with the "URL Submitted" message. The daemon is quite different.

Figure 8.16 shows the output generated after submitting the URL to the daemon. (Due to page width limitations, this version of the output includes a couple of line breaks for readability.)

```
Child 3008 started...
Child 3009 started...
PID 3000 received URL http://dev/php/html/index.html
PID 3001 received URL http://dev/php/html/preface.html
PID 3002 received URL http://dev/php/html/copyright.html
PID 3003 received URL
 http://dev/php/html/getting-started.html
PID 3004 received URL
 http://dev/php/html/introduction.html
PID 3004 received URL http://dev/php/html/tutorial.html
PID 3005 received URL http://dev/php/html/manual.html
PID 3004 received URL http://dev/php/html/install.html
. . .
```

Figure 8.16: Output after submitting a URL

The daemon immediately starts processing the pages, using up much of my free CPU very quickly. Because we index each document, the bottleneck is the writing to the index. But even so, I am processing multiple pages at a time, doing a fair number each second. Once the daemon has parsed and indexed all the pages, it generates the output shown in Figure 8.17 (again with line breaks introduced).

```
PID 3030 received URL
 http://dev/php/html/function.imagickdraw-bezier.html
PID 3029 received URL
 http://dev/php/html/function.imagickdraw-arc.html
PID 3026 received URL
 http://dev/php/html/function.imagickdraw-annotation.html
PID 3024 received URL
 http://dev/php/html/function.imagickdraw-affine.html
Data received. Optimizing index...
Optimizing Complete.
```

Figure 8.17: Output after site has been spidered

At this point, we can leave the daemon running to handle more connections or press **Ctrl-C** to get out of it. All that's left to do is to test the search on the machine. When I type in **pcntl** as my search query, I get the output shown in Figure 8.18.

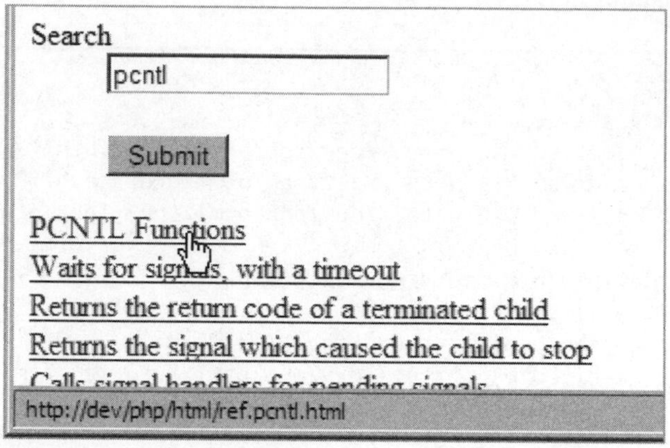

Figure 8.18: The search results

Inter-Process Communication

We could leave it at that, but there is one more thing we might want to look at, primarily because it's kind of a neat way of distributing functionality. What I would like to do is demonstrate how, by using a combination of objects and serialization, you can actually build a very compelling distributed system that can be both dumb and smart at the same time.

Let's start by defining an interface. This interface will be used by an individual worker to discover whether the received object was a **Url** object that we had previously defined or an object that contains executable functionality. We can use this interface as a sort of switch to help make that determination. Figure 8.19 shows the interface definition.

```
interface CmdInterface
{
        public function execute();
}
```

Figure 8.19: Interface for any executable functionality

Simple enough. For our example, the command that we want to build here is a command that forks another process based on the answering process upon request (Figure 8.20).

```
class CmdFork implements CmdInterface
{
    public function execute()
    {
        if (($pid = pcntl_fork()) > 0) {
            echo "New child {$pid} started...\n";
        }
    }
}
```

Figure 8.20: Class designed to fork a child

The class basically has one line of functional code. However, based on whatever functionality you need, it could have as much code as you want and as much data as you need.

We need a simple user interface (UI) to kick this off (Figure 8.21).

```
if (isset($_GET['fork'])) {
    $fork = new CmdFork();
    $serverSock = fsockopen('tcp://dev', 10000);
    $data = serialize($fork);
    $data = pack('N', strlen($data)) . $data;
    fwrite($serverSock, $data);
    fflush($serverSock);
    echo 'Request has been sent';
} else {
    ?>
Would you like to have another forked worker?
<a href="?fork=y">Yes</a>
    <?php
}
?>
```

Figure 8.21: Sending the fork command to the daemon

To implement the command, we create a new object of **CmdFork**, serialize it, and send it to the daemon. That's easy enough. The only thing left to do now is make our daemon aware of it. For that, we'll modify the **_execute()** method. Figure 8.22 highlights the necessary change.

```php
private function _execute()
{
    while (true) {
        $sock = socket_accept($this->_sSock);

        $obj = $this->_readData($sock);
        if ($obj instanceof CmdInterface) {
            $obj->execute();
            socket_close($sock);
            continue;
        } else if (!$obj instanceof Url) {
            socket_close($sock);
            continue;
        }

. . .


    }
}
```

Figure 8.22: Modifying the _execute() call to recognize CmdInterface

That is all we need to do. We start our daemon back up, click on the forking link on our UI, and send the command to the daemon. Figure 8.23 shows our output.

```
[apache@localhost Daemon]#
  /usr/local/zend/bin/php daemon.php
Child 2931 started...
Child 2932 started...
Child 2933 started...
Child 2934 started...
Child 2935 started...
Child 2936 started...
Child 2937 started...
Child 2938 started...
Child 2939 started...
Child 2940 started...
( . . . and then later on)
New child 2943 started...
```

Figure 8.23: Output after sending fork request

After I submitted the Web page, which in turn submitted the **CmdFork** object, a new process with the ID of 2943 was started. Let's take a look at our network connections (Figure 8.24) and see if this process is ready to go.

```
[root@localhost ~]# lsof -i -P | grep 10000
php  2931  apache  16u  IPv4  10891  TCP *:10000 (LISTEN)
php  2932  apache  16u  IPv4  10891  TCP *:10000 (LISTEN)
php  2933  apache  16u  IPv4  10891  TCP *:10000 (LISTEN)
php  2934  apache  16u  IPv4  10891  TCP *:10000 (LISTEN)
php  2935  apache  16u  IPv4  10891  TCP *:10000 (LISTEN)
php  2936  apache  16u  IPv4  10891  TCP *:10000 (LISTEN)
php  2937  apache  16u  IPv4  10891  TCP *:10000 (LISTEN)
php  2938  apache  16u  IPv4  10891  TCP *:10000 (LISTEN)
php  2939  apache  16u  IPv4  10891  TCP *:10000 (LISTEN)
php  2940  apache  16u  IPv4  10891  TCP *:10000 (LISTEN)
php  2943  apache  16u  IPv4  10891  TCP *:10000 (LISTEN)
```

Figure 8.24: Output after fork request

Yep. Process 2943 is sitting on the same socket as all the others, ready to handle the request.

Conclusion

The idea that is exciting here is that with this type of functionality, you can actually run PHP code as a background process by using a relatively dumb daemon. In fact, with our spidering example, we could even have written the code as a command, removing much of the functionality from the daemon itself. With that approach, the daemon would become much more multipurpose while still being able to do our spidering activity via a command instead of directly in the daemon. From a teaching perspective, I believe that the order of the ideas presented here is a better approach. But now that you have seen both possibilities, let your imagination run wild with the things you might be able to do.

Now, let's go back to my note at the beginning of the chapter. Having seen the code in this chapter, you might think this is something that a lot of organizations should be doing. I would argue that that is not the case. In most situations, the traditional PHP Web HTTP request/response approach is the proper way to write your application. Don't try to be too creative with your solutions. Be practical. Also, if you have an application that requires very high performance and a large back-end infrastructure, this might not be the approach that you want to take either. PHP running as a daemon does not have the type of ecosystem that a language such as Java or C has.

However, the vast majority of Web sites out there do not require a massive back-end infrastructure, and many of them do have needs for some kind of asynchronous processing. If you are working on one of those sites, then something like what we've covered in this chapter might be pertinent to what you are doing.

9

Debugging, Profiling, and Good Development

Permit me to rant for a moment. Not a big rant. Just a little rant. As of writing this sentence, I have been a consultant for Zend Technologies for more than three years. One of the things I do, among many others, is conduct audits of customer applications. Although it does happen, seldom are audits done "just in case." Usually, I am tasked with specific problems. More often than not, they are performance problems. Sometimes the trouble is with PHP logic, sometimes with the database, but they are performance problems nonetheless.

I'm going to let you in on the secret to why I am good at what I do. It's not because I'm special or have any type of secret knowledge. It is a button:

In case you don't know what that button is, it is the **Profile** button from the Zend Studio toolbar. That is my secret. One of the very first things I do when I look at a new application is start running profiles on it. The audits I do generally last a week, and it is imperative that I have a good understanding of what is happening in the application within the first day. It is also imperative that I understand what the main problems are by the end of the third day. I accomplish this first with the Profiler, then with the Debugger, and then by using Code Tracing.

Don't think that the problems are limited simply to the customers with whom I have worked. PHP has a reputation for being a sort of script kiddie language. Although this label is not at all true, many PHP developers haven't helped the cause by producing poor code — in many cases, really poor code. What is poor code? I remember reading a quote stating that programmers can spot bad code easily; what they have trouble doing is identifying good code. So it's a bit of a tough thing to define what "good code" looks like.

I pondered this question for a bit and did some Googling to see what others thought. Here's a list of what I found. Good code is:

1. Well-organized

2. Commented

3. Good naming conventions

4. Well-tested

5. Not "clever"

6. Developed in small, easy-to-read units

In the interest of fair disclosure, I stole this list from Stack Overflow. Someone else wrote it on December 14, 2008. I think the list is accurate. A lot of bad code misses the first item, being neither well-organized nor structured. Jackson Pollock would never have made a good programmer. Although some make it, I tend to disagree with the assertion that coding is an art form. Coding is definitely creative, but one of the purposes of art is to convey an idea via different and new mediums. Art doesn't have to be maintained by someone else. Code does, and you should not have to "study" code to discover its meaning. The meaning should be plain, and the code should be structured.

However, even a lot of code that is considered "well-architected" fails on the fifth point. Some of the worst-performing code I've seen was the result of someone trying to be too smart. The code fit all the other criteria but missed the part about not being clever. Overly clever code is, unfortunately, a bit hard to document. One example could be code that tries to guess what will be needed later in a request, front-loading program logic instead of loading it lazily. Another possibility might be using multiple levels of variable variables. Yes, you have to know how variable variables work for the Zend Certification exam, and, yes, they are useful to handle an abstraction layer. But with each level deeper that you use a variable variable, you decrease the readability of your code by an order of magnitude. Another example would be the overuse of magic methods.

Writing Good Code

To me, good code strikes a good balance between reviewed "stream of consciousness" code, or spaghetti code, and over-architected solutions. What I mean by reviewed stream of consciousness code is code written in moments of inspiration that you have then gone back over and re-examined, re-factored, and unit-tested. In the past, a lot of PHP code was written as a stream of consciousness. More recently, though, we seem in many ways to be swinging to the other side of the pendulum, making our code so complicated that it's just as difficult to work with. In addition, many modern developers seem to believe that you can click a button, run a command, or type some pseudocode and, because our computers are so powerful, have the application all but built once the command runs.

This brings me to Kevin's Framework Observation, which states that, "The effects of the law of unintended consequences are inversely proportional to the ability of a developer to build an application without a framework." Why is that? Because often when a developer starts using a framework, that developer checks his or her brain at the door. I cannot tell you how many times I've wanted to respond to people posting on one of several framework mailing lists that they'll find the answer to their question simply by reading the framework source code. You are working with PHP; therefore, you are working with open source code. If you're having a problem understanding why a framework is doing something a certain way, pull out the debugger, which you should already be using prolifically, and find out why it's doing that. As one of my colleagues noted, "You shouldn't be using a framework until you know you need a framework." Once you know you need a framework, you are much more likely to have a full enough understanding to properly harness the framework. Don't "use" a framework; harness it.

After reading that last paragraph, you may think I am anti-framework, but that is most definitely not the case. I like frameworks because I'm more productive when I use them. However, when I use a framework, I make sure I know what's going on behind the scenes. Are you using Active Record, loading up a thousand objects to do some kind of calculation, and wondering why your page is slow? Then you don't understand the concepts of Active Record.

Most of the time, the problems I see are because the developers don't know what is happening in their application. There really is no excuse for this. Two main debuggers are available for PHP: the Zend Debugger and XDebug. Both support profiling functionality, and both are free. If you are unfamiliar with these tools or do not know how to use them, *do not* read any other chapters in this book until you are proficient at debugging and profiling.

Now don't get me wrong. PHP lets you throw code at a wall and make it stick. But the developer is ultimately responsible for what gets written.

Every single one of the examples in this book has been run using the debugger. A lot of the code in the other chapters should be run by using a debugger so that you can understand the actual logic flow and variable flow for the individual method calls.

Even if you build something right the first time, it is a good idea to go through it with the debugger. Why? Because if you built it right the first time, there's probably something wrong with it. To be honest with you, if I write some section of code logic that is beyond simple variable modification and it runs the first time through, my fear is that I did something wrong. And do you know what? About half the time, that fear is correct. Always check your work. A debugger is great for that purpose.

In this chapter, we look at four different methods for gaining insight into your application and making changes more predictable: debugging, profiling, code tracing, and unit testing. We also review some steps you can take on your local operating system to get lower-level information about what it takes to get your application serving a request. All the examples use Zend Studio 7.1, but some of this functionality is also available in the Eclipse PHP Development Tools (PDT) project (which as of this writing is the most popular project on the Eclipse Web site).

Debugging

The first thing we will look at is debugging. With apologies to XDebug developer Derick Rethans, I will be working with the Zend Debugger and not XDebug, simply because I know the Zend Debugger better.

The purpose of a debugger is to give you line-by-line information about every single variable available in the current scope. In other words, before an individual line of code is executed, you can see what the variable values are and what the result of that expression will be. Take the code shown in Figure 9.1, for example.

```
$a = 1;
$a++;
$a++;
```

Figure 9.1: Starting code

With a debugger, we can stop execution on each line of this code and see what the variable's value is. Figures 9.2, 9.3, and 9.4 show the changing values of the **$a** variable in this example.

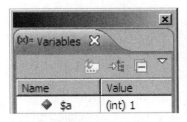

Figure 9.2: Step 1

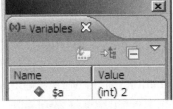

Figure 9.3: Step 2

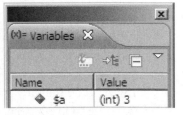

Figure 9.4: Step 3

This example may seem somewhat simplistic, and it is. However, we need to start from somewhere. If you're thinking to yourself, "That doesn't seem very useful," consider what the variable stack looks like for a simply Model-View-Controller (MVC) request (Figure 9.5).

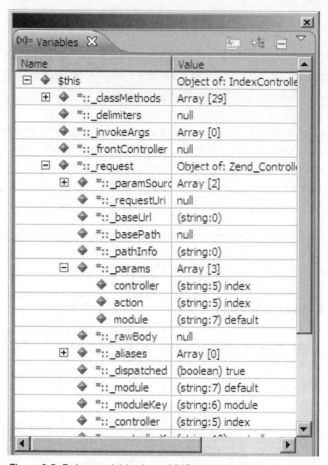

Figure 9.5: Debug variables in an MVC request

I will argue that any application that is worth spending time on is worth taking the time to use a debugger. Even if you are working with an application such as Drupal, Joomla, or SugarCRM, use a debugger to understand what it is doing.

In the past, the way PHP programmers did debugging was simply to put **var_dump()** statements into their code. This approach has several problems. First, you have no context if you have a bunch of **var_dump()** statements. Second, you could be in trouble if you deploy to production and have not removed them. Third, you need to load the page each time you need to see a different value.

To illustrate the second issue, I did a Google search for "object(stdClass)". On the second page of results, I found a page with **var_dump()** output on it. I also searched for ""array(1)" inurl:car" and ""array(1)" inurl:decorating". Why those? Because I needed to filter out the legitimate PHP questions that people asked. For these searches, I found pages in the first page of search results. And once it's in Google, it doesn't go away.

When debugging, you should be aware of several concepts:

- Step over
- Step into
- Step return
- Breakpoints
- Watch lists

The term "step over" means to execute a line but not dive into the function call, if there is one. "Step into" means that if the line you are about to execute has a function or method call on it, the debugger will dive into that function. "Step return" means that if you are in a given function, the debugger it will pause execution as soon as you have exited that function.

Breakpoints are kind of like bookmarks at which you can tell the debugger to stop. Any moderately complex application is too complex to step through on a line-by-line basis. What a breakpoint lets you do is run the program normally until that bookmarked line of code is reached. At that point, your integrated development environment (IDE) will be given control of the application, and you can inspect variables and such. Breakpoints can also be conditional. In other words, the debugger will break only if a certain condition is true.

Take the code in Figure 9.6, for example. We used it in our binary protocols discussion.

```
function printBytes($data)
{
    $len = strlen($data);
    for ($c = 0; $c < $len; $c++) {
        if ($c % 8 === 0) echo "\n";
        $hex = str_pad(
                dechex(ord($data[$c])) ,
                2 ,
                0 ,
                STR_PAD_LEFT);
        $char = ctype_print($data[$c])?$data[$c]:' ';
        echo "{$hex}={$char} ";
    }
    echo "\n";
}
```

Figure 9.6: Code to print bytes

Say we wanted to have this code break only if it finds a null character. To do that, we would create a conditional breakpoint so that if **$hex** equals **'00'** we break. First, we set the breakpoint, and then we set the condition.

But before that, let's look at the test code (Figure 9.7).

```
printBytes(
    pack(
            'a16',
            '12345'
    )
);
```

Figure 9.7: Code to print some null bytes

This code prints out the numbers **'12345'** followed by several null characters.

To set the breakpoint, we double-click on the line number for the **ctype** call and create the condition (Figure 9.8).

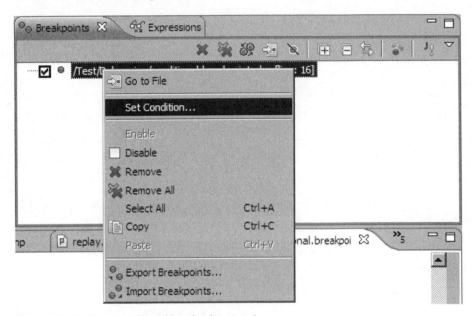

Figure 9.8: Setting a conditional breakpoint, step 1

Then, we create the actual condition expression (Figure 9.9).

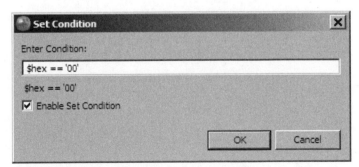

Figure 9.9: Setting a conditional breakpoint, step 2

Now when run our code, it will iterate through all the characters in the string until it reaches a null character. One thing to note, however, is that the condition must be for values that exist on the breakpoint. In other words, to make this breakpoint conditional, we need to set it on the line with **$char**, not **$hex**. When the debugger encounters the specified condition, it displays the output shown in Figure 9.10.

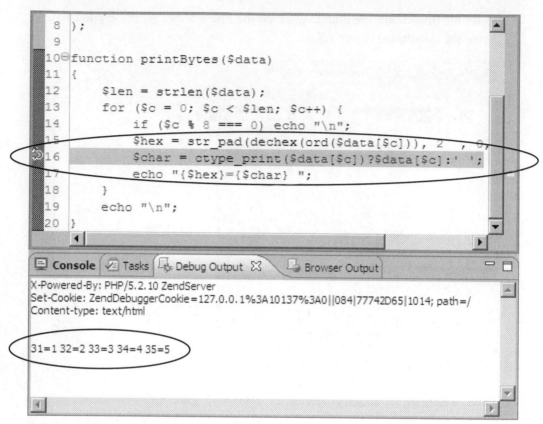

Figure 9.10: Output when the condition is reached

Figure 9.11 shows our variable stack.

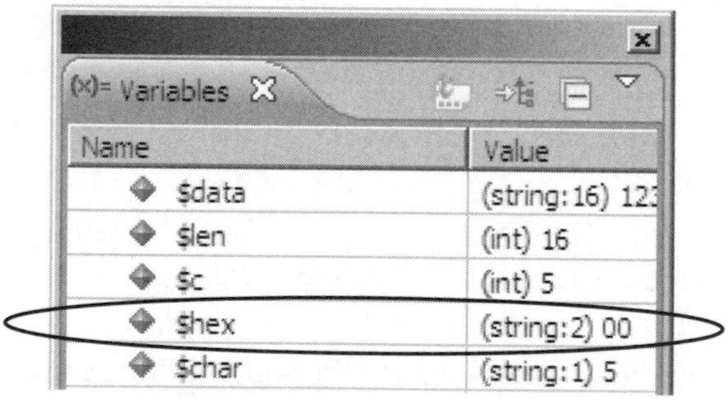

Figure 9.11: Variables current at the breakpoint condition

As you can see, the value of **$hex** is exactly what it should be, given our breakpoint.

One of the nice things about using the debugger is that you don't need to have the source code installed on your local machine. When you are debugging a remote request, your IDE will check to see whether the source code for a given file is installed locally. If it is not, the IDE will request the file from the server and let you debug against the copy installed there. However, for that reason, plus the fact that you can get runtime variable values, I highly, highly, highly recommend that you not install the debugger extension on a production system.

Profiling

The purpose of profiling is to learn where your application is spending its time for an individual request. The Profiler protocol is included with the free Zend Debugger, so if you have the Debugger, you have access to the Profiler, although you need Zend Studio to read the profile data.

The Profiler gives you the timing to each individual function call that is made, along with the execution flow. In other words, it provides the order of execution, showing all nested function calls.

The easiest way to explain the benefit of profiling is simply to present an example. The example we'll use is the structured file access code we created in the previous chapter. To profile the URL, we click the **Profile URL** button on the debugger's **Tools** menu and enter the URL. The debugger connects to the Web server, setting the cookies that the debugger extension uses to listen for a debug request and kicking off the profile.

In the resulting PHP Profile Perspective, the **Execution Statistics** tab is usually where I go first. I set it to group by function (not by file or class) and to sort by own time. Figure 9.12 shows what this output looks like. The displayed columns are **Function**, **Calls Count**, **Average Own Time**, **Own Time**, **Others Time**, and **Total Time**.

Function	Calls Count	Average Own Time	Own Time(s)	Others Time(s)	Total time(s)
● addValue	0	0.000000	0.000000	0.000000	0.000000
● getValue	0	0.000000	0.000000	0.000000	0.000000
● _findLastValueLocation	0	0.000000	0.000000	0.000000	0.000000
● _writeValue	0	0.000000	0.000000	0.000000	0.000000
● _getKeyValueLocation	0	0.000000	0.000000	0.000000	0.000000
● _appendIndexSegment	0	0.000000	0.000000	0.000000	0.000000
● _findIndexOffset	0	0.000000	0.000000	0.000000	0.000000
● _getIndexLocationForSize	0	0.000000	0.000000	0.000000	0.000000
● _freeBlock	0	0.000000	0.000000	0.000000	0.000000
● _getFirstFreeSpace	0	0.000000	0.000000	0.000000	0.000000
● _getFirstFreeSpaceOld	0	0.000000	0.000000	0.000000	0.000000
● _createNewKeyLocation	0	0.000000	0.000000	0.000000	0.000000
● _hashKey	0	0.000000	0.000000	0.000000	0.000000
● __construct	1	0.001052	0.001052	0.000123	0.001175
● _appendIndexSegment	1	0.000123	0.000123	0.000000	0.000123
● addValue	1000	0.000024	0.023748	3.140000	3.163748
● _getKeyValueLocation	1000	0.002932	2.931678	0.119999	3.051677
● _hashKey	1000	0.000008	0.007612	0.000000	0.007612
● _createNewKeyLocation	1000	0.000044	0.043816	0.068571	0.112387
● _getFirstFreeSpace	2000	0.000047	0.093587	0.040179	0.133766
● _getIndexLocationForSize	2000	0.000013	0.025991	0.014188	0.040179
● _findIndexOffset	2000	0.000007	0.014188	0.000000	0.014188
● _writeValue	1000	0.000023	0.023128	0.065195	0.088323
● (main)	1	0.000007	0.000007	0.000000	0.000007

Figure 9.12: Execution statistics

The **Function** column simply notes the name of the function that was called. It doesn't include the class name if a class was called, but in reality that doesn't matter. I use this column primarily to figure out where to look next. That typically will be either the **Calls Count** or the **Own Time** column. Without fail, looking at these two pieces of data will put you on the right track. It may not explain why you're having trouble, but it will get you moving in the right direction.

In our example, there is a clear indication of where the problem is. The call counts are around 1,000 to 2,000 calls, but that's not that bad. I remember seeing one call count of greater than 650,000 once. However, it's definitely not something I would call a best practice. Poorly performing applications frequently have high call counts on a handful of functions. It's not guaranteed by any stretch of the imagination, but there often seems to be a correlation.

In this application, though, the call count isn't that bad. However, the **Own Time** information definitely shows something. The function **_getKeyValueLocation()** takes about 93 percent of the time. Often, this is actually the way things play out. Maybe not 93 percent, but I commonly see maybe three method calls totaling about 75 percent of the execution time.

However, just seeing this number, although it's a good starting point, doesn't tell us much. It only identifies the sore spot. We still need a context. The invocation statistics can help us there. To investigate, right-click on the worst method call and select **Open Function Invocation Statistics**. This option gives us a view into the methods that called the function and tells us what functions that function in turn called. Figure 9.13 shows the invocation statistics for the **_getKeyValueLocation()** function.

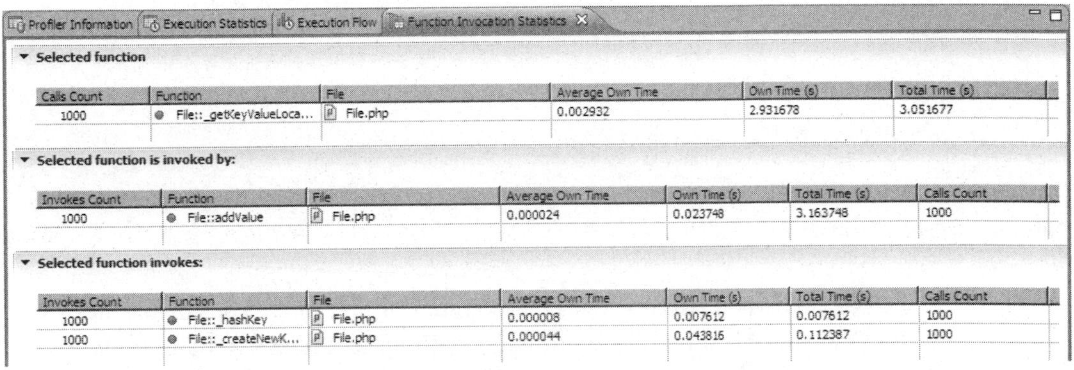

Figure 9.13: Function invocation statistics for a specific function

Looking at these statistics, we see that the only function that calls **_getKeyValue Location()** is **File::addValue()**. This is actually good. It means that we have only one entry point to consider. If your application is larger than this one, and I would expect that it is, you would want to profile several pages, examining both the execution flow and the function invocation statistics, and make sure that's the case. Profiling other pages will also let you replicate the issue. If the issue is consistent across many pages, then you have a well-replicated problem. A well-replicated problem is the best kind of problem to have because you can measure your success in beating it down.

The last tab we'll look at is the **Execution Flow** tab (Figure 9.14). This tab shows you each individual function call made to user-land and the time for each, along with its hierarchy in the call flow.

Function	File	Total Execution Time	Duration Time (ms)
⊟ ● (main)	Ⓟ Fileexec.php	93.03%	3186.87
● (main)	Ⓟ File.php	0.0%	0.01
⊞ ● File::__construct	Ⓟ File.php	0.03%	1.18
⊞ ● File::addValue	Ⓟ File.php	0.01%	0.32
⊞ ● File::addValue	Ⓟ File.php	0.01%	0.27
⊞ ● File::addValue	Ⓟ File.php	0.01%	0.25
⊞ ● File::addValue	Ⓟ File.php	0.01%	0.25
⊟ ● File::addValue	Ⓟ File.php	0.01%	0.26
⊟ ● File::_getKeyValueLocation	Ⓟ File.php	0.0%	0.15
● File::_hashKey	Ⓟ File.php	0.0%	0.01
⊞ ● File::_createNewKeyLocation	Ⓟ File.php	0.0%	0.08
⊞ ● File::_writeValue	Ⓟ File.php	0.0%	0.08
⊞ ● File::addValue	Ⓟ File.php	0.01%	0.27
⊞ ● File::addValue	Ⓟ File.php	0.01%	0.27

Figure 9.14: Execution flow

Here, we can see who called who and how much time it took. Looking at this example, you might be thinking that there's nothing that needs to be improved upon because the individual function calls are actually pretty quick. However, that's because you're not seeing the rest of it. Let's scroll down to the end of the results (Figure 9.15).

Function	File		
⊞ ● File::addValue	Ⓟ File.php	0.17%	5.74
⊞ ● File::addValue	Ⓟ File.php	0.17%	5.74
⊟ ● File::addValue	Ⓟ File.php	0.17%	5.81
⊟ ● File::_getKeyValueLocation	Ⓟ File.php	0.17%	5.71
● File::_hashKey	Ⓟ File.php	0.0%	0.01
⊞ ● File::_createNewKeyLocation	Ⓟ File.php	0.0%	0.11
⊞ ● File::_writeValue	Ⓟ File.php	0.0%	0.09
⊞ ● File::addValue	Ⓟ File.php	0.17%	5.73
⊞ ● File::addValue	Ⓟ File.php	0.17%	5.77

Figure 9.15: Drilling down on the execution flow

Look at the last column, which shows the duration time, and compare the results of the last call with those of the very first call. The last call was at 5.77 ms, while the first was at 0.32 ms. Still not bad, but it is an indication of trouble brewing. What we are seeing here is a linear increase in time as more elements are added to the file. That is the important bit of information that we could then use to determine what our next course of action should be.

Code Tracing

Code Tracing is a feature in the full version of Zend Server. I will not spend much time on it because it requires a larger financial outlay than an IDE, and my purpose in writing this book is not to provide a primer on Zend products. However, I will show you Code Tracing because it's frigging awesome.

Let me take you, in your imagination, to some time in the future. It's about 2 a.m., if you follow regular business hours, or 8 a.m. if you're an open source code jockey. Suddenly, you get a call from one of the system administrators saying that the CEO of the company (okay, so it's 8 a.m.) is on the Web site and his account is not working. Not only that, but just a few other people are having problems, and none of them are directly related to each other.

With a slight sigh, you get out of bed and turn on the computer. You bring up your browser, log in to Zend Server, and look at the most recent Monitoring events. You see a couple of events that are promising because they are generated by an **fwrite()** operation returning false. You open up one of the events and browse through the execution flow. As with the profiler, you browse through the execution flow and look to see whether the write operation is writing to the CEO's home directory (yes, you can see the parameters for each individual function call) on a specific hashed partition. You check some of the other events and see that this individual write operation is occurring on the same partition. Not only that, but you see the reason.

So you open up your e-mail and inform your sys admin (somewhat smugly, I might add) that the application error is, "The lame sys admins didn't check the free disk space on partition 'dab3d' and it is completely full" (copying the CEO on the e-mail as a professional courtesy, of course).

That is what Code Tracing does. It tracks everything in your request, *in production*, and if an event such as a failed function call, slow execution, or high memory usage (among others) is triggered, it writes all that information to the file system for you to examine at a later point in time. And it does this with a relatively low performance impact. While replicating an issue is still important, Code Tracing can in some cases actually let you fix an error without replicating it.

Interested? I thought so. That's why I included this functionality in the chapter, even though it is available only commercially.

The way Code Tracing works is that it gathers instrumentation data for each individual request as it occurs. However, it will not store that data (which is where much of the overhead is) unless a Monitoring event occurs. Monitoring watches for various conditions to occur, such as a specific monitored function call (e.g., **fopen()**) causing an error, or excessive memory being used, or a function call (e.g., **mysql_execute()**) taking too long to run. When that occurs, a Monitoring event is triggered, which stores the context of that request along with some basic instrumentation data. This information lets you replay the event in a development environment to try and reproduce the event.

However, while Monitoring lets you replay the event, replaying often is not enough. That is where Code Tracing comes in. Not only is Code Tracing attached to a specific event, such as a slow function call or slow page execution, but it contains the instrumentation data for everything that occurred. Hence the ability to sometimes fix a problem without having to replicate it. My somewhat tongue-in-cheek example of running out of disk space on a certain partition is actually quite realistic. You didn't need to reproduce that issue to diagnose and fix it.

Same thing for problems such as an SQL execution error. If you directly inject your user variables into your SQL query, Monitoring is enough for you because it shows you the function call parameters for the function that throws the error.

However, if you are following best practices and not directly injecting data into an SQL query, but are using prepared statements instead, you have a problem. If it is the execution of the prepared statement that fails, particularly if you are using **bindParam()**, then you don't really know the value that caused the error to occur. However, with Code Tracing, because the parameters for each method call are stored, you can go back in the history of the execution flow and see exactly what the parameters were. This is why I say you may not even need to replicate the issue to fix it.

There are two ways to create a code trace. The first is to attach the trace to an individual event. The second is to request one manually. Zend Server will monitor your PHP scripts for certain conditions. If those conditions arise, you can have it store that information on the disk, where you can go over it later. Figure 9.16 shows the steps involved in setting a Code Tracing event action.

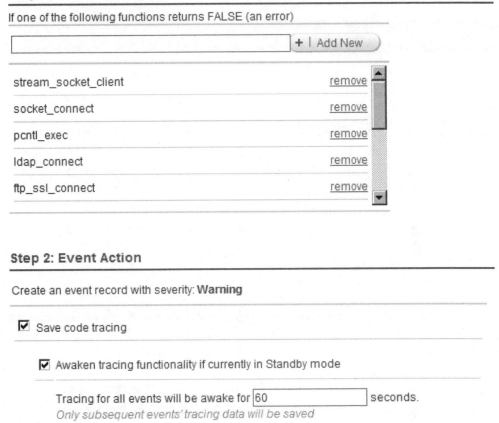

Step 1: Event Condition

If one of the following functions returns FALSE (an error)

| | + | Add New |

stream_socket_client   remove

socket_connect   remove

pcntl_exec   remove

ldap_connect   remove

ftp_ssl_connect   remove

Step 2: Event Action

Create an event record with severity: **Warning**

☑ Save code tracing

    ☑ Awaken tracing functionality if currently in Standby mode

      Tracing for all events will be awake for 60   seconds.
      Only subsequent events' tracing data will be saved

Figure 9.16: Setting an event action

Code Tracing exists in two modes: on and standby. "On" is self-explanatory. What standby mode does is keep trace data from being gathered until a certain event occurs. This feature lets you set a certain event as the trigger. Once the event trigger has been hit, code tracing will be turned on and the tracing data will start being gathered. At that point, all events are eligible to dump a trace.

So what do you get with a code trace? Let's take a look. We'll use our asynchronous example.

Let's say that, for some reason, the browser is taking a long time to process a credit card transaction. If a condition occurs that causes a Code Tracing enabled event to occur, or if we make a request manually, we get output similar to that shown in Figure 9.17.

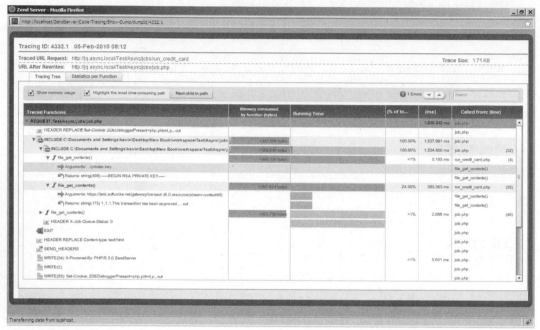

Figure 9.17: Highlighting the path consuming the most time

You can see timings for each individual function as well as the arguments that were used for each. You can also see the inclusion functions and **header()** calls.

Not a bad bit of functionality to have in your arsenal.

Unit Testing

In recent months, I have drunk the unit testing Kool-Aid. I am not one who embraces new things easily. Not because I am stuck in my ways but because new things have not been tested. Our beloved IT industry is horrendously vulnerable to fads.

Take, for example, design patterns. The concept of a design pattern is great. Have a problem? Describe it, solve it, name it. Factory, Singleton, Active Record. All useful descriptions. But the problem is that now everything is a design pattern. To quote Top Dollar (from *The Crow*), "The idea has become the institution." What? You don't know what the "Bit Sensitive Primitive Element Design Pattern" is? How amateur are you? About as amateur as me. Change is good only if change is positive.

So, if I am so resistant to change, why am I now a fan of unit testing? Because the change is positive. The premise behind unit testing is that if the parts work, the whole works. Although this principle may not apply well to Psychiatric Social Study, it applies well to computers. This is because a computer, if given the exact same input, will provide the exact same output. There is no answer to "1 plus 1" other than 2, unless there is a serious error in your CPU. So if the parts work, the whole works.

Another reason why unit testing is positive is because it is repeatable and scriptable. You break down each test into its disparate parts, including database structure. When you start a test, you start with a clean slate and run tests against the functionality in a given unit of code. If it doesn't work, either the test is wrong or your code is wrong, and it's probably your code. So change your code, and run the script again.

When building unit tests, you generally do it against a specific unit of code. That unit of code could be a function library or a class. Unit tests *can* be done against output, but such tests are not as important as having the underlying functionality working. That's not to say that unit tests on output are not important; they're just not as important as your library.

What I've heard said about unit testing is that you build your tests first and then write your code to pass the tests. I am not sure I agree with that philosophy 100 percent. If I'm building to an API where a third party is expecting data in a certain format when certain data is provided, then, yes, I agree with it. But if I'm writing original code, I've found that writing my unit tests alongside my regular code suits my development style a little better. Some people like writing out their architecture in nice fancy diagrams. I like to write out out my architecture in code. To me, that's a more natural method of development. Sure, there may be flow charts and such to describe where stuff is going, but coding lets me more easily see problems that I don't see in a graphical architecture. Some people see it in the visual architecture, but I don't, and I don't think that there is necessarily a "correct" order to it. Consistency and repeatability are more important than order, in my opinion.

However, because books are linear things, I need to cover one thing before the other, and so I will demonstrate it in the "ordered" manner.

So, first up, a skeleton of a class that will represent a credit card transaction (Figure 9.18).

```
class CreditCard
{

    public function setCreditCardNumber($ccNum)
    {

    }

    public function setCreditCardDate($date)
    {

    }

    public function charge($amount)
    {

    }

    public function refund($amount)
    {

    }

}
```

Figure 9.18: Empty class for setting up a unit test

Next, we create our unit test. I use the unit test generator available in Zend Studio. The generator takes a library item, such as a file with global functions or a class, and automatically creates stubs for each piece of functionality in there.

However, we need to add some additional stuff. On top of making sure that you get back the correct value when a certain value is provided, it is also a good idea to make sure you test any error conditions. If you have boundaries, such as upper and lower limits, test both the upper and the lower limit. It will take you 30 seconds to write the test but will add years to your life by reducing the stress caused by making stupid programming mistakes, which all of us do. Experience doesn't mean that you stop making mistakes; you just anticipate them better. Plus, you might not be the one maintaining the code five years from now.

So what would that unit test code look like? Figure 9.19 provides the answer.

```php
class CreditCardTest extends PHPUnit_Framework_TestCase {

    /**
     * @var CreditCard
     */
    private $CreditCard;

    protected function setUp() {
        $this->CreditCard = new CreditCard();
    }

    public function testSetCreditCardNumber() {
        $this->assertTrue(
            $this->CreditCard->setCreditCardNumber(
                '4012000010000'
            )
        );
    }

    public function testSetCreditCardNumberFail() {
        try {
            $this->CreditCard->setCreditCardNumber(
                'abcdefg'
            );
            $this->assertTrue(
                false,
                'An invalid credit card number
                should throw an exception'
            );
        } catch (CreditCardException $e) {}
    }
}
```

```
public function testSetCreditCardDate() {
    $this->assertTrue(
        $this->CreditCard->setCreditCardDate(
            '1202'
        )
    );
}

public function testSetCreditCardDateFail() {
    try {
        $this->CreditCard->setCreditCardDate(
            '121212'
        );
        $this->assertTrue(
            false,
            'An invalid credit card date
            should throw an exception'
        );
    } catch (CreditCardException $e) {}
}

public function testCharge() {
    $this->assertTrue(
        $this->CreditCard->charge(
            100
        )
    );
}

public function testChargeFail() {
    try {
        $this->CreditCard->charge(
            -1
        );
        $this->assertTrue(
            false,
            'An invalid charge amount
            should throw an exception'
        );
    } catch (CreditCardException $e) {}
}

public function testRefund() {
    $this->assertTrue(
        $this->CreditCard->refund(
            100
        )
    );
}
```

```
public function testRefundFail() {
    try {
        $this->CreditCard->refund(
            -1
        );
        $this->assertTrue(
            false,
            'An invalid refund amount
             should throw an exception'
        );
    } catch (CreditCardException $e) {}
}
}
```

Figure 9.19: Building the credit card unit test

(One point to note here: **CreditCardException** just extends **Exception**. The **PHPUnit** framework handles errors by throwing an exception. If you catch *all* exceptions, you will also catch the failure exception, which makes it look like your test passed when it did not.)

It seems like a lot of code, but it's not. I copied and pasted most of it, and it took me about five minutes. So to make this worth our while, I need to be able to save five minutes. The way to test our classes in a non–unit-tested environment is to go to the Web page, enter the data, hit submit, and note any errors. Then go back and fix them. With unit tests, we click a button. Figure 9.20 shows what we get.

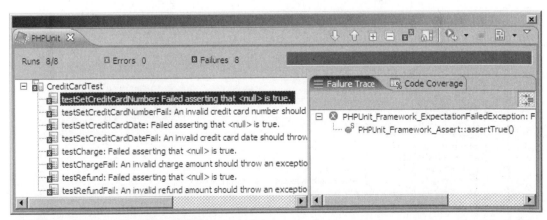

Figure 9.20: Output of the failed unit tests

What we see here is that out of the eight tests that ran, all eight failed. Now we can start writing our code. For the sake of brevity, we'll write only the code to handle credit card failures (Figure 9.21).

```php
public function setCreditCardNumber($ccNum)
{
    $valid = new Zend_Validate_Ccnum();
    if (!$valid->isValid($ccNum)) {
        throw new CreditCardException(
            'Invalid Credit Card Number'
        );
    }
}

public function setCreditCardDate($date)
{
    if (strlen($date) === 4) {
        $yearTime = date('y');
        $mon = (int)substr($date, 0, 2);
        $year = (int)substr($date, 2);
        if ($mon < 13 && $mon > 0 &&
            $year >= $yearTime) {
            return;
        }
    }
    throw new CreditCardException(
        'Invalid Credit Card Date'
    );
}
```

Figure 9.21: Implementing some of the class code

Figure 9.22 shows what we get when we click our button.

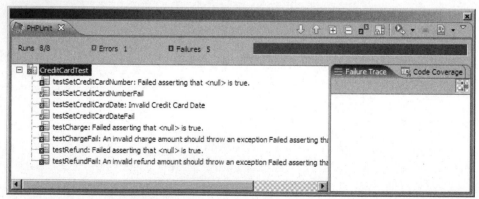

Figure 9.22: Passing a few tests

Two of our failures are now gone. But there is more as well. If you look on the right side next to the **Failure Trace** tab you also see **Code Coverage**. The code coverage function provides a report that shows you which lines of code were actually executed. Figure 9.23 shows the result for our test.

```
public function setCreditCardDate($date)
{
    if (strlen($date) === 4) {
        $yearTime = date('y');
        $mon = (int)substr($date, 0, 2);
        $year = (int)substr($date, 2);
        if ($mon < 13 && $mon > 0 && $year >= $yearTime) {
            return;
        }
    }
    throw new CreditCardException(
        'Invalid Credit Card Date'
    );
}
```

Figure 9.23: Output of code coverage

The output shows that even though we set a credit card date length of four characters, we did not run the **return** expression. That is because the test we wrote had an expiration date in the past. This is one of the reasons why code coverage is so good. If there is code that is not being run, you can see it and write tests for it. This is also why writing unit tests to test for error conditions is important. Nobody in their right mind writes an application that intentionally fails within the context of the application. However, you can do that here. Simply write a test that checks the error condition. Or, in our case, add a valid test that makes sure that the line of code is run. Figure 9.24 shows such a test.

```
public function testSetCreditCardDate() {
    $this->assertTrue(
        $this->CreditCard->setCreditCardDate(
            '1212'
        )
    );
}
```

```
public function testSetCreditCardDateInvalid() {
    try {
        $this->CreditCard->setCreditCardDate(
            '1202'
        );
        $this->assertTrue(
            false,
            'An expired credit card number
             should throw an exception'
        );
    } catch (CreditCardException $e) {}
}
```

Figure 9.24: A unit test to test an error condition

When we run the unit tests again, we get the output shown in Figure 9.25.

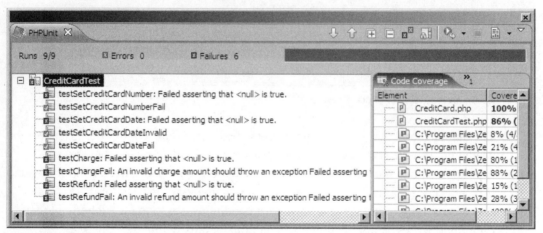

Figure 9.25: Output of a successful error test

We still get a failure, but that's because we haven't actually written the logic to handle it (book brevity and all). And our code coverage report now looks as shown in Figure 9.26.

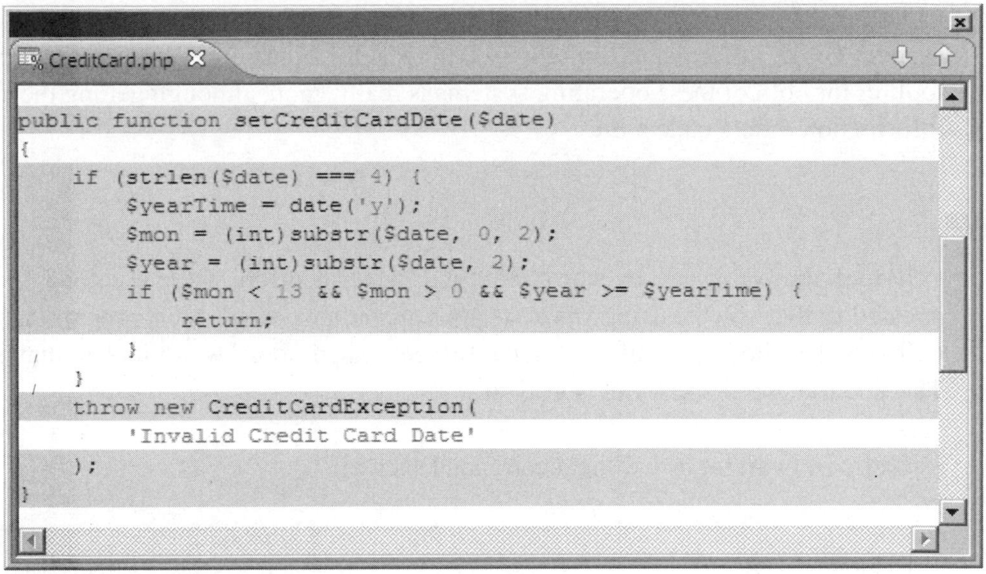

Figure 9.26: Code coverage output

System-Level Diagnostics

A decent portion of PHP developers are acquainted with most or all of the tools we've looked at here. But very few developers are familiar with some of the system-level diagnostic tools available. One of the things I often scold developers about is a lack of understanding of the impacts of the code they develop. In other words, when developers write code, they often do so without regard for the impacts their decisions will have on the people who must manage those applications. System administrators are people, too.

You know those **require_once()** calls that you do? They have an impact on performance. All those database calls on the primary key? They impact performance, too. All those writes you do to the file system? They impact performance. All those writes you do to the file system in the document root of your Web server? They have a massive impact on security. Security isn't really part of this discussion, but it is worth mentioning because it ties in with my earlier claim that many developers build their applications with very little operational impact in mind.

Clearly, the tools available for use will vary widely based on your operating system. For this discussion, we will look at tools for Linux and Windows. The tooling for both of these operating systems is really good, although getting the information differs quite a bit.

Linux

PHP took the Web world by storm through Linux. Therefore, there is a good possibility that you are using Linux as your operating system. Most programmers will be at least a little familiar with the **top** command, so we won't look at that one. The first tool we'll check out is **vmstat**.

I usually run **vmstat** by calling a command such as:

```
vmstat 1 100
```

or

```
vmstat 1 1000
```

These commands instruct **vmstat** to report instrumentation data once a second either 100 times or 1,000 times. When the system is idle, the results will often look like those shown in Figure 9.27.

```
[root@localhost ~]# vmstat 1 100
procs ---------memory---------- ---swap-- -----io---- --system-- -----cpu------
 r  b  swpd   free   buff  cache   si   so    bi    bo   in    cs us sy id wa st
 1  0     0  60596  20996 345224    0    0  1498    78  529   193  5 10 70 15  0
 0  0     0  60596  20996 345224    0    0     0     0 1024    63  0  0 100  0  0
```

Figure 9.27: Output of vmstat

Let's review what this data represents:

- **procs**:

  - r — This is the run queue for the system. This number is the number of processes that are waiting for processer time. So, if you have a dual-core machine and you have three processes running that are running very efficiently (no disk usage, minimal memory usage, and so on), you would likely see a run queue of 1. Note that this is not necessarily a bad thing. However, I have found, as a very general rule, that once you reach a run queue of **numcpu-1**, that is when performance starts to drop off. For example, if you have eight CPUs and your run queue is **7**, you are generally fine, but if you get to **8** to **10**, performance begins dropping off. This is by no means a hard and fast rule, but it often seems to happen like that.

  - b — This is the number of processes that currently are in blocking operations that cannot be interrupted. This can be things such as network I/O or disk I/O.

- **memory**:

  - **swpd** — This is the amount of swap space that is currently being used. This number, while important, is not as important as the **so** and **si** fields that we will look at in a bit. However, minimizing your swap usage is never a bad thing. You usually do this simply by adding RAM.

  - **free** — This is the amount of inactive RAM — in other words, RAM that has not been allocated. How large this number should be depends on the memory usage of your PHP application, but suffice to say that if it is at or near zero, the **swpd** value will go up as information is paged to the disk, or the operating system will refuse to execute your process and throw an error.

  - **buff** — This is the amount of data that is used for storing meta information about block devices, so things such as inodes, directory trees, and so on. If you go to the root directory and type **du -h -max-depth=1** while watching **vmstat**, you will notice that the **cache** value (the next item we'll look at) will stay the same but the **buff** value will go up as you traverse more of the file system.

- ○ **cache** — This shows the amount of memory that is used to store disk page caches in RAM. When you read a block from a disk, that individual block may be stored in RAM for faster access at a later time. This is why a file loads more quickly a second time. Linux usually does a good job of balancing this with other RAM requirements, but if you have a lot of disk reads in your application, seeing a high number here is a good thing.

- ● **swap**:

  - ○ **si** — This is the amount of memory that is being loaded from the disk. It indicates that data stored in swap is being loaded into memory.

  - ○ **so** — This is the amount of memory that is being taken from RAM and paged onto the disk. Seeing a lot of this activity is an indication that your system is low on RAM for your current tasks.

- ● **io**:

  - ○ **bi** — This is the total number of blocks read in from all block devices on the system, measured in blocks per second. This can include both data and metadata. In other words, it is measuring actual hardware throughput. If this number peaks and you have a high I/O wait time, there is a good chance that your system is suffering from I/O contention.

  - ○ **bo** — This is the number of blocks being written to any block devices on the system. If this number is high and I/O wait time is high, you might be able to improve performance by buffering your data and only writing in chunks that match or are larger than the size of a block on the disk.

- ● **system**:

  - ○ **in** — This is the number of interrupts per second. When working with peripherals outside the CPU, you could iterate over each of the individual devices and tell it to do something and then wait for the response. This is quite inefficient. So what it does instead is tell the hardware to do something and then it goes on to do something else. Then when the hardware is done, it sends an interrupt back to the CPU to say that it has finished. The number of interrupts per second will generally be a relatively high number. My laptop, idle, is about 1,000 interrupts per second.

o **cs** — Even in today's world of multi-core CPUs, there is a great need to have CPUs shared by multiple resources. Even an 8- or 16-core machine can have more than 8 or 16 individual processes running at a given point in time. So when a task needs to be executed, the current task will be stored elsewhere and the new task will be executed, and then back again so each process gets enough of the CPU time. The act of moving the current task out and switching another task in is a relatively expensive task that cannot be eliminated. However, if the number is quite high, it is a good indication either that your logic is taking a long time to run, so CPU time is spread across a good number of processes, or that you have a lot of places in your application where the CPU sees it can do something else during the request. Having a process in some kind of a wait state can give the OS a reason to switch it out.

- **cpu**:

  o **us** — This is the amount of time, as a percentage, that is spent doing non-kernel processing, or user time. Your PHP script is an example of this. You want your server to be as high here as possible. That is because the purpose of having the server is to do your work. If this number is not high, the server is having to do other things. That said, having this number at 100 percent or thereabout is probably an indication of an infinite loop.

  o **sy** — This is the amount of system time spent, as a percentage, running kernel-level code, so things such as disk IO, context switching, and so on.

  o **id** — This is idle time — the time spent, as a percentage, doing nothing.

  o **wa** — I/O wait time. Think of this as the amount of time spent waiting for synchronous disk I/O. This is definitely something you want to have on the low side. I have seen this as a significant problem on more than one occasion. Network I/O is not included in this number.

  o **st** — This is the amount of time that is stolen from the virtual machine. It is primarily, if not exclusively, related to hypervisor activity when running as a virtual machine.

The next tool I use when working with Linux is **strace**, a tool that lets you perform system call tracing. Any time your application needs to do something that is system-level, that call will show up in the trace.

We will look at **strace** in two ways. The first will be on the command line. Then I'll show you a quick trick for how to run it on the server.

Figure 9.28 shows the code for our test.

```
$fh = fopen(__FILE__, 'r');
$data = fread($fh, 1024);
echo $data;
```

Figure 9.28: Test code for an strace

To get an **strace** of this code, you must execute the command **strace php test. php**, where **test.php** is the name of the file where the test code resides and **php** is whichever PHP interpreter you are running (of course). When you run the command, you will get several thousand lines. My run had about 4,300 individual function calls.

Because we are running **strace** in command line interface (CLI) mode, the output includes all the start-up routines as well. However, you can scan the output or pipe to less (or more) to locate the PHP script entry point. The way to find it, for a small script, is go to the end and work backwards. If you start seeing calls to system devices and such, you've gone too far. Scan back until you see an **open()** call on your file name. That's where your script starts. Technically, the execution will have started earlier because PHP will have called **RINIT** on the installed modules, but that is where your code starts. In our example, that point in the output looks something like Figure 9.29.

```
open("test.php", O_RDONLY)               = 4
fstat64(4, {st_mode=S_IFREG|0644, st_size=74, ...}) = 0
mmap2(NULL, 4096, PROT_READ|PROT_WRITE,
      MAP_PRIVATE|MAP_ANONYMOUS, -1, 0) = 0x401000
read(4, "<?php\n\n$fh = fopen(__FILE__, 'r'"..., 4096) = 74
_llseek(4, 0, [0], SEEK_SET)             = 0
time(NULL)                               = 1263993173
fstat64(0, {st_mode=S_IFCHR|0620, st_rdev=makedev(136, 1), ...}) = 0
fstat64(0, {st_mode=S_IFCHR|0620, st_rdev=makedev(136, 1), ...}) = 0
fstat64(0, {st_mode=S_IFCHR|0620, st_rdev=makedev(136, 1), ...}) = 0
```

```
mmap2(NULL, 4096, PROT_READ|PROT_WRITE,
      MAP_PRIVATE|MAP_ANONYMOUS, -1, 0) = 0x402000
_llseek(0, 0, 0xbfa31e38, SEEK_CUR)     = -1 ESPIPE (Illegal seek)
fstat64(1, {st_mode=S_IFIFO|0600, st_size=0, ...}) = 0
fstat64(1, {st_mode=S_IFIFO|0600, st_size=0, ...}) = 0
fstat64(2, {st_mode=S_IFCHR|0620, st_rdev=makedev(136, 1), ...}) = 0
fstat64(2, {st_mode=S_IFCHR|0620, st_rdev=makedev(136, 1), ...}) = 0
_llseek(2, 0, 0xbfa31e38, SEEK_CUR)     = -1 ESPIPE (Illegal seek)
getcwd("/root"..., 4096)                = 6
time(NULL)                              = 1263993173
lstat64("/root", {st_mode=S_IFDIR|0750, st_size=4096, ...}) = 0
lstat64("/root/test.php",
        {st_mode=S_IFREG|0644, st_size=74, ...}) = 0
ioctl(4, SNDCTL_TMR_TIMEBASE or TCGETS, 0xbfa2fe08) = -1
 ENOTTY (Inappropriate ioctl for device)
read(4, "<?php\n\n$fh = fopen(__FILE__, 'r'"..., 8192) = 74
read(4, "", 4096)                       = 0
read(4, "", 8192)                       = 0
close(4)                                = 0
munmap(0x401000, 4096)                  = 0
time(NULL)                              = 1263993173
open("/root/test.php", O_RDONLY)        = 4
fstat64(4, {st_mode=S_IFREG|0644, st_size=74, ...}) = 0
lseek(4, 0, SEEK_CUR)                   = 0
read(4, "<?php\n\n$fh = fopen(__FILE__, 'r'"..., 8192) = 74
read(4, "", 8192)                       = 0
write(1, "<?php\n\n$fh = fopen(__FILE__, 'r'"..., 74) = 74
close(4)                                = 0
close(2)                                = 0
close(1)                                = 0
close(0)                                = 0
```

Figure 9.29: Output of an strace

The **open()** function returns a file handle of **4**. This file handle is used to read from the individual file when the script is compiled. That's why, a few lines down, we see the **read(4, ...)** call that reads up to 4,096 bytes from the string but returns only 74. The compilation stage goes until the **close(4)** call, a little further down in the output.

The next time we see an **open()** call, it is to the same file, but this time it is the **fopen()** call in our code. But you can see that the file handle number is being reused as **open()** returns **4**. We do a read on file descriptor 4 up to 8,192 bytes, even though we specified **1024**. That's the buffer length that PHP reads, even if you specify a different length.

When we reach the end of the file, we do our echo, which writes to file descriptor 1. What? We didn't open a file descriptor 1. This file descriptor is actually **STDOUT**, which is the console. After that, we enter into **RSHUTDOWN**, and because we didn't explicitly close the file, PHP now does it for us; then it closes down **STDERR (2)**, **STDOUT (1)**, and **STDIN(0)**.

That covers running **strace** using CLI, but this method is really not all that useful because most PHP development occurs on the browser. To do an **strace** on a browser-based request, we need to know which Apache process is the one that will service the request. Then we run **strace -p**. This command causes **strace** to attach to the process and start dumping data.

We have a problem, though. How do we know which Apache process will be used? We don't. There is, however, a way to find out.

When a browser opens a connection to a Web server, it tries to keep that connection open after the end of the request, thereby reducing overhead for subsequent requests. In case you are not familiar with this concept, it is called an HTTP KeepAlive. You can actually use this feature to your benefit if you need to do an **strace** on a Web server (which you should not do in a production environment unless you have absolutely no other way to get this data). You do so in conjunction with another command, called **lsof**. The **lsof** command prints a list of all open file descriptors on your operating system. A network socket is also a file descriptor, so you can use this technique to determine which process will serve the request next.

To start, make just a regular request to Apache. It can be a GIF, JPEG, or PHP file; it really doesn't matter. All you want to do is initiate the connection. Immediately after making the request, issue this command:

```
lsof -i | grep httpd | grep ESTA
```

This command runs an **lsof** on IPv4 or IPv6 files and network sockets and greps for **httpd**. Then, for each of the **httpd** finds, it greps for established connections.

With a very small bit of luck, you will get output similar to what Figure 9.30 shows.

```
httpd     2944   apache   20u   IPv6   10389       TCP
192.168.129.218:http->192.168.129.1:13666 (ESTABLISHED)
```

Figure 9.30: Catching an HTTP KeepAlive

If you don't, make sure you have KeepAlive turned on with a **KeepAliveTimeout** setting that's high enough for you to type in the process ID (PID). I set mine at 60 seconds. Do not, however, use this timeout in a production environment; in production, you are using the timeout for different purposes and should probably restrict it to 2 to 3 seconds.

In the grep output, the second number is the PID of the Apache process with the open connection to your browser. Once you have this number, quickly type in the following command, replacing **<PID>** with the number:

```
strace -p <PID>
```

The **strace** will sit at something similar to

```
poll([{fd=20, events=POLLIN}], 1, 60000)
```

That is Apache simply waiting for you. When you request the page that you're looking to get, your screen will be filled with far fewer **strace** lines, but still a good number (Figure 9.31).

```
read(20, "GET /test.php HTTP/1.1\r\nHost: de"..., 8000) = 471
gettimeofday({1264035372, 383681}, NULL) = 0
stat64("/var/www/html/test.php",
        {st_mode=S_IFREG|0644, st_size=74, ...}) = 0
open("/.htaccess", O_RDONLY|O_LARGEFILE) = -1
 ENOENT (No such file or directory)
open("/var/.htaccess", O_RDONLY|O_LARGEFILE) = -1
 ENOENT (No such file or directory)
open("/var/www/.htaccess", O_RDONLY|O_LARGEFILE) = -1
 ENOENT (No such file or directory)
```

```
setitimer(ITIMER_PROF, {it_interval={0, 0},
        it_value={60, 0}}, NULL) = 0
rt_sigaction(SIGPROF, {0x12b1df0, [PROF], SA_RESTART},
 {0x12b1df0, [PROF], SA_RESTART}, 8) = 0
rt_sigprocmask(SIG_UNBLOCK, [PROF], NULL, 8) = 0
getcwd("/"..., 4095)                    = 2
chdir("/var/www/html")                  = 0
setitimer(ITIMER_PROF, {it_interval={0, 0},
        it_value={30, 0}}, NULL) = 0
rt_sigaction(SIGPROF, {0x12b1df0, [PROF], SA_RESTART},
 {0x12b1df0, [PROF], SA_RESTART}, 8) = 0
rt_sigprocmask(SIG_UNBLOCK, [PROF], NULL, 8) = 0
time(NULL)                              = 1264035372
open("/var/www/html/test.php", O_RDONLY) = 21
fstat64(21, {st_mode=S_IFREG|0644, st_size=74, ...}) = 0
read(21, "<?php\n\n$fh = fopen(__FILE__, 'r'"..., 8192) = 74
read(21, "", 8192)                      = 0
read(21, "", 8192)                      = 0
close(21)                               = 0
time(NULL)                              = 1264035372
open("/var/www/html/test.php", O_RDONLY) = 21
fstat64(21, {st_mode=S_IFREG|0644, st_size=74, ...}) = 0
lseek(21, 0, SEEK_CUR)                  = 0
read(21, "<?php\n\n$fh = fopen(__FILE__, 'r'"..., 8192) = 74
read(21, "", 8192)                      = 0
chdir("/")                              = 0
close(21)                               = 0
setitimer(ITIMER_PROF, {it_interval={0, 0},
        it_value={0, 0}}, NULL) = 0
writev(20, [{"HTTP/1.1 200 OK\r\nDate: Thu, 21 J"..., 299},
    {"<?php\n\n$fh = fopen(__FILE__, 'r'"..., 74}], 2) = 373
read(20, 0x8b28960, 8000)               = -1
 EAGAIN (Resource temporarily unavailable)
write(13, "192.168.129.1 - - [20/Jan/2010:1"..., 79) = 79
poll([{fd=20, events=POLLIN}], 1, 60000 <unfinished ...>
```

Figure 9.31: strace of a "caught" connection

You might notice that a lot of file I/O is going on just to get this request. We have three **open()** calls for **.htaccess** files from the current working directory down to the root. The **test.php** file is also opened several times.

Often, the amount of data produced by **strace** is just too much, or you really don't need to know what every system call is doing. In that case, you can use the **-c** flag and get a count of all the system calls that were made. When you run **strace**, it will sit there until you press **Ctrl-C**. So, start up **strace**, make your request, and then hit **Ctrl-C**. You should get a summary similar to the one shown in Figure 9.32.

```
Process 3301 attached - interrupt to quit
Process 3301 detached
% time     seconds  usecs/call     calls    errors syscall
------ ---------- ----------- --------- --------- ---------------
 99.13   0.000342         171         2           close
  0.29   0.000001           0         7         1 read
  0.29   0.000001           1         1           gettimeofday
  0.29   0.000001           1         1           poll
  0.00   0.000000           0         1           write
  0.00   0.000000           0         5         3 open
  0.00   0.000000           0         2           chdir
  0.00   0.000000           0         2           time
  0.00   0.000000           0         1           lseek
  0.00   0.000000           0         1           brk
  0.00   0.000000           0         3           setitimer
  0.00   0.000000           0         1           writev
  0.00   0.000000           0         2           rt_sigaction
  0.00   0.000000           0         2           rt_sigprocmask
  0.00   0.000000           0         1           getcwd
  0.00   0.000000           0         1           stat64
  0.00   0.000000           0         2           fstat64
  0.00   0.000000           0         1           fcntl64
------ ---------- ----------- --------- --------- ---------------
100.00   0.000345                    36         4 total
```

Figure 9.32: Cumulative strace

Because we're examining system calls, let's look at an interesting demonstration of what an opcode cache such as the Alternative PHP Cache (APC) or Zend's Optimizer+ actually does. We will use a basic Zend Framework application and run **strace -c** on it before and after an opcode cache and see what the difference is.

Figure 9.33 shows the output for a request without an opcode cache.

```
Process 3302 attached - interrupt to quit
Process 3302 detached
% time     seconds usecs/call  calls errors syscall
------ ---------- ----------- ------ ------ --------------
 47.57  0.003903           2   1588    217 lstat64
 15.04  0.001234           4    300    220 open
 14.04  0.001152           4    301        time
  8.65  0.000710          71     10        brk
  4.63  0.000380           2    211      1 read
  3.28  0.000269          90      3        setitimer
  3.25  0.000267           3     80        close
  2.04  0.000167           2     75        getcwd
  1.46  0.000120           2     80        fstat64
  0.01  0.000001           1      1        gettimeofday
  0.01  0.000001           1      1        poll
  0.00  0.000000           0      1        write
  0.00  0.000000           0      2        chdir
  0.00  0.000000           0      4        lseek
  0.00  0.000000           0      1        access
  0.00  0.000000           0      1        writev
  0.00  0.000000           0      2        rt_sigaction
  0.00  0.000000           0      2        rt_sigprocmask
  0.00  0.000000           0      2        stat64
  0.00  0.000000           0      1        fcntl64
------ ---------- ----------- ------ ------ --------------
100.00  0.008204                2666    438 total
```

Figure 9.33: strace of Zend Framework request without an opcode cache

Figure 9.34 shows the output for a request with an opcode cache.

```
Process 3384 attached - interrupt to quit
Process 3384 detached
% time     seconds usecs/call  calls errors syscall
------ ---------- ----------- ------ ------ --------------
 62.30  0.000917           7    129     18 lstat64
 23.44  0.000345         345      1        writev
  7.95  0.000117           8     14        getcwd
  5.64  0.000083           5     17     12 open
```

```
  0.34   0.000005          0      59          stat64
  0.14   0.000002          1       3          brk
  0.07   0.000001          0       5       1  read
  0.07   0.000001          1       1          gettimeofday
  0.07   0.000001          1       1          poll
  0.00   0.000000          0       1          write
  0.00   0.000000          0       5          close
  0.00   0.000000          0       2          chdir
  0.00   0.000000          0      29          time
  0.00   0.000000          0       4          lseek
  0.00   0.000000          0       3          setitimer
  0.00   0.000000          0       2          rt_sigaction
  0.00   0.000000          0       2          rt_sigprocmask
  0.00   0.000000          0       5          fstat64
  0.00   0.000000          0       2          fcntl64
 ------ ---------- ---------- ------ ------ --------------
100.00   0.001472                 285      31  total
```

Figure 9.34: strace of Zend Framework request with an opcode cache

As you can see, the number of system calls dropped 90 percent, and the **open()** calls dropped by an order of magnitude.

Windows

If you are not familiar with the Windows Sysinternals utilities, you should really get to know them. The amount of data you can get out of the various tools is really quite good. On more than one occasion, I have been able to pinpoint performance problems using the System Internals Process Explorer. Process Monitor is another tool that is quite useful.

Figure 9.35 shows a snapshot in time of an individual process handling a request. This display shows you many different points of data that can be pertinent, from memory size to disk reads.

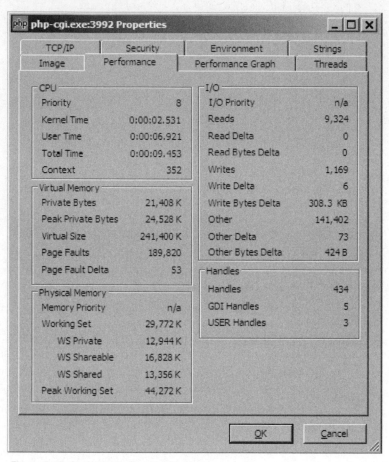

Figure 9.35: Sysinternals Process Explorer

You can also get excellent overview information about the state of your machine by looking at the System Information view (Figure 9.36).

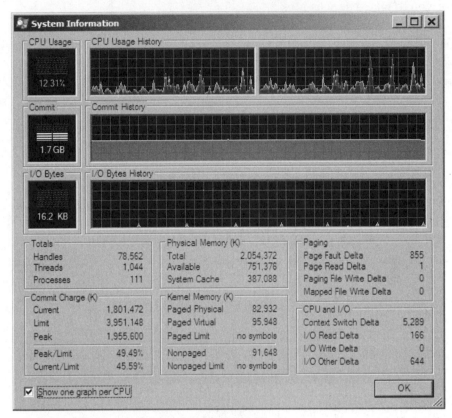

Figure 9.36: Process Explorer system information

That is a brief look at Windows, yes. Many PHP developers who work on Windows are not familiar with these tools. If you are not, I suggest spending some time getting to know them. Many of the same principles that we examined on the Linux operating system can be applied here as well.

Conclusion

That brings us to the end of our chapter on good development. As with anything else in this book, the examples are simpler than what you will see in real life. But my hope is that you can glean from this discussion some good information to go and make yourself a better programmer. The techniques I've shown here are virtually required, especially debugging, profiling, and unit testing. Code Tracing, if you have the budget and are running critical Web applications, is another thing for you to take a serious look at.

Also, take some time to get to know your operating system. How you structure your application will have an impact on how the operating system behaves because, well, you're running on it. Get to know the environment for which you are building, and learn to read some of the warning signs. They probably won't save your life, but they might save your job.

CHAPTER 10

Preparing for Success

Ironically, preparing for success and preparing for failure require very similar disciplines. But before we go into the technical details, let's define what success is and what failure is. As I'm sure you can see where I'm going here, success and failure can actually be the same thing.

Success is when you've spent oodles of your own "free" time developing some kind of Web site that you think will be kind of cool. The first couple of days see some pretty decent traffic, and you're relatively happy that people like what it is you've done. A few weeks pass, and your servers are happily chugging along. You experience some minor load issues, but nothing that an additional server or two can't handle.

Then, for some reason, you start having trouble sleeping. It could be because you're starting to become less sure about the stability of your system. Or maybe it's because that fracking beeper keeps going off because another machine has crashed.

Congratulations. You are now successful. This is where the failure starts.

In light of that unfortunate reality, let's look at a few things you can do to be successful that also permit you to get a full night's sleep. I present these steps in no particular order. More important, none of them will guarantee that you won't have problems. Why? That question brings us to our first point.

Expect Failure

The question is not *if* hardware (or software, for that matter) will fail, but *when*. I even read an article several months ago in which the author stated that RAID will eventually fail. Always. That's because as disk capacity grows, the amount of data that needs to be re-imaged on one disk failure will actually exceed the error tolerance of the new disk.

I don't know that I take *that* pessimistic of a view, but it makes for interesting thinking. Do you have enough redundancy that you can still handle load under failure? A common approach is to have two servers. That way, if one system goes down, your Web site remains up and running. I believe this to be the wrong approach. If your Web application is business-critical, you need *at least* three machines for each separate application.

There are a couple of reasons for this rule of thumb. The first is maintenance. Your machines will need maintenance. They *will* break. They *will* need updates. When you take a machine off your load balancer, you need to continue to have redundancy. What if the maintenance you're doing is emergency maintenance because your motherboard or backplane went out? The machine is already shut down, and you have to drive to the data center — during rush hour, of course. You yank the machine out of the rack and replace the motherboard (or have your hardware support person do it for you). When you plug it back in, nothing happens. After 20 minutes, you find out that's because when the motherboard got fried, it took a few memory chips with it.

Thankfully, your hardware support person had some memory chips in the back of the van (you would have remembered to bring them yourself just in case, right?), and so the memory issue is quickly solved. You boot up the machine, and it comes up just fine. Except for the network. You realize that, in your haste, you forgot to unplug one of the network cables when you pulled it out of the rack, thus damaging the network card. This time, the hardware support person doesn't have the right one.

So now your support person is racing back to the warehouse to get a new network interface card (NIC), and you're sitting in the data center reading XKCD to try and find some humor in the world. Two hours later, the support person returns with the proper network card and installs it. The system boots up fine.

But the application doesn't run. Turns out your application is hardware-locked. It's Sunday night, and you won't be able to get a new key until the next day.

Did I mention that tomorrow is Cyber Monday?

Three servers. Minimum. If you are concerned about cost, buy three smaller ones rather than two medium ones. I hope you never need to learn this lesson the hard way. I am grateful that I learned it the easy way; someone smarter than me told me.

Partition Your Data

If you are building something that needs to scale beyond a few Web servers, perhaps half a dozen to a dozen, consider partitioning your data. What partitioning basically means is that you separate your data into distinct systems. These systems may have the ability to talk to each other, but they do not replicate data to each other. So what we're *not* talking about is anything to do with replication.

However, before you say to yourself, "Okay, I'll just partition my data," you need to examine your application. Do you have a lot of dependencies across a wide range of tables? You might need to look at setting up a system where you have a master machine that is eligible only for writes. Reads cannot go to that machine. Then you use simple replication to replicate all the writes on the master to as many slaves as you need to handle your load.

But shouldn't you have three masters, as I noted before? Nope. Use one, if performance allows, so that you have a single access point. If that machine goes down, and it will, promote one of the slaves to be the master until you have the master back up.

I must really be confusing you. I started out talking about how you should partition your data and then gave reasons why you should not. The reason I did that is because partitioning is not a cure-all for scalability. Partitioning should be toward the end of your list. I hate to break it to you, but your site will probably not be Google, Facebook, or Yahoo. If it is, simple partitioning won't be sufficient anyway.

But if you are an upper-middle player with decent load requirements, partitioning your data can be a viable way to increase the scalability of your site. Using a single master will help you scale to a decent level, but at some point replication is going to starting making slave writes more common than reads. If that starts looking probable in the future, then partitioning becomes a virtual necessity.

Calculate Before Writing

Say you have some kind of social networking application where people can post status updates and other people can read them. If I see a query like the one in Figure 10.1, we're going to need to have a little talk.

```
SELECT m.* FROM messages AS m
INNER JOIN relationships AS r
    ON r.user_relationship_key = m.user_key
WHERE r.user_key = 836272
ORDER BY m.posted
LIMIT 10
```

Figure 10.1: Bad SQL for high-scale social networking application

Every time someone refreshes the page, this query is going to be run. The query may be lightning fast, but it a) does not allow for partitioning (if you end up needing it), and b) well, with at least 836,272 members who are interrelated, how big do you think the **relationships** table would be? Given 836,272 members, each with 100 relationships, we get a total of 83,627,200. So, you'll have 836,272 members hitting a table with 83 million rows maybe once every 10 seconds at peak? Have fun.

No. Instead, calculate ahead of time. And what we have here is a *perfect* opportunity for partitioning. Set aside a database or two (or 10) that have tables such as **mq2**, **mqf**, and **mq8**, and when a new status update is given (and therefore a write to the database), do something similar to the solution shown in Figure 10.2.

```
$select = 'SELECT user_relationship_key
    FROM relationships WHERE user_key = ?';
$stmt = $db->prepare($select);
$stmt->execute(array($_SESSION['user_key']));
```

```
foreach ($stmt->fetchAll(PDO::FETCH_ASSOC) as $row) {
    $hash = sha1($row['user_relationship_key']);
    $dbName    = 'db' . $hash[0];
    $tableName = 'mq' . $hash[1];
    $db->changeDb($dbName);
    $db->insert(
        $tableName,
        array(
            'first_name'  => $_SESSION['fname'],
            'last_name'   => $_SESSION['lname'],
            'message'     => $_POST['message'],
            'user_key'    => $row['user_key']
        )
    );
}
```

Figure 10.2: Partitioning your data across multiple databases and tables

Then, when the people who have the relationship check back, they would do something like what you see in Figure 10.3.

```
$hash = sha1($_SESSION['user_key']);
$dbName    = 'db' . $hash[0];
$tableName = 'mq' . $hash[1];
$db->changeDb($dbName);
$select = 'SELECT * FROM '
        . $tableName
        . ' WHERE user_key = ?
            ORDER BY posted DESC
            WHERE posted > ?';

$stmt = $db->prepare($select);
$stmt->execute(
    array(
        $_SESSION['user_key'],
        $_SESSION['last_check']
    )
);
foreach ($stmt->fetchAll(PDO::FETCH_ASSOC) as $row) {
    // etc.
}
```

Figure 10.3: Retrieving data from across multiple databases and tables

Clearly I'm taking some shortcuts here, but what this code does is allow for individual machines handling data for 52,267 users, with each table holding data for just over 3,000 users. This means that you can hold data in the primary message tables for longer than if it were stored in one table. What I mean by that is that say 50,000 users don't log in for a week and they each have 50 status updates from their friends (because you arbitrarily limit the display of the last 50). In the previous setup, you would have 250,000 rows of data in one table that you'd have to keep for when the users log in a week later. This new setup would mean 200 rows per table instead.

By pre-building your data on writes, you have been able to scale much more easily, using a system that is much more fault-tolerant.

Process Asynchronously

Are you a bank or a stock broker? No? Then your visitors can wait a minute or two before getting their status updates. Use a queue. To continue using our previous example, what happens when someone has 5,000 friends? That person will get a timeout any time he or she posts something. Instead, take that small task (submitting a status update), which will become a big task (to 5,000 friends), and run it when you have free CPU cycles. The Job Queue in both Zend Server and Zend Platform lets you do this, or you could use something such as Gearman to achieve something similar.

By offloading high write tasks to an asynchronous process, you gain a couple of things:

- The ability to throttle expensive writes to the database

- Higher throughput on the front end (the front end isn't waiting for 5,000 inserts; it's waiting for 1)

Don't Poll

Are we there yet? Are we there yet? Are we there yet? It's annoying to Web servers, too, and it sucks up bandwidth and Apache processes. Consider using some kind of HTTP messaging solution for your front end. We looked at an example in the asynchronicity chapter; try doing something like that. Being able to handle a large number of sleeping connections will be easier than handling 10 times the number of active connections (assuming that every 10 poll actions results in data being returned).

Use Ajax

One of the things that's kind of annoying about Web sites is that you have to redraw the entire user interface (UI) any time someone clicks a button. JavaScript needs to be reloaded and executed. Cascading Style Sheets (CSS) needs to be downloaded again. Ditto for images. It's all kind of a big waste when, most of the time, only the main content container needs to be loaded.

Instead, try to minimize the full page reloads that you need to do by using partial-page Ajax calls. Doing so offers two primary benefits:

- Significantly reduced HTTP traffic — One of the biggest causes of poor performance is not slow PHP code but ancillary HTTP calls. Reducing the number of HTTP calls increases what I call the "perception of performance." How fast your Web site is really doesn't matter to the end users. What matters is how fast they *think* it is.

- Significantly reduced logic execution — Often, the UI has a fair amount of functionality that needs to be called to make it render properly. By calling only the pertinent layout code for a specific action, you can significantly reduce the amount of logic you need to execute. Note, however, that this approach will limit browser bookmark functionality.

Remove Single Points of Failure

Network File System, I'm looking at you. I don't know what it is, but NFS (or any remotely shared file system) as a deployment platform never seems to go away. NFS is great for aggregating data, such as log files, but you should never, ever use it as the document root for your production application.

But, I hear you saying, "Our NFS server is rock solid; it *never* goes down."

silence

Not only will it go down at some point, but when it goes down it will take your entire system down with it. We're talking massive, catastrophic failure. Never, ever depend on something that can take down your entire application if one part of it goes down.

So, how do you deal with information that needs to be clustered?

First, application data: your source code, application images, CSS files, JavaScript, and so on. These should all be deployable, static items. In other words, there is no reason why these items cannot exist as multiple copies on multiple servers. Rsync is a common mechanism used for deployment for this type of data. Other options exist, too, and it really doesn't matter which one you use, but whatever you use, it needs to deploy locally.

Next, user data. This is a more complicated beast, but we actually get to fix two issues at the same time. A lot of applications have user-supplied content with which people can interact — forum posts, images, and so on. Forum posts go to the database, so you should not have many issues there, but items such as images are a little more difficult. You *could* store them in the database, but unless you have gobs of money that you want to waste, storing them on the file system is a much better option. However, there is a problem here. The Web server should never have write access to the file system, except for log files and temp directories.

"What?" You heard me. A Web server should be able to write only log files to the file system. Many of the exploits I have seen on Web sites happen because people are able to write to the file system and then execute the Web page from their browser.

But if the Web server cannot write to the file system, how do you handle user-supplied content? You have them upload to a temp directory. From there, you use another process, running under a different user — presumably the one that your deployer uses — and have it move the content to a live directory.

There's another option, one that is better for sites with more than average traffic. Say you have a site with more than three Web servers, to use an arbitrary number. At that point, having any of your static content delivered from your Web servers running PHP may not be the best idea. This is because Apache is a relatively heavy process when it houses the application server. It is by no means slow or anything like that, but you need to have a lot of processes hanging around to deliver content.

Instead, it is a good idea to have a static cluster using a lightweight Web server to serve static content. The way things are today, it's not uncommon to have 50 or more additional HTTP requests for one PHP request. Those 50 requests are tying up your PHP server. A good example of a lightweight Web server is lighttpd.

To get user-supplied content to your static content cluster, you could use a similar deployment script or deployment daemon that either would run X number of seconds to see whether new content is available or could be pinged when new content is available and then download it to the content server cluster. It would, of course, run under a different user than your lightweight HTTP server as well.

Note here that none of these processes would actually use shared storage. When a user uploaded an image, he or she would do it to a local temp directory. Once that occurred, the application would notify a deployment mechanism, which would then move the image to shared storage. From there, the deployment mechanism would notify the static servers that new content was available, and they would each download and deploy the content locally for the local static Web server to serve. Figure 10.4 depicts this type of solution.

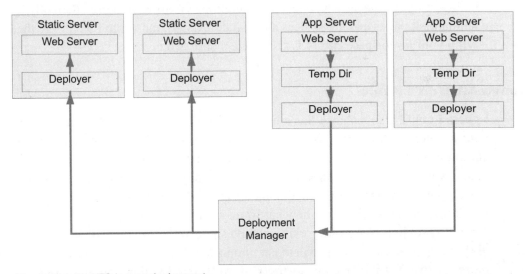

Figure 10.4: No NFS in your deployment

Does this waste your hard drive space? Actually, no. "Waste" occurs only if you use space you don't need. You use this space to maintain uptime, reduce security vulnerabilities, and make your application run faster.

Max Out Your Memory

Only after disk space is memory more expensive. And disk space is cheap. So memory is just less cheap. I won't go into all the reasons why this circumstance is good, but I will give you a bit of information. Memory is, of course, faster than disk. So if you can put your data in memory, it will be faster. This is why people use Memcache instead of a distributed disk array for important data.

However, there are some things you should not store in Memcache. Things such as application settings or partial page caches. Anything that is global in nature but that can be a couple of seconds out of date from the rest of the cluster belongs in a local cache. A local shared memory cache will always be faster than Memcache. Under heavy load, even a Time To Live (TTL) of one second can drastically reduce load, although your TTL should be somewhere around what the typical time between clicks is for sensitive data and however long you are comfortable with for non-sensitive data.

Maxing out your memory also lets the operating system work more efficiently by caching disk pages and file system metadata in RAM. And while I won't say that having your swap space empty is preferred, it sure is nice.

Above All, Don't Panic

I guess I could also rephrase this advice as, "Don't make hasty decisions." *Examine* your problems. Don't say, "We need to add more servers," unless you know that adding more servers will solve your problem. Simply adding more RAM won't help if you do a recursive directory scan of your application for each request. Use the diagnostic tools that I detailed in the chapter on debugging and good practices. Don't just immediately throw new hardware at the problem if you don't know what the problem is. A fallacy exists among some Web developers that says that diagnosing a performance problem isn't important because you can just throw more hardware at it. There are a variety of words that I will not put into print concerning that approach.

Also, don't *assume* that caching will solve your problem. Caching is a very valid solution to scalability problems, but it should be your *last* solution. If one of your developers comes to you and says, "There is this shiny new design pattern that everyone is using. It doesn't scale and it performs very poorly, but we'll solve that by caching," send him back to remedial programming. *Think* about what you need. Does the shiny new design pattern actually solve your problem? Yes? Use it. No? Don't try to be hip and cool. Practicality is one of the best tools to have in the programmer tool belt.

Index

NOTE: **Boldface** indicates illustrations and code; *t* indicates a table.

NOTE: **Boldface** indicates illustrations and code; *t* indicates a table.

NOTE: **Boldface** indicates illustrations and code; *t* indicates a table.

NOTE: **Boldface** indicates illustrations and code; *t* indicates a table.

NOTE: **Boldface** indicates illustrations and code; *t* indicates a table.

NOTE: **Boldface** indicates illustrations and code; *t* indicates a table.

NOTE: **Boldface** indicates illustrations and code; *t* indicates a table.